SIBER

A RECORD OF
TRAVEL, CLIMBING AND EXPLORATION

BY

SAMUEL TURNER, F.R.G.S.

WITH AN INTRODUCTION BY BARON HEYKING

Illustrated from Photographs by the Author

LONDON

T. FISHER UNWIN
Paternoster Square
MCMV

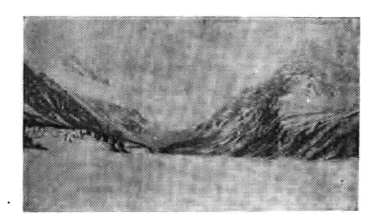

CONTENTS

CHAPTER I

CONTENTS

PAGE

Beauty of the view—Measurements of the mountains—
I begin the return—Am thoroughly exhausted—A
Kalmuck humorist—We sleep in the open—An ibex
hunt—An ibex dinner—Kalmuck appetite—The horns
of the ibex.

CHAPTER VII

I decide to climb Belukha—Difficulties with the hunters,
who turn back—I pitch my tent in a snowstorm—An
unpleasant shock—Making soup in a portable tent—
Sleep and dreams—Morning—No sign of the hunters—
I decide to continue alone—Among the boulders—
Hardness of the ice—Apparition of one of the hunters
four miles away—The ascent—A snow-slip—I narrowly
escape—The descent—Difficult progress—I make up to
the hunter—Taken ill—I reach the camp with difficulty
—Inflammation of the eyes—Compelled to abandon
attempt—Striking our tents—We miss our track, but
arrive at Kalmuck hut—Shelter and warmth—On the
way again to Katunda—Crossing the Katun—Advice
to future explorers—Climbing—Akkem Valley—Climate
—Mountain formation—Fauna and flora.

CHAPTER VIII

Katunda church and priest—We visit a hunter's establishment—Beneficent efforts on the part of the Government—
Steam-boats required to relieve the traffic—An inspector
of forests—Extent of Altai forests—We leave Katunda
—The coming of the great thaw—Ouemon—A good
night's rest—Thriftlessness of the peasantry—Compelled
to continue our journey on horseback—Triumphant
"tarakans"—A sledge drive—Abbi cemetery—An
obstinate driver—Kalmucks—Horsemanship—We break
down—Are rescued—Kirlick—Shooting wild fowl—
Ouskam—On the way to Chorni-Anni—Returning to
civilisation—The Easter fair at Chorni-Anni—A drive in
the dark—Solonishini—A letter from Prince Khilkoff—
An Easter service—Chiranchanka creamery—Lejanovo—

CHAPTER XI

LIST OF ILLUSTRATIONS

xvi LIST OF ILLUSTRATIONS

PREFACE

THE progress of geographical exploration in all parts of the world has been more rapid during the last few years than at any previous period of the world's history. How far this is to be attributed to George Stephenson's epoch-making invention it is difficult to say, but the greatest tribute to the memory of that great man, to my mind, is the enormous stretch of 6466 miles of railway from St Petersburg to Vladivostock, which spans the gulf between the Eastern and Western worlds and is steadily peopling and developing Siberia—a country which covers one-thirteenth of the land surface of the Globe. It is impossible to over-estimate the importance of this development from an international point of view. The exploration of the Highlands and Steppes of Siberia has been successfully carried out by able Russians and Siberians, leaving very little virgin ground for explorers of other nationalities; but the highest Siberian mountains, for want of mountaineers, remain almost unexplored.

The Siberian trade route to Mongolia has occasionally

been traversed by sportsmen who have passed through the Altai Mountains in search of wild goats (*Ovis Ammon*), but, so far as the mountains themselves are concerned, no previous English-speaking explorer has been there, and there is no English literature on the subject, although the Altai Mountain district covers 144,140 square miles, an area nine times as large as Switzerland.

The present volume claims no more than to give an account of a winter exploration of the Altai Mountains. It makes no scientific pretensions, beyond recording the ascertained altitudes of the mountains, describing the passes and glaciers, and placing on the map those of the mountains which it was my privilege to discover and ascend. The remaining portion of the book records my personal impressions of the journey across Siberia.

My main object in visiting Siberia was business, but, business concluded, and the journey having carried me within 400 miles of the highest Altai Mountains, I decided to devote the remainder of my stay to the exploration of that unknown region which includes the highest mountain range of South Central Siberia—Katunskië-Belki (Alps). Eventually it was my privilege to stand on the summit of the highest-discovered mountain in Siberia.

It is my conviction that exploration and commerce should be in intimate relation, and that the explorer who fails to do something towards promoting the trade of the country he visits falls short of the main purpose of exploration. I propose, therefore, to describe Siberia's chief industry—the dairy industry—which owes its rapidly-growing prosperity to the unique geographical conditions of the country: mountains for the grazing of cattle more ideal than those of Switzerland; a rich virgin soil and succulent grass of the steppes richer than that of any Canadian prairie and more valuable than the gold mines of Klondyke or South Africa.

The views and opinions to which I venture from time to time to give expression are offered with all humility. Having thought and read extensively about Russia and Siberia, and having been in the very favourable position of conversing with more than a hundred Russian, German and Danish merchants residing in Siberia, besides having made short stays with English families in different centres of the country—most of my informants have lived in Siberia several years,—I have compared their views with the results of my own observations.

Whatever shortcomings this book may have, therefore, it contains at least the conscientious opinions of an unprejudiced Englishman, who has had the advantage of good sources of information. Nations, like individuals, should be judged with some reference to their own ideals and modes of thinking, and not by our pet personal standards of right and wrong. Instead, for instance, of looking to Siberia for a perennial crop of exaggerated exile horrors, we should, I venture to believe, be better employed in studying its vast commercial possibilities. We should then be led to admire a nation, which, instead of imprisoning its convicts, has sent them to Siberia, to help in the development of a country which is already producing enormous supplies of food for the ever-growing populations of Western Europe, and the potentialities of which it is at present almost impossible to gauge.

I should like to mention that some of the statistics have been taken from the *Siberian Railway Guide* and the most recent Goverment Blue Books on Japan and China. Finally,I wish to express my indebtedness to Baron Heyking for the brief outline of Siberian history which forms Appendix II. p. 367.

S. T.

INTRODUCTION

I REGARD it as a compliment to have been invited by the author of this work to write a few words by way of introduction to the narrative of his travels in Siberia, which country he visited for the purpose of studying local conditions of trade and the possibility of importing produce therefrom into Great Britain.

In my capacity as Russian Consul for Scotland and the Northern Counties of England I have, for some time, been endeavouring to arouse the interest of British capitalists, merchants and manufacturers in Russia, her resources, products and export trade. These efforts have been most fruitful of results in the present case, in which so well-known a firm as that of Messrs Willer & Riley sent one of their directors to European Russia and Siberia as a pioneer of Anglo-Russian trade relations. It is to be hoped that the pleasant nature of Mr Turner's experiences in the Russian Empire, the breaking of new ground in the export trade from Siberia to Great Britain, and the publication of the present work, will contribute to the development of trade relations between the two countries.

The chief obstacles in the way of such development are to be looked for in the facts that very little indeed is known about Russia in Great Britain, and that what little is known is often distorted by an unfortunate racial animosity and by the too-ready credence that is given to sensational stories by the great mass of the public. It is maintained, for instance, that a lack of civilisation in Russia, as compared with Western Europe, hampers trade relations with Great Britain, and renders it difficult, if not impossible, for foreign merchants or capitalists to conduct business operations within the limits of the empire of the Czar.

There are necessarily points of difference between the two countries. Thus, it may be true that Great Britain has an advantage in her spirit of enterprise, the strength of her public opinion, the mutual confidence of her subjects —resembling the *publica fides* of ancient Rome—the interest that every one takes in public affairs—in short, her more advanced stage of civilisation. These are precious flowers which only grow up in the course of centuries, and require, for their perfection, the fruitful soil of uninterrupted peaceful development. Thanks to her insular position, which has preserved her through hundreds of years from the incursions of foreign enemies, it has been possible for England to arrive at this advanced stage of development. Russia has been less fortunate, it having been her office to shelter European civilisation, even until recent times, by receiving the shock of successive Tartar, Chinese and Japanese invasions. Acting, so to speak, as the buffer of Western Europe, her efforts have been largely absorbed by struggles and wars; but she has not remained a barbaric country. Thanks to the autocratic form of her government it has been possible to advance Russia in civilisation and progress more quickly and successfully than could have been done under any other system. Owing principally to the enlightened reforms of Peter the Great, Catherine the Second and the first two Alexanders, Russia has become an entirely European country. The administration of the empire has been remodelled on the European system; serfdom has been abolished; the juris-

diction of the courts of justice has been made independent
of the Government; the principle of trial by jury has been
established; the laws are codified; local self-government
exists in the towns and villages; education is spreading
steadily among the lower orders; the trade in alcohol has
been regulated and restricted during the reign of his
present Majesty, Nicholas II., through the introduction of a
state monopoly of the traffic in alcohol; in the same reign
a series of successful financial reforms has been introduced, such, for instance, as the adoption of a gold standard
for the currency, which have rendered Russian financial
affairs stable and secure. Add to these important changes
the entire separation of justice from the executive, a series
of important reforms in the economic conditions of the
peasantry, and the prospective convocation of an assembly
of representatives of the whole Russian nation, and it will be
apparent that a new era of progress has begun in Russia.

It is not my intention to enumerate all the reforms
which have contributed to convert Russia into a civilised
European country. I only wish to point out that the
necessary conditions are present which would enable
British business men to establish trade relations with
Russia on the same lines as those which exist between
other civilised countries, the more so as an extensive and
mutually advantageous exchange of commodities between
the two countries would seem to be in the natural order of
things. Great Britain is chiefly an industrial country,
while Russia's principal products are agricultural; the one
being, so to speak, the necessary complement of the other.
It would, therefore, be only in keeping with the economic
requirements of the two countries if the commercial,
industrial and financial relations subsisting between them
were on a much larger scale than has been the case
hitherto. Englishmen would find in Russia a profitable
field for commercial enterprise, advantageous investment,

and the cheap purchase of raw materials, food stuffs and half-finished products. A country such as Russia, which is seventy times as large as the United Kingdom, has a population three and a half times as great, and is endowed with almost unlimited and hardly touched natural wealth, should not fail to be attractive to any Englishman who can appreciate his opportunities and who possesses the necessary energy and enterprise.

There are few better ways in which an Englishman could seek to promote the extension of commercial and trade relations with Russia than that selected by the author of this volume, of making himself acquainted with the country at first hand by travel and residence within its borders and afterwards publishing a record of his experiences and impressions. In addition to the narrative of his trip, Mr Turner gives interesting statistics of the economic conditions of Siberia and records interviews with officials and experts in many branches of trade and commerce. His observations merit the attention of the British public, as representing the conscientious opinions of an unprejudiced English man of business, who is anxious to give his countrymen trustworthy information about the country. It is worth noting that the author believes England to be making " one of the biggest political and commercial blunders in not cultivating the friendship of the Russian Empire." The narrative of his mountaineering feats does him credit as an expert Alpine climber, while the numerous and unique photographic views add attractiveness to the book. I have therefore much pleasure in congratulating him on the results of his travels, the opening out of new commercial relations with Russia, and the publication of his book, which will form a useful addition to English literature on the subject of the Russian Empire.

A. HEYKING.

SIBERIA

A Record of Travel, Climbing and · Exploration

CHAPTER I

ST PETERSBURG—MOSCOW—*EN ROUTE* FOR SIBERIA

Object of the exile system—and of the Great Siberian Railway—Growth of agriculture in Siberia—Object of the author's visit to Siberia—A letter from Professor Sapozhnikoff of Tomsk University—Departure from London —The Kiel Canal—In the Baltic—Riga—Yuryeff—Peterhof—St Petersburg—Idiosyncrasies of the Russian "jarvey"—The Nevsky Prospect— St Isaac's Cathedral—The Neva—The Fortress of St Peter and St Paul— Moscow—The Great Siberian Railway Station—Booking for Siberia— Railway comforts—Across the Steppes—The "verstman"—Dinner on the cars—Sleeping arrangements—Crossing the Volga—Iron and steel industries of Ufa—Zlatoust, the Russian Sheffield—The Orenburg gold fields—Cheliabinsk—The Government of Tobolsk—Climate—Immensity of the country—Kourgan—Bazaar and Easter fair—Sensational journalism— Exile to Siberia.

A DOMINANT theme of writers on Russian subjects appears to be the banishment to Siberia of Russia's undesirables. Whatever may be said, however, either for or against the system, it is clear that its introduction was the outcome of a desire to people and open out a vast, sparsely-populated country, to which, partly on account of the severity of the Siberian winter, and partly owing to the enormous distances involved—the old overland trail represented a journey of from eighteen months to two years. —the Russian peasant was extremely loth to emigrate.

What the exile system began, the Great Siberian railway is completing, for, since it was opened, the banishment of convicts to Siberia—with the exception of murderers who are still deported to the island of Sakhalin —has been abolished. Villages are springing into towns, and Siberia is developing at a rate that is only paralleled by a few of our own colonies. The promulgation, since

A

the Siberian railway was opened, of a host of new laws, the object of which is to encourage by every possible means the emigration of peasants to Siberia, shows clearly enough, to my mind, that "the world's longest" iron-way was built mainly with a view to promoting the development of the vast agricultural regions of Siberia and the interchange of commodities between the Eastern and Western worlds. Nor have some of the nations of Western Europe been slow to take advantage of the facilities offered. The Russian nation is, therefore, justified in regarding the new railway as a very promising commercial asset.

Since the line was opened the produce of agricultural and dairy farms has increased from insignificance to vast importance, and the prices of such products, and more particularly of butter, on the world's markets, including that of London, have been revolutionised, despite the fact that Siberia recently experienced a three years' drought. This enormous development was the reason of my prolonged visit to the innermost regions of Siberia.

As members of a leading English firm of provision importers with an annual trade of about three millions in dairy products from nearly all parts of the world, it was only natural that my colleagues and myself, having an eye to future trade relations, should seek to increase our knowledge of Siberia and its potentialities. My fellow-directors having selected me for the journey, on the score that as an Alpine climber the wolves would find me too tough to devour and the Siberian cold too hardy to freeze, the end of the winter of 1903 was fixed upon for the trip. Like most Britishers, all I knew of Siberia was that it had an intensely cold climate, the mere mention of the place being sufficient to make me feel chilly on the hottest day. I pictured to myself, on the Siberian steppes, the traditional pack of wolves devouring the horses which the hotly-pursued travellers had cut away from the sledge, and, so vivid was the picture, that when purchasing a revolver I found myself pondering whether it would be safe to buy one without a self-extractor—in case there should be more than six wolves in the pack.

One of my colleagues, who maintains that I suffer from "mountain fever," having suggested that it was rather a good thing that there were no mountains to climb in Siberia, as I would not be tempted to risk my neck, a train of ideas was started in my mind which resulted in a visit to the Royal Geographical Society. I found that all the literature the Society possessed which dealt with the Altai Mountains consisted of a few lines translated from the Russian Geographical Society's Journal, to the effect that Professor Sapozhnikoff had climbed 13,300 feet of the south side of the Belukha, and from that elevation had determined the altitude of the mountain to be 14,800 feet, which is the height of the Matterhorn.

Belukha is the highest known mountain in Siberia, so, wishing to learn more about it, I consulted a Russian map and found that it is situated about 300 miles from Bysk, the most southerly town I was to visit on business. I determined, therefore, instead of making my annual ascent of the Swiss Alps, to humour my "mountain fever," after completing my business, by exploring this little-known group of mountains, making glacier observations and climbing and measuring Belukha.

One or two Asiatic travellers whom I consulted questioned the fact that the Altai range contained so high a mountain. Two others condemned my expedition at that time of the year as impracticable, owing to the condition of the roads in March and April; they had, themselves, been within 250 miles of the mountains in their travels.

I wrote to the British Commercial Agent at Moscow on business and made incidental inquiries about the mountains. He kindly referred me to Mr Oswald Cattley, F.R.G.S.; Novo-Nicolaëvsk. This gentleman was good enough to assist me greatly, endeavouring to find out something about the mountains, but he earnestly dissuaded me from going out in March or April because of the bad state of the roads and the probability of a thaw, which would render them impassable. He, however, gave his son permission to accompany me, and communicated with Professor Sapozhnikoff, of Tomsk University, from whom he received a letter, of which the following is a translation :—

"TOMSK UNIVERSITY,
"TOMSK, 28/8 *April* 1903.

"DEAR SIR,—In regard to Mr Turner's proposed trip to the Altai, I shall be glad to give him the benefit of my experience. From the town of Bysk post horses can be had as far as the village of Altaiskoë. Thence to Katunda village, a distance of 400 versts, the journey must be done by free horses. Horses are generally easy to procure. Select as light a drosky or sledge as possible, as there are swamps to cross. It is also possible to travel by stages, changing vehicles at each stage. Beyond Katunda the travelling will have to be done on horseback. The journey from Bysk to Katunda takes about five days. The nearest route to Belukha by the north approach is along the valley of the Akkem, three days' journey from Katunda. It is also possible to reach the source of the Katun river from the south, but this takes about five days.

"I can recommend a hunter, one Innokenti Matai, at Katunda, and another, the Kalmuck, Sollinka, who lives in the valley of Kochourli, 12 versts from Katunda. One rouble per day is fair pay for your man, but he will also require 50 kopecks per day, free of food, for riding or driving horses.

"English saddles are quite useless, you will require cavalry or Altai saddles, and these you can buy in the Altai, or from the merchant Oshlikoff, at Nishni Ouemon, a village 17 versts this side of Katunda. Rusks can be bought from the Kalmucks—the hunters will be able to make the necessary arrangements. Tinned foods must be brought with you, also sugar, tea and coffee. Do not forget to take a kettle, teapot, spoons, knives and all English accessories for climbing on ice, if Mr Turner intends to do this. Three weeks is too short a time in which to do the Belukha, especially so early in the spring. The end of March and the beginning of April I hold to be a very bad time of the year, as there are still large quantities of snow everywhere, and I doubt whether it will be possible to get further than Katunda, except on snow shoes, and even this is by no means easy in the mountains and will be slow work. The best time for visiting the Altai is in June or July. From Katunda, however, it would be possible to climb up the Saptam or Kyzyl mountains and obtain a view of Belukha in the distance—about 40 miles away. To get to Belukha itself in April will be very difficult, and at this time of the year it would be necessary to travel partly by sledge even to reach Katunda."

This letter proved my best guide.

I bustled about London for a fortnight, collecting information, procuring nine letters of introduction and my all-important passport, buying a fur coat, warm clothing and other articles. These arrangements completed, I embarked at Millwall Docks on the 5th of March.

In the North Sea we passed a number of fishing smacks and were prompted to moralise feelingly on the rough and hazardous life of the fisherman. We did not slacken speed until the time came for us to take on board the German pilot, whose business it was to guide us up the Elbe and into the Kiel Canal, and there to hand us over to the canal pilot. The journey through the canal occupied eight hours. A little way through we made fast to allow a German man-of-war to pass; the sailors on board were drilling. A peep through the porthole as the vessel left the canal was rewarded by the sight of the Emperor William's statue looking towards Russia across the Baltic Sea. The water of the Baltic appeared to me to be much darker than that of the North Sea. The revolving light-ship on the reefs served to remind one that the treacherous Baltic has the worst character for shipwrecks of any sea in the world. There was a fair amount of traffic, the captain calling my attention to the only ten-mast ship I have ever seen. A small bird, not unlike a duck in appearance, flies about in flocks; it is, however, too strongly flavoured with fish to be palatable. Forging our way through the broken ice near Riga, we passed a fort in which the soldiers were singing the Russian National Anthem as they marched. The Russian Customs officials have a reputation for being unmercifully strict, and I was, naturally, rather anxious as to what my experience of their treatment would be. The Customs boat came alongside and several officers took charge of the luggage—and of refreshments, the latter being, apparently, an indispensable part of the programme. Our passports were handed by the captain to the Chief Customs Officer. The latter carefully scrutinised each passenger and, on our arrival at Riga, handed our papers back to us. My bags were then opened and everything pulled out. Besides my personal luggage I had an Alpine outfit, including a tent, an assortment of tinned foodstuffs, an aneroid barometer, a prismatic compass, a Zeiss binocular, a photographic camera, 30 spools of films, a revolver, 200 cartridges and other things necessary for my expedition. I explained to the officer in bad Russian that I was bound on a mountaineering expedition and he at once ordered my things to be put back. In this manner my first impression of Russian officialdom left nothing to be desired. Driving to the Hotel de Rome I had a good view of part of the town. Many of the buildings are very old and include a castle built by the Swedish kings—whose domains once included Riga—some 700 years ago. The remaining buildings are more modern and of rather handsome architecture. They include a huge cold storage warehouse large enough to store 8600 tons of butter. The population of Riga (300,000) consists of Russians, Germans and Letts.

A glance at the thermometer outside the hotel windows helps one to bear the excessive heat registered by the ones inside. Thermometers are to be seen everywhere—both inside and outside almost every window. In summer the climate is sufficiently warm, but in winter the thermometer sometimes registers 63° Fahr. below zero. It frequently happens that a hard spell of frost during the night will imprison a merchant ship in the harbour, and then the services of the ice-breaker are required to open a passage to the Baltic. Shipping is on the increase and steamers sail from Riga to most parts of Europe. The people of Riga take life easily, as, in fact, they do in nearly all parts of the Empire. It may be that the frequent saints' days and holidays have something to do with this. It was a holiday when, two days after my arrival in Riga, I took train for the capital through Livonia. The train progressed at the leisurely rate of about 12 or 14 miles an hour, causing me to speculate whether either the driver or the engine had been affected by the holiday. Foot-passengers crossed and re-crossed the line, contemptuously indifferent to the approaching train, as though it were a country road.

We stopped at Yuryeff, formerly Dorpat, a fine agricultural centre with one or two going agricultural concerns. The province is partly German and the town still contains the once so famous university. Nearing St Petersburg we passed one of the Czar's palaces, that of Peterhof, which looked very pretty from the railway line. The Znamensk farm near Peterhof is noted for enormous numbers of pheasants in a semi-wild state, which belong to the Czar.

We arrived at St Petersburg early in the morning. An isvostchik, in the quaint, old-fashioned garb of his class, shouted and whipped his horses into a break-neck pace, while the small wheels of the drosky raced over the round stones with which the broad streets of the capital are paved. I held on to my luggage, though with difficulty, while the driver tried to make a fresh bargain with me. Failing, he drove me to two wrong hotels and wasted considerable time. I tried to stop him by poking him in the back with my umbrella, but he only replied, "seychas," which means "immediately," and continued his wild career. Finally, he landed me at my hotel, where I took good care to pay him his exact fare, making a mental comparison between him and the average London cabby, which was very much in favour of the latter.

The porter and manager of the Hotel d'Europe both

PALACE OF THE CZAR, PETERHOF.

speak English. I had many interesting conversations with the latter, who is a Swiss. His face shone when I related incidents of my climbs in his native Alps. He introduced me to a Frenchman, an African explorer, who told me that he was the first to discover the African pigmies. He agreed to spend a night with me and relate his adventures, but the Czar gave him an audience that day, so that I was disappointed.

The Nevsky Prospect is the fashionable thoroughfare of St Petersburg. One is struck by the German character of the handsome, well-stocked shops. The street itself is véry broad and constitutes the main thoroughfare of this great city ; but it contains no feature to denote that it is Russian. St Isaac's Cathedral, an imposing structure not far from the end of the Nevsky Prospect, deserves a visit. Its four lofty porticoes are supported by magnificent granite monoliths from Finland. These monoliths are 112 feet in height. The church is surmounted by a cupola-shaped dome of brightly-burnished gold. The inside is of Italian and French marble, and is luxuriously decorated. The golden screen, called the " ikonostas," which separates the inner sanctuary from the body of the church, is beautifully decorated with pillars of malachite and *lapis lazuli*. Several of the pictures are skilfully worked in mosaic. Gold and precious stones abound, one ikon in particular having two large diamonds in place of eyes. Russian churches have, usually, no seats, and the singing is unaccompanied by instrumental music. Candles, generally of wax, are used—gas and electricity are uncanonical. Leaving the church I turned to photograph it, and included a group of students in the picture. They were quite willing, and all raised their uniform caps and moved on as soon as the operation was completed.

Hailing a drosky I drove along the broad thoroughfare and across one of the many bridges that span the Neva to Prince Khilkoff's offices. The Neva is lined on either side by granite embankments. The granite comes from Finland. It is composed of felspar, mica and quartz, differing only in one constituent from that of Egypt, which is closer grained. Two sphinxes from Thebes have been erected in front of the Academy of Arts on the Vassili Island and serve admirably for purposes of comparison. The supports of the Nicolai Bridge, the oldest stone bridge across the Neva, are of grey granite obtained from the small islet of Serdobol in Lake Ladoga. The caryatides which support the portico of the historic Hermitage founded by Catherine the Great and now the repository of priceless art treasures, are of the same material. These caryatides are magnificent in proportions and execution, and highly polished. It is marvellous how they have withstood the winter cold, which has transformed the numerous statues in the Summer Garden, for instance, into an assemblage of melancholy cripples in all stages of disfigurement.

I was received by the officials at Prince Khilkoff's offices with marked courtesy, and the desired letter of

GROUP OF STUDENTS OUTSIDE ST ISAAC'S CATHEDRAL, ST PETERSBURG.

introduction to the authorities in Siberia was duly forwarded to my hotel.

I afterwards took a long drive past the historic fortress of St Peter and St Paul. Here lie interred the remains of the Czars and Czaritsas of Russia from Peter the Great to the father of his present Majesty. The fortress also contains the mint and serves as a prison for political offenders.

The view along the embankment is most attractive. It is lined with palaces, stately mansions and Government buildings, the continuity being broken here and there by spacious squares and parks. The ice is railed off in places for skating. Electric trams run across the ice, and here and there men were at work removing huge blocks for the ice-cellars of the inhabitants. These blocks are usually six to eight cubic feet in size.

My business being further afield I was not able to spend very much time in this fascinating capital, which the inhabitants affectionately term the northern Palmyra.

A few business calls completed my visit, and having been joined by an English friend bound, like myself, for Siberia, I took a drosky and set out for the railway station. The train accommodation was excellent, but although we offered to make it worth the "conductor's" while to let us have a compartment to ourselves, our blandishments proved all unavailing. The north of Russia is rich in forests, and as we looked through the windows of the carriage they presented a noble sight. The journey, which took us through forests and over lovely frost-bound country, occupied about thirteen hours.

We arrived in Moscow at 9 a.m., having left St Petersburg at 8 p.m. the previous evening. The 400 miles have been done in a little over thirty miles an hour by the express which forms the through connection with the Siberian express train, leaving Moscow for Siberia the same afternoon at 2.30. We decided to take that train, so we made the best of the few hours we had to spend in Moscow by visiting the British Consul and doing some necessary shopping.

Reminiscences of what I had heard and read of this ancient capital crowded through my mind as we drove through the narrow, old-fashioned streets: Napoleon's disastrous march and the heroic burning of the city, and the still earlier destruction of the "city of white stones" by the Moguls under Batou in the thirteenth century. I determined to pay the town a second visit on my return journey and spend a few days there.

The town impressed me as a compact good Russian centre—the Manchester of Russia. The narrow streets made it easy to get about, and were a great contrast to those of St Petersburg, but the round stones with which they are paved are quite as hard, and their effect on the anatomy of the uninitiated quite as discomposing. The round stones serve, no doubt, to prevent snow-slides, by

THE SIBERIAN RAILWAY STATION, MOSCOW.

enabling the deep layers to obtain a firm grip of the roads. The weather was colder than at St Petersburg, although the latter is farther north.

Accompanied by an English friend who spoke Russian like a native, it was unlikely that I should experience any difficulty in finding the British Consul, yet, with the assistance of a particularly dull driver, we managed for a time to get hopelessly lost, so that after our interview we had little time to spare, but drove straight to the railway station. This is a particularly handsome building. The winter snow was being removed from its wide approach. It looks what it is—a busy terminus, with numbers of droskies waiting outside for fares, and an army of stalwart porters, wearing badges and dressed in blue shirts tied round the waist, hovering about like vultures on the lookout for passengers with luggage. Entering the huge doors we found ourselves in a spacious hall with the interpreter's offices on one side, the booking-office on the other, and the offices of the station-master and his staff further along.

When booking for Siberia it is well to remember that the greater the distance you go at one booking the cheaper is the mileage charged. Passengers are at liberty to break the journey, but the ticket only allows a few days over the time which the train takes to go the whole distance, and any miscalculation renders the ticket void. It is therefore advisable to distribute the visits to towns on the way by taking half of them going out and the other half coming back. In addition to the extra charge for travelling by the express train — which runs four times a week in summer and three times in winter— travellers to Siberia require a " place " ticket, which reserves the berth, according to the number on the door of the compartment, and is valid to the first town where the journey is broken.

The cheapest route, first class, is : London to St Petersburg in summer, or Windau in winter, by the Lassman line of steamers, or by those of Helmsing & Grimm to Riga, which costs about £10—return. Hence, by rail to Moscow direct and over the Siberian line by the express, which copies the International Wagons-Lits Company's trains, which are slightly dearer. German and sometimes French is spoken by the guards or " conductors," and occasionally even English.

Having taken our tickets, we passed into a second large hall to take lunch. Everyone seemed to have plenty of time on his hands. There was nothing to resemble the

feverish rush noticeable at our big English railway
stations. It was more like the landing-stage of one of
the great liners sailing to South Africa. The passengers
had been there for hours, while a number of emigrants
might well have been waiting for a day or two, seated or
reclining on easy couches, their goods and chattels piled
around them on the floor. Nobody hurried, and it looked
for all the world like a holiday. After lunch we made for
the train, which was drawn up alongside the station, but
not under a roof as in our English stations. The smoke
from the engine could rise into space without blackening
the windows or clouding the whole station. Iron roofs,
a little higher than the train, sheltered the platform.
The result was that the platform was airy and clean,
and the station buildings and halls in keeping · with
them.

We secured a first-class compartment with two berths,
our luggage being easily contained by the racks, which
hold fully five times as much as those in English railway
carriages. One advantage of travelling first is that one's
luggage is not excessed, although it may exceed the legal
weight by as much as half a hundredweight. In a
second-class carriage—such, at least, was the experience
of one of my friends—the luggage would have been
excessed. We found an Irish friend on the platform who
was endeavouring, in very eloquent Irish, to convince the
station-master, who only spoke Russian, that his tickets
were in perfect order. My companion went to his assistance, when it was discovered that the Irishman had
forgotten to provide himself with a "place" ticket. As
the bell had already sounded once he was permitted to
take his seat, the officials agreeing to assess him on the
train. The bell sounded twice, and an immediate change
took place in the expressions of those saying "Good-bye."
There were merchants, emigrants, officers of the Army
and Government officials, all bound for the Far East.
Everyone seemed to feel that Siberia is a long way off,

and the country so vast that people proceeding thither are taking no inconsiderable step. I am not sure whether the passengers looked upon the journey with anything like apprehension; I. rather think the feeling was similar to that which an Englishman might experience when leaving his native country for South Africa or Australia. One couple—evidently man and wife—embraced each other with an expression bordering on agony on their faces; others, who were bidding farewell to friends or relatives, dragged themselves away with sad faces and moistened eyes as the whistle blew and, all on board, the train started slowly on its long journey. Having no friends of our own to bid us a tearful farewell, we were merely spectators. I admit, however, that I felt rather sad myself as I stood at the window and watched the sorrowful faces on the platform growing farther and farther away as we left the station behind us. After glancing at the glittering domes and spires of Moscow's many churches disappearing in the distance, I sat down and gave myself up to dreams of what the journey had in store for me. A beautiful sunset ripened my thoughts and gave tone to the cold steppes. We passed by long, straggling villages and occasional patches of forest land —the rest was ice and snow, and again ice and snow. The signalmen, armed with green and red flags, and stationed every two-thirds of a mile, seemed a long chain of humanity stretched across this lonely country to relieve it of its cold lifelessness. There are 9000 of these men stationed along the entire route from Moscow to the Eastern Ocean. What a post in the Siberian winter! Standing at the back of the train the signalman will be seen to cross into the middle of the line as soon as the train has passed him, and stand there until it passes the next verstman.* He then returns to his cabin (numbered with the distance from Moscow in versts), where, if he is married, his wife, and perhaps a baby,

* One Russian verst is equal to 0·66 mile.

await him. These men are usually exiles. The lonely
verstman was often in my thoughts.

We made our way to the dining-car for dinner and
were surprised at the luxurious equipment of this compartment, with its easy chairs and lounges upholstered in
Russian leather. A piano at one end and a library containing many books in English and other languages at the
other add to the comforts of the journey. The dinner
was equal to that provided by a good English commercial
hotel and the charges were very moderate.

After dinner everyone became very sociable. Parties
were made up at cards and dominoes. Some played
chess; one of the passengers possessed a phonograph, and
a concert or two helped to pass the evening very
pleasantly. On retiring to our compartment we pressed
an electric button marked "attendant" and asked for our
beds. The attendant raises the back of the seat, opens it
out and presses certain electric buttons; short steel
supports spring out of the side upon which the bed rests.
Having spread the clean linen he announces that the bed
is ready, and with a polite "Good-night" leaves us to
decide who shall take the top bunk. Before retiring to
bed I went to the back of the train and stood for some
time looking across the silent steppes.

The train threaded its way through the darkness with
huge lanterns on the engine, and I noticed that the verst-
men had lanterns showing green. The stars were unusually large and brilliant, the pale moonlight bathing the
steppes in a light that made them appear almost unreal.
I returned to our compartment feeling very well satisfied
with my first day on the steppes.

By turning over the little tables in this compartment,
the legs of which are made like a step-ladder, it is convenient to climb to the top bunk, The electric lamp can
be taken off the table and fixed in a clip just above the
top bunk, in a convenient place to enable the occupant, if
so inclined, to read before going to sleep.

When we awoke next morning it was to find no change in the landscape of the previous evening.

Shaving was easy owing to the smooth running of the train, but there was very little water in the two lavatories at each end of the carriage, and, all the passengers seeming to wash at once, we wasted half an hour. At an early hour we stopped for a few minutes at Visokovo. The small station was almost buried in the snow and the trees were thick with hoar frost. The effect was very striking.

We crossed the Volga by the Alexander Bridge—seven-eighths of a mile in length. The Samara-Zlatoust railway commences at Batraki on the right bank of the Volga, and the bridge is about five and a half miles further. At eleven o'clock we reached Samara, 744 miles beyond Moscow and very conveniently situated in a bend of the River Volga. The Volga is frozen over four months in the year, which is about two months less than the rivers of Central Siberia.

The country about Samara appeared very fertile and the vegetation rich. It is not only an important agricultural centre, but is also one of the principal grain, cattle and tallow markets in the Empire. Between Samara and Ufa the country reminded me somewhat of the south of Ireland. Ufa is reached after crossing a bridge over the Belaya river, nearly half a mile across. It is a pretty little town with a population of about 52,000, and is situated on the right bank of the river. It is well provided with religious and educational establishments. Ufa is the capital of the Government of the same name, which is two-thirds the size of Great Britain, and is one of the most fertile of the central Volga Governments and rich in forest land. Mining is the principal local industry as it is situated within easy distance of the Ural range of mountains and on a river which flows into the Volga and therefore serves as a convenient means of traffic. The town is also a forwarding station for grain cargoes, helping to swell the ever-flowing transports down the Volga.

B

Between Ufa and Zlatoust we passed through the chief centre of the iron and steel industry of the Empire. Zlatoust is the Russian Sheffield, and the cutlery runs that of Sheffield very closely in point of quality. I bought a set of chased knives, the workmanship of which was as skilful as it is possible to find anywhere else in

UFA, 1000 MILES BEYOND MOSCOW.

the world. Three thousand men are employed in this industry.

After leaving the pretty town behind us we commenced to ascend the Ural. The town is visible nearly two miles from the station. The prospect of seeing the Ural Mountains appeared to elate the passengers as much as if the spectacle they were about to behold was as sublime as that of the Swiss Alps. In point of fact, however, the scenery is not unlike that of the Derbyshire Peak district. After several curves we reached the station at the summit, called Urzhumka, remote from all habitation, where the

Ural ridge opens into a cavity among the wide and lofty
rocks of the principal chain. A stone monument bearing
an inscription marks the boundary line between Europe
and Siberia. Here the engine shuts off steam and the
train rushes down the sides of the mountains at the rate
of from forty to forty-five miles an hour by its own weight,
entering.Asia by a zig-zag route. The Orenburg Govern-

MONUMENT MARKING THE BOUNDARY BETWEEN EUROPE AND ASIA.

ment, in which we now found ourselves, is larger
than the British Isles, and is situated partly in Europe and
partly in Asia. While the western slopes of the Ural
range are rich in iron ore, those on the east are noted for
their gold-fields. The total quantity of gold procured
from the Urals is over 9 tons per annum. Of this
quantity 40 per cent., or 10 per cent. of the total production of the Empire, is found in this one Government.
Several varieties of precious stones are also found in this
region, which is hilly and very fertile.

It was not long before we emerged once again into the
steppe land, this time in the Cheliabinsk district, which
is noted for its numerous lakes. The station at Cheliabinsk is about 3 miles from the town itself, which has a
population of about 19,000. The town was founded in
1658 and has been the scene of a rising of the natives.
For some time it has been an important *étape*, or station
for convicts and emigrants, the emigrant station being
situated just outside the town and containing accommodation for from 1500 to 2000 persons. Over 1,000,000
emigrants, or one-eighth of the total population of Siberia,
have passed through this centre during the last five years.
There is an important branch line from Cheliabinsk to
Ekaterinburg.

Passing through the forest regions, we practically
leave the iron industry behind us and enter the agricultural and cattle-breeding districts, while 133 miles
east of Cheliabinsk we cross the administrative frontier of
Siberia and enter the Government of Tobolsk. We are
now speeding over a vast plain, the beginning of Siberia
proper. There is no mistaking it; the country, as far as
one can see, is as flat as a billiard-table—an ideal country
for a wolf-hunt. It contains about 1600 lakes of various
sizes and is very swampy, owing to its uniform flatness.
In the extreme north the swamps merge into the frozen
tundras. The lakes and swamps, many of which are bitter,
exhibit a rather strange peculiarity in that they frequently
dry up altogether in a most inexplicable manner and
again fill with water and fish after a lapse of many
years. As a result of this curious phenomenon many
cultivated spots and fertile meadows periodically lose
their fertility, to recover it after a more or less considerable lapse of time.

The climate is very severe and the mean temperature
considerably below that of places situated in the same
degrees of latitude in European Russia. The winters are
colder and the extremes of temperature more pronounced

than in the countries lying to the west of the Urals. The vegetation is different, birches being very much in evidence, with a percentage of aspen and willows in damp places. In the southern regions of the Government forest fires are of frequent occurrence, sometimes destroying the woods over an area of many hundreds of square miles. Many parts which were once thickly wooded are now quite denuded of trees.

The train runs with so little vibration that it is at times possible to forget that one is moving at all. It is possible to write at ease and to walk the corridors without being shaken from one side to the other. Even shaving is a comparatively easy operation. This cannot be said of the 60-miles-an-hour rate of progression by train in Europe and America; in fact, I believe it is quite possible to travel 2000 miles on the Siberian line and experience as little fatigue as during a run from London to Manchester and back.

One of the most striking features of this wonderful country is its immensity. The Governments into which it is divided for purposes of administration must be imagined in terms of countries of the size of France and Germany. Thus, the Government of Tobolsk is four times the size of Germany, yet it is only a little more than one-half of Western Siberia, while Eastern Siberia is three times as large again as the Western portion and twelve times the size of Germany. The north-west portion of the Asiatic steppes is the smallest, being nearly twice as large as Germany, while the Amur-Littoral region, which includes the Trans-Baikal and the convict island of Sakhalin, is more than twice as large again.

The climatic conditions of the various parts of Siberia vary more than those of Europe. On the authority of a member of the Royal Geographical Society the coldest place in the world is in Central Siberia, where the temperature has been registered at 83° Fahr. below zero. This is 30 degrees colder than Mr Harry de Windt's coldest place in the world, north of Yakutsk. These figures are the result of observations made over a considerable period during the winter months by Mr Cattley, F.R.G.S. Contrary to the popular idea, it is one of the hottest countries in the world in the summer. Although it is a mistake to suppose that Siberia enjoys an abnormal monotony of cold weather, it is true that, latitude for latitude, it is the coldest country in the world, and its rivers and lakes freeze to the bottom from four to six months of the year, according to the locality. By a beneficent provision of Nature the coldest days are also the calmest, so that, the air being still and very dry, it is possible, if sufficiently warmly clothed, to feel quite comfortable. Many of my Siberian friends asserted that a cold, damp day in London was vastly more disagreeable than the frostiest weather in Siberia.

The enormous distances to which I have already referred exercised an extraordinary influence upon me, so that I would gaze for hours at a time across the steppes in a vain endeavour to grasp the magnitude of the country, just as, standing on the summit of the Matterhorn, I had failed to realise anything except my own insignificance.

If travellers in America think little of travelling long distances, the Siberians think even less, journeying for two and three weeks at a time for distances of 600 to 1000 miles, and over the roughest sledge roads.

The sparsity of the population is very noticeable—a thoroughfare like that of London Bridge being something undreamt of. The Siberian railway line, with its verstman stationed every two-thirds of a mile, may serve as a gauge of the density of the population. The country is quite forty times the size of Great Britain, yet it only contains one-sixth of the population, or somewhat less than that of Greater London. By way of comparison I may state that the mean density of the population of

the British Isles is 666, and that of the United States 50
for every two square miles, while that of Siberia is only
three.

We very often passed sledges going in the same direction as our train, and sometimes, when the horses took
fright at the engine, they maintained the same speed as
the train for considerable distances, frequently terminating
the race by overturning the sledges and scattering their
occupants.

Throughout the entire length of the line strong wooden
railings are placed across the steppes to prevent the
snowdrifts covering the permanent way. In the severe
winter the engine-drivers, the fuel used being wood,
have great difficulty in keeping the engines going. The
Siberian winter has added a new difficulty to those
peculiar to railway lines, in that the cold causes the rails to
swell and the joints to bulge up. The engineers have only
recently reported the phenomenon, although they have
known of it for some time ; they were afraid to appear pre-
sumptuous. In the meantime there can be little doubt
that it is dangerous to traffic.

We were glad when we arrived at Kourgan, 1532 miles
beyond Moscow. This is the nearest town of importance
to European Russia. It is situated on the River Tobol, and,
although the population is only 19,000, exercises an influence equal to that of towns five times its own size in
countries which are not so purely agricultural. It is an
important forwarding centre for a very large district situated north and south of the Siberian railway. Kourgan
boasts quite a number of substantial buildings, stone
churches and spacious educational establishments.

It is usually insisted that the Russian and Siberian
authorities are indifferent to the educational requirements
of the people. In the nine towns which I visited the total
number of schools and other educational institutions was
181, the population amounting to 221,464, and, as the
majority of these are immigrants and adults, the

children cannot exceed one half of this number. I am not acquainted with any other agricultural country where the educational facilities are greater; at the same time the necessity for education is not so obvious in an agricultural country like Russia as it is in great industrial and commercial centres like the great cities of England and America. The peasant is pretty much the same every-

CHURCH IN MAIN STREET, KOURGAN, FIREMAN'S WATCH TOWER IN THE DISTANCE.

where. I have travelled in other countries among farmers, on business of the same nature as that on which I visited Siberia, and have noticed that they are all remarkable for a disinclination to work any more than is absolutely necessary, and are, as a class, almost utterly devoid of education. The occasional exceptions prove the rule.

One of the most intelligent Siberians it was my good fortune to meet lived some 400 miles from the Siberian railway line, at Bysk, and had never seen the railway.

He spoke fairly good English, was an excellent musician, and in his dress and general demeanour might have passed for an average Briton. There are, of course, others like him, and, not infrequently, remarkably intelligent men are met with among the peasantry. It is not my desire to dispute the value of education to the agriculturist, my contention is, that education is less essential to success in that sphere of life than it is to the artisan or the commercial man, to those, in fact, who dwell in city and town. I have, however, met men of very little education in the ordinary sense of the word, who were excellent business men, and I have, again, met men whose education left nothing to be desired, yet who were devoid of the tact and commonsense which are so essential to a successful business, career. Whatever the sphere of activity, a good "school" education can never be more than a highly desirable adjunct to the natural qualifications which are essential to success. The Siberian peasant possesses many of these qualifications in a very marked degree. To sum up, moralisers on Siberia and its ways should remember that education does not create intelligence, but, at best, can only teach the individual how to use it to the best advantage.

A thoughtful study of the peasantry of the Kourgan district will persuade the student that, in agricultural matters at least, he has very little to learn from other countries. A proof of this may be found in the system of co-operative dairy-farming, which has been introduced with quite phenomenal success. The dairies are handled in a rational, business-like manner; the Government gives the peasantry every possible assistance, both financially and by providing expert teachers of agriculture, and the peasant shows his appreciation of his opportunities by purchasing the best American harvesting machinery, almost regardless of cost. It is astonishing how easily these people adopt new ideas and methods. Five years ago they were completely ignorant of the butter trade—to-day they

are skilled commercial men who always know where to
obtain the highest market prices, and who will run all over
the town before they consent to sell their produce, rather
than forfeit an extra 5 kopecks * per pood † (4d. per cwt.).
And what is true of the butter trade is true of every other
branch in which the peasantry have made a commencement. Every Saturday they assemble at the bazaar,

DROSKIES LOADED WITH BUTTER, NEAR KOURGAN. MERCHANT'S
WAREHOUSE.

bringing with them supplies of grain, meat, etc., etc. The
bazaar is an interesting trade centre, where the produce is
exhibited in rows of wooden huts, each class of goods
being kept separate. As in some of our own country
villages, the barter system is common, the seller taking
goods of equal value in exchange for the commodities he is
offering for sale. The annual Easter fair is a most inter-

* 1 rouble = 100 kopecks = about 2s. 1½d.
† 1 pood = 36·11 lbs. avoirdupois.

esting sight to witness. Peasants arrive from all parts of
the Empire, bringing with them every variety of goods,
including articles of gold and silver, silks, etc. Many
articles are sold at such low prices as a farthing or a half-
penny each. Gipsies are conspicuous among the traders,
the women telling fortunes, and much shouting and
clamouring is indulged in. The mixture of races at
Kourgan is at all times considerable, but during the Easter

A MIXTURE OF ELEVEN RACES—KOURGAN.

fair it is particularly varied. Russians, Siberians, Kirghiz,
Tartars, Cossacks, Caucasians, Gipsies—all are represented.
There are four annual fairs, and the aggregate turnover is
estimated at £500,000. In addition to the town itself the
railway station at Kourgan is in direct communication
with 132 settlements, with a population of 68,000. The
principal products are grain, tallow, flesh-meat, game
and butter. The latter article has attained such importance that I propose to deal with it exhaustively in the
following chapter, most of the facts having never yet seen
book form.

I was not unaware that the sensational journalism of my native land had grossly libelled and misrepresented this country. I was, therefore, not at all surprised to learn that my preconceived notions of wolves and their habits, of convicts, the "knout," exiles who fainted or fell dead while on the march, and many other blood-curdling characteristics of the country and its people were altogether erroneous. It is certain that if these occurrences are real they rarely, if ever, come under the notice of the people among whom they are supposed to occur. Business is carried on pretty much the same as everywhere else, and peace and serenity are the order of the day. It may be, though I don't insist upon it, that the journals in question refrained, from motives of humanity, from sending their best men to Siberia, and that the misleading reports one so frequently reads are the natural consequence. The result, however, is, that an inherently fair-minded people like that of Great Britain has been trained to misjudge and traduce a nation with whom it should, for the best of reasons, be on terms of amity and peace. I was told at Kourgan of an English journalist in search of "copy" who visited the place without knowing a single word of the language and without a solitary introduction to anyone who could have furnished him with information. It is not at all wonderful, under the circumstances, that the mental picture which the average Briton possesses of Siberia should be so exceedingly unprepossessing. Any falsehood is apparently good enough for the British public, and the more grotesque and sensational it is the more readily it is swallowed.

The influence of the railway, which is rapidly converting insignificant villages into prosperous towns, and the constant flow of immigrants, has done away with the terror of the exile system. At one time, exile to Siberia involved genuine hardship. The journey to Eastern Siberia, which now occupies a few months, then meant a weary, painful tramp which lasted nearly as many years. The Siberians repeatedly petitioned the Central Executive against the system, which they rightly regarded as a menace to their safety and well-being, and, in 1898, a Commission was appointed to inquire into the matter, a tour of inspection was organised, and all the prisons and exile colonies visited, even to the remote island of Sakhalin. As a result of the labours of the Commission, a law was promulgated, which came into force in 1900, abolishing banishment for criminal offences. Henceforth transportation to Siberia will be confined to political and religious offenders, and to vagrants whose identity the police is unable to establish. The average annual number of prisoners transported under these three heads is about 400. Criminals of other categories will be imprisoned instead of being transported. The cost of this reform to the Government will amount to about £85,000 per annum.

CHAPTER II

THE internal development of Siberia will have to be
enormous before the new railway can be made a success
from a financial point of view, as the cost of construction
amounted to more than £78,000,000, while the annual
expenditure on the working of the line is nearly
£5,000,000. To make the line pay it would have to carry
about 10,000,000 tons of goods per annum at the present
rates, or three times as much as was conveyed last year
and the year before.

The value of the line, however, cannot be estimated by
the direct results, as there are numbers of indirect ways in
which this gigantic undertaking confers benefits on the
country and the people. Grain is the principal article on
the list of goods transported. In consequence of bad
harvests the quantity of grain conveyed over the line
during the last four years only averaged about 350,000
tons. This is grown in the western regions, in the
neighbourhood of the section between Cheliabinsk and
Petropavlovsk, and principally in the districts of Ishim and
Kourgan of the Government of Tobolsk. Barley and rye
are grown in the central parts of the same Government,

and oats, which are of very fine quality, in the vicinity of
the railway. The Governments of Tobolsk and Tomsk
yield about 40 per cent. of the annual total of crops.
Beside the Siberian route, grain is transported by the
Perm-Kotlas railway to Archangel, and thence abroad ;
about 25,000 tons being exported in this manner every year.

One of the most striking direct results of the opening of

CASKS OF BUTTER (MISCHKINO STATION) WAITING FOR
REFRIGERATOR WAGGONS.

the western section of the railway has been the exceptionally rapid progress made in the production and exportation
of Siberian butter.   Prior to 1893 no butter whatever was
either produced or exported.   The first person in Western
Siberia to engage in the manufacture of butter in accordance with European methods was an Englishwoman
married to a Russian, whose dairy farm at Chernaya
Rechka, in the district of Tiumen, is to this day a well-
known model of its kind. In 1896 this was the only

dairy in Siberia. In 1893 a Russian, near Kourgan, opened the first dairy which produced butter for export abroad, but the progress made during the first four years was painfully slow. The manufacture of butter was then taken over by the Government, which granted the dairy farmers a substantial initial subsidy, to which a further grant of £200,000 was added in 1903, for the purpose of assisting the formation of co-operative dairies, by which means it was made possible to produce butter of better and more uniform quality. At present the population is almost entirely engaged in agricultural pursuits, the ranks of the workers being constantly recruited by immigrants, who are drawn almost exclusively from the peasant class. The quantity of butter exported to-day is about double that of wheat, and, from the point of view of international trade, the dairy industry may well be said to hold the first place.

In view of the foregoing it will be sufficiently obvious that the construction of the Great Siberian railway had for its object the welfare of the Russian nation at large, and that the development of Siberia is the contemplated and necessary result. The value of the line from a military standpoint is a matter of altogether secondary importance, although real enough in itself. We may point to a parallel in the case of the control by Great Britain of the Suez Canal, a route which, however important it may be in time of war, has proved of enormous value for purposes of peaceful intercourse and trade.

The part which the railway plays in assisting emigrants from European Russia to Siberia has already been referred to. The Government has promulgated a series of laws exceedingly favourable to immigration. Land surveyors and qualified agents have been appointed, whose duties consist in assisting the local authorities to distribute the immigrants throughout the country, care being taken to apportion to each immigrant unit an allotment as similar as possible in quality and kind to that which he has left behind him in European Russia, each male immigrant to Siberia being allowed 40½ acres of land in perpetuity, and free of all taxes for the first three years of tenure. On the expiration of this period, however, a nominal tax is imposed. Emigrants to Siberia are, further, exempt from the obligation to serve in the Army during the first three years of settlement—no trifling advantage in a country where conscription is strictly enforced.

The Government has already spent some £72,000 in aiding emigrants, by granting them cheap railway fares, cheap food and medical assistance, and by distributing them on the land from the thirty emigrant stations, of which the most important is that of Cheliabinsk. The quantity of land apportioned out in this manner between 1885 and 1899 exceeded 19,000,000 acres.

In 1901, 55,233 emigrants returned to European Russia, of whom 18,019 were pioneer emigrants sent by groups of intending settlers. It would, however, be premature to assume from these figures that immigration is on the decline, as the years 1901 to 1903 were years of bad harvests, when relief was required and obtained from European Russia, and the temporary decrease in the number of emigrants to Siberia must be attributed to that fact. The development of the butter industry, however, will not fail to add to the general material well-being of the Siberian peasant, who, at present, is practically financed and trained by the Government.

A professor of agriculture is appointed by the central authorities, whose duty it is to make himself acquainted with the latest discoveries and improvements in the science and art of butter-making all over the world. He afterwards publishes the results of his researches in book form, and these are used as guides by the trained teachers —University men—at the Siberian dairy schools established at Kainsk, Omsk, Kourgan, Smernagorsk and Barnaul, important centres of the industry. An "agronom" (professor of dairy-farming) has the control of each dairy, and a peasant of average intelligence and industry, after three months' tuition at one of these practical dairy-schools, is qualified to undertake the management of a dairy, and is accordingly hired by an "artel" (co-operative group) of peasants, to convert their milk into butter.

While undergoing the prescribed course of training at the dairy-school farms, the peasants are instructed how to feed cattle scientifically on preserved fodder, a most important matter during the long Siberian winters. That the instruction thus imparted to them is of very high value is proved by the fact that during the last winter the best stall-fed Siberian butter was sold to the British public at the same price as the best Colonial, and was declared by experts to be scarcely inferior to it in quality. German experts—usually from the Baltic provinces—and skilled Danish butter-makers—every one of whom is required to be the holder of a Government diploma before he can qualify as a teacher—supplement the training received by the peasants at the schools by visiting the several dairies, giving practical demonstrations in butter-making and pointing out any errors that may come under their notice. Each of these instructors has ten creameries under his immediate supervision. The organised groups of peasants—"artels"—are encouraged in every way by the Government to form co-operative dairies on the system which has placed Denmark in the front rank of butter-producing countries, a position which she has held for the last twenty years. In point of quality alone Siberian butter has improved enormously during the last three years, so much so, indeed, that, in winter stall-fed butters, the best dairies can easily compete with those of our Colonies, while in a few more years they will run Danish very close all the year round. The uninterrupted production of butter, winter and summer, moreover, will give Siberia a decided advantage over our Colonies and Ireland, which can only supply butter during seven months

of the year. The quantities supplied have, already, reduced the price of butter to the British public by quite
3d. per lb. since the first appearance of the Siberian product on our market, and it is abundantly evident that,
within the next four or five years, a further reduction
is bound to take place, when the British working man
will be able to buy good, wholesome butter at 8d. per lb.
Money has already been lost in Siberian butter, owing
to the fierce competition of Danish and German firms, in
consequence of which the purchasing prices of the commodity were raised until no margin of profit was left to
anyone but the Siberian producer. It is probable, too, that
fortunes will be lost in consequence of the downward
tendency of the prices during the next four or five years,
unless, indeed, the present war has the effect of taking
away a large number of dairy hands and consequently
reducing the quantity of butter produced, or unless a
repetition of the German drought takes place. When I
returned from my expedition last year it was clear to me
that the imports of Siberian butter into Great Britain
would be much greater in 1904 than they had been the
year before and for the first time I gave the figures of
some of the previous years in a paper in which the
butter trade is interested ; but, owing to the war, the
demand upon the dairy hands interfered with the natural
increase and turned it into a decrease.

The following figures show the advance that has been
made in this new Siberian industry since the opening of
the railway :—

Year.				Number of Dairies.	Exports in Cwts.
1898	.	.	.	140	48,360
1899	.	.	.	334	86,730
1900	.	.	.	1107	354,670
1901	.	.	.	1800	599,720
1902	.	.	.	2035	685,500
1903	.	.	.	2500	695,488
1904	.	.	.	2630	681,857

The Barnaul and Altai regions, in particular, have increased their output enormously. In 1899, Obi Station, or Novo-Nikolaëvsk, which serve this district, only

REFRIGERATOR WAGGONS.

despatched six truck loads, containing 738 cwts., while, in 1902, the export amounted to 995 loads, or 161,000 cwts. Altogether, between three and three and a-half million sterling worth of butter is now exported annually from Siberia, which is more than double the value of the

total quantity of wheat exported in 1900, the year of the
last good harvest.

The following facts go to prove that there are good
grounds for my assumption that much larger quantities
of butter will be produced in Siberia in the immediate
future. In the first place, the industry provides the
peasant with an easy source of revenue through the sale
of milk to the dairies, which, in their turn, are able to do
good business by converting it into butter. Cattle-rearing
is general throughout Siberia, on account of the abundance of rich pasture land and cheap and plentiful fodder
for the winter months. Owing to the cost of transport
cattle fodder cannot, at least under existing conditions, be
profitably exported. For this reason it will continue to
be cheap within the country, and, by its cheapness, permit
the Siberian peasant to maintain his stock of cattle. In
the southern steppe districts individual families own,
on the average, five horses, three cows, and about a
dozen sheep each ; but in the butter-producing districts
the number of cows kept is considerably greater. At a
rough estimate the total number of cows owned in Siberia
at the present moment is about 25,000,000. The breed
of cattle presents no remarkable features. The animals
are of average size, dark brown in colour, and when I saw
them, towards the end of the winter season, appeared to
me to err on the side of leanness, showing much of the
bony part. The supply of butter naturally depends
on the quantity of milk that is available, which, in its
turn, depends on the number of cows and, to some extent
also, on the quality of the harvest. If the harvest is a
poor one fodder may be scarce and expensive, in which
case it may not pay the peasant to keep his cows. The
price of a cow varies from £2 to £3 in the beginning and
from £3 to £4 at the end of the winter months. At
these prices the animals are bought by butchers,
slaughtered, and the meat forwarded to Russian towns.
It is very lean and poor in quality and is sold very cheaply.

The development of the dairy industry has, as might be expected, resulted in a considerable increase in the number of cows. Thus, notwithstanding the recent famine, which lasted three years (1900 to 1902), the number of milch cows in Siberia was doubled. It can easily be conjectured how great the increase would be after a few years of rich harvests. The industry is, therefore, obviously bound to grow very rapidly, the more so as it is the only one which permanently benefits the peasant, for the grain harvests cannot always find a profitable market. The natural conditions of the country, moreover, are precisely the ones requisite to constitute Siberia the best country in the world for the production of the highest quality of butter. The soil is rich, black and loamy, and the climatic conditions such as to combine with the soil in the production of a very rich, succulent grass. The cattle eat this and drink little, so that the milk contains an exceptionally high percentage of fat. Cattle diseases are practically unknown, owing, probably, to the clear dry air and the purifying cold of the winter. The average age attained by a cow in Denmark is from seven to eight years; in Siberia the cows usually live to the age of ten years, the extra two years, no doubt, helping the cattle to increase in number. The meat is too lean to be exported in any considerable quantities, and of too poor quality to render its exportation a profitable undertaking. Owing to its exceptional richness, 19 lbs. of Siberian milk in winter, and 22 lbs. in summer, are sufficient for the manufacture of 1 lb. of butter, whereas in Denmark 28 lbs. of milk are required to produce the same quantity. This exceptional richness, moreover, renders the milk peculiarly suitable for the production of butter by means of the hand-separator. The owner of cows is able to make a good average profit on each animal, by selling its milk to a creamery. If he is not a landowner himself, he can hire grazing ground from the village council. The rent for such grazing ground

averages 7s. 6d. to 8s. 6d. per acre, per month.   If
he owns grazing land he pays a tax upon it amounting to
about 4d. per acre per annum.   During the famine the
monthly rent of grazing ground rose to about 17s. per
acre, and the price of a cow was then from 21s. to 32s.;
but after the famine, and during the good harvest of
1903, the rent was only 8s. 6d., while the price of a cow
advanced to £3 and £4.   The Siberian peasant can make
better butter in his dairy than a Dane settled in Siberia, a
fact which was confirmed to me by several Danes.   This
may probably be due to the circumstance that the Dane
is accustomed to machinery driven by steam and is not at
home with the hand-separator, while the reverse is true of
the peasant.   Whatever the reason, however, we have
here one of those combinations which, with very cheap
labour, is bound to work wonders in the prices of dairy
produce.

Cheap and abundant labour is one of the essentials of
the dairy industry, and it is one of the most important
factors in favour of the Siberian dairies that labour is
cheaper there than in any other butter-producing country
in the world, the labourer receiving about one-twelfth of
the wages paid for·the same class of work in Canada.
Official reports speak of £7, 8s. 9d. as the annual wage of
a good Siberian workman, while inferior labour is paid as
little as thirty roubles per annum (£3, 3s. 9d.).   This
annual wage is about equal to the sum earned by a
Canadian workman in one month.   The growth of the
dairy industry will, however, have the effect of raising
wages considerably above the standard mentioned above.
Thus, I was informed by a Danish expert, who had opened
dairies in Southern Siberia, that he paid one rouble
(2s. 1½d.) per day of twenty-one hours for dairy hands
in June, July and August, when the milk is most plentiful,
and half a rouble (1s. 0¾d.) per day of twelve hours
during the remaining nine months.   The exceptionally
cheap labour, which works out at about 7s. per week of

six days (seventy-two hours), will be a very important item in favour of the Siberian dairies, and will give them an immense advantage over those of other countries. As things are at present, the peasantry, according to their own modest notions, are prospering exceedingly, and, if we look into the matter a little more closely, we will see that they are, indeed, doing very well at the business—a sure guarantee of increase in the production. A cow earns from 8d. to 9d. per day by supplying one vedro * of milk, that being the average price. During the winter months the quantity is reduced to three-quarters of a vedro. This represents from 3s. 6d. to 5s. 3d. per week, or 14s. to 21s. per month. In times of famine it barely pays to keep cows, but in ordinary seasons, when food is plentiful, after deducting 7s. 6d. to 8s. 6d. per month for grazing, the peasant cattle-breeder is able to show a profit of from 6s. 6d. to 12s. 6d. per month on each cow.

There are, however, peasants who, for one reason or another, refuse to sell their milk or to turn it into butter. The owner of a farm not far from the station of Tagai was asked by a Danish friend why he did not sell the milk from his three hundred cows to the neighbouring dairy. He replied that his grandfather and his father had not sold milk before him and that he saw no reason why he should do so; he was sure the Lord would not like it. This is only one of a large number of similar cases and enables one to imagine how great the output will be when the peasantry are convinced that there is no wrong in selling their milk, but rather that it is to their advantage to do so.

It is only two years since the farmers of the Altai spoke of the separator as the " devil " and blamed it as the cause of the famine. It had so happened that the year in which the dairies were opened and separators introduced was also the first of the three years of famine. Towards the end of that time the peasants broke into the creameries,

* One vedro = 2·70 gallons.

and, having captured the separators, threw them into the nearest river or pond. Several of the Danish dairy-men were obliged to defend their creameries at the muzzle of the revolver. As is so often the case, a coincidence helped to convince the peasants of the justice of their accusations, for the year after the crusade against the separators the harvest showed a marked improvement. This is one of the factors that has militated against the otherwise inevitable large increase in the quantity of butter produced, another being the unfortunate three years' famine, which occurred at a time when peasant immigration was at its highest, viz., over 200,000 a year. The peasant will soon learn the commercial value of his milk and the advantages of the separator. Immigration will increase. Between 1893, the year in which the making of butter was first recognised in Siberia as a money-making industry, and 1901, the railway committee distributed 1,318,000 emigrants. In 1899 the annual figure had risen to 225,000, an average which will be exceeded as soon as the bad impression produced by the three years' famine has worn off. It is a matter of general knowledge that Russia's natural wealth lies waiting to be tapped in Siberia. With this knowledge to guide them the authorities are sparing no pains to induce the peasantry of European Russia to emigrate east, assisting them to establish co-operative dairies, in the proportion of one to each village, by advancing loans of about £300 at 4 per cent. for five years to those village councils who own a sufficient number of cows to guarantee the amount. Each peasant is, therefore, his own butter producer, and shares in the profits of the dairy in proportion to the quantity of milk he supplies.

There are over 250 of these co-operative dairies and they are largely on the increase. In course of time they will spread over the whole of Siberia, until every peasant will benefit by them and all who possess cattle will be butter producers and dairy owners. It is estimated that the village councils, the members of which are usually the largest cattle-owners, will be able to pay back the Government loan, with interest, in five years.

To facilitate this the Government should brand the name of the dairy on each cask, and appoint a sole agent for Great Britain, who should be qualified for the task of distributing the produce where it would be most appreciated. By this means the Russian producer will learn one of the secrets as to the methods by which such high prices are obtained for Danish butter on the European markets. He will also be able to put his produce before the public quickly and in good condition—a most important consideration. It would be advisable, further, to distribute the butter through the agency of an English representative well acquainted with the idiosyncrasies of the English market.

The impartial reader will perceive that the paternal Russian Government, at whose methods in our insular complacency we are so apt to smile, has already effected much for the peasantry, and will effect more. As a mere matter of fact it has done more for Siberia than our own enlightened Government has done for the sister island, with her glorious agricultural possibilities. The Irish were first instructed in the art of producing butter of uniform quality on the Danish principle about twelve years ago by Father Black, of Milford in the south of Ireland. Other priests of the Roman Catholic Church have lent their aid towards the creation of a dairy industry, and, during the last three or four years, their efforts have led the Irish farmer to recognise the value of the co-operative system of dairy-farming ; so much so, that several of our extensive English butter merchants have been compelled to sell their Irish creameries at considerable loss to the very farmers who had refused to supply them with milk and had thus prevented their working them at a profit. The priest is doing for Ireland what the British Government should have done long ago in order to prevent the wholesale emigration from the "distressful country."

The parrot-cry that "Russia is keeping the peasant down and not educating him" is absurd. Far from such being the case, Russia has wisely selected a practical and beneficial method of education and one admirably suited to the necessities of the case. She is gradually introducing the Siberian peasant to the means of obtaining a better livelihood and so achieving all and more than our Western methods have accomplished in the case, say, of the half-educated, intellectually-misdirected products of our Board School system.

These subsidised co-operative dairies manufacture an article of very uniform quality, while the quantity fluctuates between 15 and 30 cwts. per week, representing the amount of cream supplied by from five to ten skimming stations. The method of working is similar to that of the dairies of New Zealand, our leading colony for quality. The separator used is also similar in type to that used in New Zealand, the favourite pattern being the "Alfa Laval"; but the New Zealand creameries use a much more expensive apparatus, giving much larger results, the largest factories producing as much as 250 cwts. per week. The system of Pasteurising the milk, as applied in Denmark, has also been introduced in the Siberian co-operative dairies. Denmark will have to reckon with Siberia before long both as regards price and quality. The inevitable result of increased production of the Siberian dairies will be that other countries, not being able to make their dairies pay, will reduce their production, and, in time, like Germany of recent years, instead of exporting butter to Great Britain, will finish by importing large quantities from Siberia themselves. At present Denmark imports enormous quantities of the best Siberian butter and, by doing so, is enabled to export very largely of the produce of her own dairies, besides exporting the Siberian article both to Great Britain and Germany. The Copenhagen market has, in fact, received at times as much as 300 tons per week. The same is true of Sweden and Norway, which countries, by importing the Siberian article, are enabled to sell more of their own produce to Great Britain.

The bulk of the Siberian butter which reaches the London market is bought direct from the dairies, 1000 tons having been delivered in London in one week. What is more noteworthy, however, is the fact that during one week in winter between seven and eight thousand casks of Siberian winter stall-fed butter were placed upon the London market, an article which, strange as it may appear, our Irish dairies have not yet learnt to make. So much for the backward, ignorant peasant of Siberia.

At the present moment Canada is the most promising wheat-growing country in the world next to the U.S.A., and she will continue to hold a high position as a wheat-exporting country as long as the carriage on cereals from Western Siberia is too high to allow the Russian grower to compete in the Western markets ; but she is certain to drop out of the butter-making business and use her milk in the manufacture of cheese, unless, indeed, she is assisted by an occasional opportune drought like the one that occurred in Germany during the current year. New Zealand will be obliged to follow her example, more particularly in the case of the dairies producing the poorer kinds of butter, and the price of milk all over the world will be lowered in consequence, a state of affairs which cannot fail to benefit the Siberian peasant, who will thus, before long, be able to get as much out of his land as any other farmer in the world.

I have endeavoured to foreshadow as briefly as possible the probable future of the Siberian peasant. The State has, practically, taken him into partnership, with a view to realising the hopes that prompted the construction of the great railway. Last year the carriage on butter alone contributed £250,000 towards the expenses of the line, while the value of land situated in the vicinity of the railway has risen as much as 200 per cent. in some places and will rise higher still.

Peasants who establish creameries on their own initiative, and without the aid of the Government, generally hire a wooden hut at a rental of about £1 per month, which they furnish with an ordinary " Alfa Laval" plant costing anything from £5 to £27. A peasant is then engaged who has gone through the course of Government training described, and, with the help of a Government instructor, the separator is started, much to the astonishment and awe of the peasants. Notwithstanding cheap labour and inexpensive plant, however, failures are very far from being unknown, as the dairies cannot afford to pay more than 35 or 40 kopecks (8¾d. or 10d.) per vedro of milk, in order to realise a profit; competition may, therefore, easily kill a nursling venture of this kind. Before the advent of the cheap native dairy-man, Danish companies commencing operations in Siberia were accustomed to employ Danish managers and instructors at what were, proportionately, enormously high wages. The consequences were that the manager's salary usually ate up the whole of the profits. I know of two Danish firms and one Russian one, all of which were at first worked on this plan but were compelled to alter their methods in order to avoid insolvency. It is, moreover, a rather dangerous undertaking to put up a creamery unless the proprietor is guaranteed a sufficient number of cows to keep it going, as otherwise he will be entirely in the hands of the peasants from whom he purchases his milk. In this way the firm that is most likely to outlive the rest is the one that is backed up by a Government subsidy, usually the village council, who are also the owners of most of the cattle and can therefore be trusted to dispose of their milk to the best advantage.

Only a few years ago the whole of the Siberian butter trade was in the hands of Russian and Danish merchants, who had offices in all the leading butter centres; but during the last three years at least eleven large London importers have entered into direct business relations with the Siberian dairies, importing butter without any intermediaries. In consequence of a provision of the Russian law which prohibits foreign firms from conducting operations within the Empire unless at least one member of the firm is on the spot to take all responsibility,

KOURGAN BUTTER MERCHANTS.

the name of the British firm's local manager is used. This is generally a Dane who, from long residence in Siberia, possesses some knowledge of the language. Ignorance of the Russian language, in fact, has interfered with the possibility of many a good English manager being appointed to one of these butter-buying depôts, whereas British capital is every bit as truly invested in the country through Danish agents as that of Danish firms, while the British importer is actually buying more extensively. These facts go to show that our countrymen are not altogether so backward in realising the possibilities for trade with Siberia as some writers would have us believe. One of these gentlemen has gone so far as to say, that "The Dane rules a Butter Kingdom of 160,000 square miles, or an area about equal to that of Germany." This may have been true at one time, but it is ancient history now. It is British enterprise that rules the Siberian markets to-day, and it is, moreover, the British capitalist who has, during the last year or two, had the honour of losing the most money in the trade.

This is one of those truths which are stranger than fiction, and the cause of such a state of affairs is to be looked for in the insane competition of the purchasers, thanks to which, the peasant dairy-farmer has them entirely in his hands, and, notwithstanding his reputation for ignorance and stupidity—which should rather be taken to mean business tact and ability—is enabled to squeeze the highest prices out of them. As an illustration I may point to the fact that, as I write, there are 7000 casks of Siberian winter butter being delivered on the London market, 5000 of which were bought at prices running 4s. and 5s. per cwt. higher than this week's London market price. It must, however, be remembered that there are only about eleven firms engaged in this interesting and exciting pastime, and of them we can say, as we say of the Australian Cricketers, that they are an excellent eleven and play a splendid losing game. I do not wish it to be understood that all provision merchants act in the same way. There are "elevens" in the trade who can play a waiting game and come on the market at the eleventh hour with the air of men "who know," favouring the importer by picking out his best qualities, and smiling complacently as they pocket his sale-note at 4s. to 6s. below cost price. There is no standard of quality in this line of trade, and buyers are frequently able to persuade the importer (who is eager to cut out a competitor) that they have been offered equal butter at 2s. and sometimes 4s. below the price fixed by him. If the buyer is not a very good judge of butter, or is in the habit of forgetting the quality of the lot he has just inspected, and the importer is aware of the fact, he sticks to his price ; but, if it happens that the buyer is an adept in the gentle art of persuasion, though he, too, may have forgotten the taste of the quality he is talking about, the importer may be inveigled into accepting the price offered; the price gets known among his brother importers, the market is broken, and more money is lost than there is any real reason for. All of which goes to show that there are ups and downs in the butter trade as in all others.

Notwithstanding these drawbacks, however, the firms engaged in importing butter into this country, like a certain character in one of Dickens's novels, are profoundly confident that, sooner or later, something is bound to "turn up," to recoup them for their losses and to justify their courage and enterprise. In the meantime they have some consolation in the knowledge that, after all, "it is the quantity that pays," as one far-seeing member of the butter trade remarked some time ago.

In the matter of large imports the British merchant is an easy first. There is a gentleman who has realised a fortune in the provision trade and is now spending a large portion of it in the attempt to carry away the Cup from the American Yacht Club, a feat which it is to be hoped he may accomplish ere long. The Siberian butter trade appears to me to be a somewhat similar hobby to international yacht racing. Perhaps it had its origin in a humane feeling of pity for the ill-used and neglected Siberian peasant, who, having been exiled to Siberia, is now being persuaded to accept more for his butter than can be realised for it on the London market.

Some British merchants are in favour of what is known as the "consignment" method of doing business, which consists in the importer advancing from three-quarters to seven-eighths of the value of the goods—after careful inquiries as to the solvency and commercial standing of the shipper—and remitting the balance, if any, less commission and expenses, after the butter has been sold. This arrangement is usually made with merchants who buy from the peasants, and the amount of the advance varies from thirty-four to forty-two roubles per cask, according to the season of the year.

There is another method of doing business which is termed the "buying agent" arrangement, which consists in appointing agents to buy butter on the spot. The majority of these agents are good, trustworthy buyers; but I have heard of cases where the agent at the same time sold separators to the peasants, guaranteeing that with their aid the peasant would be able to produce butter of the highest quality, for which he undertook to pay the best prices. It would often happen that, in order to avoid any injury to the sale of his separators through the peasants talking to each other, he would continue to pay the full market price for very inferior butter, while the peasant, being fully alive to the strength of his position, never troubled himself to improve the quality of his product. This method of doing business is, however, declining very rapidly, and the buyer now rarely pays the highest market price for anything but the very best quality of butter. English importers must make certain that they engage the services of honest buyers, as otherwise the bribery and sharp practice which are possible, and which sometimes actually go on, between buyer and peasant, are quite extraordinary. A recital of them would fill a volume. It must be remembered that the majority of the merchants are foreigners and not Siberians, and that a fair percentage of them are honest and trustworthy. The Danes in Siberia are very reliable as a whole, and are, undoubtedly, the best buying agents, as they are usually experts in the trade.

When the Russian Government recognises the fact that British importers are willing to pay the peasant hand-

somely for his produce, it will be encouraged to promote
the still more rapid development of the industry.
£10,600 have recently been spent on a dairy school at
Omsk, and others are to be established at Tomsk and
Kourgan. The industry has now spread east of the Obi
river as far as Krasnoyarsk and Yenisei, and 800 miles
from the railway in a southerly direction in the Altai
district. In the latter the industry is still at a very primitive
stage, but the district is an ideal one for cattle-grazing
and is bound to have a great future as soon as ever the
means of transit are sufficiently improved to obviate
delays and admit of the produce being conveyed to the
distributing centres with a minimum risk of being spoiled
in transit. I have tasted the finest butter I ever saw in
the Altai, but, owing to the delay in conveying it to the
London market, its quality has deteriorated by as much
as 2d. per lb. This is a tremendous loss to the peasant,
and, indirectly, to the country. The projected railway
through Barnaul, the business centre of the Altai butter-
producing region, will be a splendid thing for that vast
country. It would also be well worth while going to the
cost of constructing light railways to convey the cream
from the skimming stations to the central creameries and
the projected railway line. The lack of speedy means of
transit and communication is the country's greatest
drawback, as the enormous advance made by the towns in
the neighbourhood of the great railway abundantly
proves.

Owing to the abundance and consequent cheapness of
all forms of fodder, horses are very cheap and plentiful,
the price of a farm horse being from £2 to £4. Every
farmer owns between five and seven horses, which, when
not employed on the farm, are taken long journeys with
sledge or drosky, being frequently away from home for
four or five days at a time in winter, conveying butter to
the various centres. The longest of these journeys are
from some parts of the Altai district to Bysk, 300 miles.

Long caravans, consisting frequently of as many as 100 sledges, led by one or two men, bring the butter 400 miles further to the Siberian line, being joined by still larger caravans half-way at Barnaul. The sight of these crawling caravans of butter in the endless steppes is unique. The road is only wide enough for sledges to advance in one direction, so that all traffic proceeding in the opposite direction is compelled to pull to one side into the deep snow to allow the endless procession to pass.

The Russian horse is fairly good as a racer. It is on record that, at one race meeting, a Kirghiz horse ran 20 versts (14 miles) at the rate of one verst (or two-thirds of a mile) in a minute and a half. We travelled behind one in the Altai district which drew our sledge 40 miles, trotting all the way and only resting for a brief half-hour. The horses are not very extravagantly fed, but the air is very bracing and invigorating. A Government publication dealing with Siberia states explicitly that the Siberian horse is not particular as to food.

So far as the railway is concerned it has been arranged that a weekly service will be run of from seven to nine butter trains, if necessary, each train to consist of thirty-five carriages. These trains will take from ten to twenty-one days to convey the butter to Moscow from the different Siberian centres. The rolling stock includes 1080 refrigerator waggons, with a carrying capacity of 15 tons each. These are painted white and are cooled by ice, which is taken from the rivers in winter and stored in suitable ice-houses situated at stated intervals along the line. From Moscow the butter is conveyed to Windau and Reval, which are ports of shipment all the year round, and also to Riga and St Petersburg during the summer. Two regular lines, of three steamers each, fitted with refrigerator plants and owned respectively by Messrs Lassman Brothers and Messrs Helmsing & Grimm, and which sail under the Russian flag, carry the butter to London. Messrs Helmsing & Grimm's boats sail twice a

week and Messrs Lassman Brothers' once a week. They
have reduced the freight from 27s. 6d. to 15s. per ton, or a
little higher in winter—so much for competition. The
freight on the 1000 miles' voyage from the Baltic Ports is
about half as much as is paid on butter brought from Ireland.
The total cost of conveying a hundredweight of butter
from Siberia to London is from 5s. 3d. to 6s. 7d. The proprietors of Hay's Wharf, Tooley Street, Southwark, have
spent thousands on the construction of a new landing-
stage and in dredging the Thames, and have shown the
old-fashioned, slow-moving port of London how to save
lighterage to the importer and reduce by about twenty
hours the time wasted in docking and loading barges.
The curious, by visiting the wharf during August, may
see lots of 15,000 casks of butter landed, which will be
sold by the importers for what it is—*i.e.*, Siberian butter—
frequently within three days after arrival.

The trade is already a large one. During the two
years which ended with the winter of 1903 Siberia
exported more than all our Colonies put together, and
the industry is as yet in its infancy. The quantity produced and exported annually is a little over 80,000,000 lbs.,
while the cows owned by the peasantry are capable
of producing more than fifteen times as much, or,
roughly, 1,200,000,000 lbs., which is as much as our
imports of butter and cheese from all our possessions.
It will not be many years before these vast quantities are
brought within the reach of the British working man, and
the effect will be felt by the butter importers of many
other countries. On the other hand, the slump in the
dairy trade of the whole world may be averted if, as is
not impossible, the enormous multitudes of the East should
add butter to the list of their articles of diet.

My reason for this detailed information about Siberia's
chief industry is that it is becoming as important as all
the Siberian industries put together.

CHAPTER III

KOURGAN—PETROPAVLOVSK—OMSK

In addition to being the pioneer butter-exporting town,
Kourgan possesses granaries for the storage of wheat, flour
mills, a distillery, a brewery, a sugar factory, a tallow
factory, a glass works and a starch factory. The railway
station, besides serving the town itself, forms the nucleus
of a region which includes 132 settlements with a population of 68,000. The vicinity is rich in game, which is
killed, and, together with meat, tallow and grain, is
dispatched direct to the seaports and markets of European
Russia. Fifteen thousand tons of oats and 16,000 of
barley, peas, wheat meal, rye meal and bran, together
with 1536 tons of hemp seed, linseed and other seeds used
in the manufacture of oil, were dispatched to the West from
this station during 1898.

An immigrant station has been established, from which
immigrants are drafted to the north-western portions of
the Akmolinsk territory.

I was not sorry when it came to my turn to emigrate
from the Kourgan hotel. The bedroom accommodation at

that establishment is extremely poor, and, in order to secure a good night's rest, a plentiful supply of insect powder is essential. The hotel is all on the ground floor and the greater part of the space is occupied by the billiard-tables and refreshment-bar, at which the merchant or peasant is supplied with "vodka "* or enabled to gamble away his savings during the long winter nights. The

EMIGRANTS' CHURCH, PETROPAVLOVSK.

result has been that the proprietor has succeeded in putting together a very respectable fortune.

On the way to the station the sledge we occupied raced with that of our friends. These small express sledges travel at a good speed and the drive through the keen dry air is pleasant and exhilarating. The thermometer registered 50 degrees below freezing point, Fahr., in March, but it frequently falls to 110 degrees in the winter

* Brandy, usually made from barley or rye. A cheaper kind is made from potatoes.

months. In the summer, however, it rises as high as 114 degrees. The early frosts in the autumn and the morning frosts in spring have a most disastrous effect on the crops. The temperature is often very low in September, but the coldest months are December, January and February.

The railway runs through flat, uninteresting land until it reaches Petropavlovsk, which is approached by a bridge over the Ishim. The town is situated on the right bank of the river and is about one and a half miles from the railway.

Leather tanning and tallow refining are the principal industries, the town being noted as the most important centre for the sale of hides and skins in Siberia. The animals are brought from China, Turkestan and Persia, as well as from other parts of Siberia, as many as three to four hundred thousand heads of cattle being brought to the town and slaughtered annually. The various branches of the industry give employment to some fifty different establishments, and the value of the products is estimated at about three millions per annum. Half a million worth of skins, chiefly of the goat, are shipped every year to America, other skins being also sent to England and Germany. A trade in flesh meat is anticipated with England and America, and it would certainly pay anyone who was disposed to examine its possibilities. An average of 2½ cwts. of meat is obtained from each cow.

The population of Petropavlovsk numbers about 26,000. The town is quite Asiatic in character. Caravan routes extend in a southerly direction into the very heart of Asia, chiefly along the identical river basins which, as is shown by ancient tombs and the ruins of towns dispersed along the road, were the highways along which the Asiatic hordes proceeded in their march to Europe in the days when history was young. Stone images, which the Russians call "babas," and which are found in considerable numbers in Central and New Asia, testify further to this line of migration. Beyond doubt, besides its glorious commercial possibilities, Siberia possesses a rich field for ethnographical and archæological research.

The earliest settlers from Russia were cut off from all intercourse with their European kindred for three whole centuries, during which time they intermarried freely with the aborigines. The result has been the creation of a hybrid race differing from the tall, well-knit Russian; these hybrids being of shorter stature and darker complexion. The nomads of Siberia have managed to retain their racial individuality, their numbers and habits having prevented their absorption by the immigrant race. The Siberian differs considerably, both in his mental and in his moral characteristics, from the peasant of European Russia. His moral standard is lower, polygamy is tolerated, and the benefits of Western civilisation are not usually either understood or appreciated. The Siberian, however, is much the more striking character. Having never known serfdom, he exhibits a fine sense of independence and considerably greater individuality of character than his brother of European Russia. If he could be induced to recognise the nobility of labour he would be able to effect wonders with the country.

Besides the hybrid population mentioned above, there is a small proportion of from 8 per cent. to 9 per cent. of exiles, or the descendants of exiles, and a very considerable contingent of immigrants from Europe, which, in course of time, is bound to outnumber all the others.

Criminals exiled to Siberia generally take to the roads, escaping in the spring and creeping back into the town prisons in winter. Householders are in the habit of leaving food and drink in the open bathhouses, which are usually situated in one corner of the yard, for convicts who may be prowling in the neighbourhood. This is not so much an act of charity as of policy, for it often secures the house, and perhaps the whole village, against the danger of being set on fire, the convict tramp frequently revenging himself for not finding food in the village by setting alight to conveniently-situated buildings. He usually journeys by night, sleeping in the forest during the day. These interesting worthies are so numerous in spring as to constitute a real danger to travellers. When I told a Siberian friend that I carried a revolver as a protection against wolves, I was promptly informed that I had much more reason to fear the human wolves I might encounter, and this I found was a general view of the case. About one-third of the criminal exiles escape all control. Armed with a stick, to which is attached a strong piece of cord or cat-gut, they will approach the unwary traveller from behind, throw the cord round his neck, and quietly strangle him by twisting the stick, to rob him at their leisure of whatever he may possess, or to secure his passport in order to make their escape from the country.

There being only one police-officer to every 10,000 of the population, sparsely distributed over immense areas, the authorities are practically powerless to suppress these outrages. If a convict is caught red-handed, therefore, he is very commonly shot out of hand. Like the beggars, the garrotting robbers usually travel in groups; crime is prevalent, murderers are to be met with in nearly every town and village, and robberies with violence and burglaries are of everyday occurrence. Shortly before I reached Omsk the office of a resident Dane had been visited by three burglars, who relieved him of the custody of some £10 worth of goods. He reported the matter to the police and was advised to shoot them if they should come again. Some time afterwards they did come again, and their Danish host showed his appreciation of their courtesy by shooting two of them and afterwards reporting to the police, who were rather pleased than otherwise to be rid of them. So long as a burglar or foot-pad is shot in front the authorities do not make much trouble, but if he is shot in the back an explanation becomes necessary, as it is assumed that if he had his back turned he must have been running away, and it is only allowable to shoot a robber in self-protection. On the other hand, horse-stealers are very often shot. The Danish and German residents are attacked so frequently that the very first advice they gave me was: "If you see a man approach you too closely in the dark shoot him; you can scarcely make a mistake." The above remarks apply to convicts who have been exiled for murder or other criminal offences. These are a source of endless trouble and anxiety and are totally undeserving of sympathy or pity.

The political exile is, however, a very different type of man. These unfortunates numbered 700,000 in seventy-five years, and included some of the most enlightened of the Tsar's subjects. Two-thirds of them, accompanied by their wives and families, settle peacefully in the country and supply the intelligence of the place. The development of Siberia is due in no small measure to the enlightened efforts of this section of the population. But in view of the fact that Russia's worst criminals, to the number of many hundreds of thousands, have been set loose in Siberia, it is surprising that crime is not more prevalent there than it is, and that business can be conducted as peacefully and methodically as in European Russia—the export trade reaching a figure somewhat in excess of £3,800,000. This is in dairy produce, principally butter, most of which comes direct to London. There is no robbery on the way to speak of, the occasional petty pilferings scarcely exceeding in value what daily takes place on our British railways.

As regards the place itself and the dread of being compelled to live there, Germans and Danes look upon Siberia as a kind of El Dorado, where money can be earned quickly and easily. The firm to which I belong frequently receives applications from young men in Denmark and Germany requesting to be sent to Siberia, while Germany, in particular, has furnished a number of individuals anxious to be introduced to the official who has the responsibility of appointing dairy instructors, a circumstance

which is owing to the fact that the dairy industry in
Germany is being slowly crushed by that of Siberia.

The inhabitants are very well to live with, and the
conditions of life quite endurable. A Russian and several
Danes of my acquaintance, at present living in London,
have repeatedly told me that they would rather live in
Siberia than in London; and a Siberian merchant, residing
about 300 miles from the Siberian railway, in the course
of a conversation on a foggy day in London, declared that
he would not live in London for the equivalent of £1000
a year. This man had come over from Siberia to arrange
the sale of a gold mine and to settle the preliminaries for
the purchase of 7500 tons of Siberian butter during the
ensuing year for a prominent London firm. It is now becoming quite common for Siberian merchants to visit
London, so that, as the people of Siberia are constantly
coming into closer contact with this country, it will be
impossible shortly to circulate foolish and malicious reports about the country and the Government without the
risk of their being authoritatively contradicted.

The mixed peoples of Siberia are destined one day to
become a very powerful nation. They possess considerable
originality, and are supported and encouraged by a far-
seeing and energetic Government.

From Petropavlovsk to Omsk, a distance of 186 miles,
the railway runs parallel to the ancient frontier, from
which steppe highways and caravan routes lead to the
centres of the steppe regions, including the territories of
Akmolinsk and Semipalatinsk. The territory of Akmolinsk
occupies the northern portion of the steppe region. It is
divided into five districts—Petropavlovsk and Omsk are
two of them—and comprises 9902 square miles. It is
bounded on the north by the Government of Tobolsk, on
the west by the Government of Orenburg, and on the east
by the territory of Semipalatinsk, 9138 square miles in
extent, the extreme south-east of which adjoins the Chinese
Empire and the western spurs of the Great Altai range.

The mountain ridges of this region contain untold mineral wealth, which has as yet hardly been touched, and at the foot of these mountains there are extensive deposits of coal. The coal is easily procurable, and will, some day, be utilised to work the various mines by steam. There are, further, gold, silver, copper, lead and iron. Granite of very fine quality is quarried in the vicinity of Semipalatinsk. The bridge over the Irtish at Omsk is built of this stone.

After leaving Kourgan the journey began to tire me. I found myself wishing for a sharp run of 60 miles an hour as in England or America. This speed, however, would be impossible on the Siberian railway, as the rails only weigh 18 lbs. to the foot, and, although as well laid as possible, the soil of the steppes is too loose to afford them a sufficiently stable foundation. It will be necessary to build with stones and cinders until the foundation is made sufficiently secure, when heavier rails can be laid and a greater speed maintained. There is at present a project on foot to lay another line parallel to the existing one.

The organisation of the line for traffic has hitherto been magnificent. It was currently believed that during the present war the increase of traffic would result in the line being blocked. Far from such being the case, the whole stretch has worked very well indeed. The bulk of goods, with the exception of butter, were sent by the ordinary post road, as in pre-railway days, but the authorities evidently regard the butter trade as of the first importance to the country and have never ceased to run seven to eight trains per week during the whole period that the war has been in progress, conveying enormous quantities. Butter coming to the railway from distances of five and six hundred miles reaches the English market with little or no delay, and one of the most southerly towns of Western Siberia—Semipalatinsk—sent large quantities of produce to this country. Although the

British public has displayed considerable sympathy with the Japanese in the present struggle, British merchants have not lost faith in the Siberian business man and Russian trade, as they have opened credit accounts with the banks in all the leading towns of Western Siberia. These banks have been conducted in a highly creditable manner, and the trade is rapidly acquiring full confidence in them; so much so, that British buyers do not hesitate to advance 90 per cent. of the value upon butter bought by them in these remote parts.

The territory of Semipalatinsk is well supplied with lakes and rivers. The Irtish, which takes its source in the Chinese Empire, flows through the territory for a distance of 766 miles, and is navigable throughout its entire course. Of the lakes, the most important is Lake Balkash, which is situated at an elevation of 500 feet and covers an area of 10,196 square miles. Lake Marka-Kul is 200 square miles in extent and lies in a mountain hollow, surrounded by high ridges, at an elevation of 5700 feet. These are two of the largest lakes, and as they contain large quantities of salt in solution the salt industry centres in their neighbourhood. Over 100,000 tons of the best quality of lake salt are taken from Lake Koriakiv annually. The climate of the Kirghiz steppe border is much milder than that of the neighbouring cultivated zone of Western Siberia, the average temperature being quite 5 degrees Fahr. higher, while the temperature during the warmest month is not infrequently as high as 100 degrees Fahr.

Tigers lurk among the reeds of Lake Balkash; the lynx dwells in the mountains; wild boars are met with on the steppes; and, on the borders of rivers, the famous *Ovis Argali*, a variety of wild sheep, and the real *Ovis Ammon* are met with. In Mongolia, more especially south of Semipalatinsk, there is the two-humped or Bactrian camel, a species of deer, the maral (*Cerous Elephas*), the roebuck, the wolf, the bear, fox, marmot, the jumping hare and others. The rivers and lakes are abundantly stocked with sturgeon, sterlet, nelma, roach, lote, pike, carp and several species of fish peculiar to Siberian waters.

The Kirghiz are the last representatives of the Turko-Mongolian hordes, who, at one time, used to make incursions into more civilised countries, threatening Western Europe with conquest. They constitute 80 per cent. of the total population, speak a Turkish dialect and profess the Mohammedan belief, while practising a form of Shamanism. They are nomadic in their habits, and from the first days in spring till late in the autumn live on the steppes in light, portable tents called "yurtas," wandering with their herds in directions which have been determined by ancient custom. The door of the "yurta" usually opens towards the north-east, in a direction opposite to the point to which the Mohammedan addresses himself when engaging in prayer. This arrangement also serves another purpose, viz., to avoid the winds from the south and south-west, which are so prevalent in the steppes. The Kirghiz live in wooden huts in the winter, which huts form the basis of their land tenure, although all land belongs *de jure* to the State. The possessions of the nomads are fixed either on the basis of previous occupation or in accordance with ancient custom or hereditary descent.

The Cossacks forming the Siberian troops were the first colonists of the Kirghiz Steppes and at present represent about 10 per cent. of the population of the Semipalatinsk territory. The Siberian Cossack contingent is located in the Akmolinsk and Semipalatinsk territories and the Bysk district of the Government of Tomsk. The settlements of the Siberian Cossacks are disposed in a more or less unbroken line, which commences at the boundary of the region occupied by the Orenburg Cossacks, continues along the fringe of the Kirghiz Steppes through the town of Petropavlovsk eastward to Omsk, and thence in a westerly direction along the banks of the Irtish. This portion is known as the Irtish line and another, the Bysk line, runs through the Government of Tomsk. Three Atamans, under the control of a chief Ataman, constitute a board of Military Affairs and command the whole of the Siberian Cossack troops. The chief elements of the military section of the population are immigrants from European Russia, and only a small fraction of them are recruited from native Siberians. Their principal sources of wealth are agriculture, fishing and the breeding of cattle. Fisheries will, at no very remote date, be of the first importance in Siberia.

Under the organisation which exists at present, the contingent of the Siberian Cossack troops is divided into the following classes: a preparatory class, consisting of young Cossack boys enrolled from the age of eighteen for a period of three years; a second class, which comprises Cossacks enrolled from the age of twenty-one years for a period of twelve years' active service; and lastly, a reserve, the members of which serve another five years, or till the age of thirty-eight, when they are discharged. The number of troops in the country prior to the war was 16,752, with 192 officers. These men are admirably trained and are the equals of any cavalry in the world. During the early part of the war with Japan the Siberian Cossacks furnished a contingent of nine cavalry regiments of 600 each, or fifty-four sotnias, and three reserve sotnias of 100 men each, in addition to ordinary reserves.

With a view to opening out the country in the neighbourhood of the Siberian railway, land was selected for the Russian peasants within 350 miles of the line, in the Omsk and Petropavlovsk districts, of a quality most suitable for present and future colonisation, and great progress has been made in that direction since. In 1879 eighteen villages contained a population of 1749, while in 1896, 132 villages had increased the number of inhabitants to 99,399. The tide of immigration showed a slight diminution in 1897, but increased again in 1898 and 1899.

The vast pastures of the steppe region combine with the favourable conditions of soil and climate to render cattle-breeding a very lucrative occupation, while the nomadic habits of the Kirghiz make it the most suitable business for them to engage in. Cattle is the standard of value, and the Kirghiz, when they meet, hail each other with the inquiry : "How is the cattle thriving?" The stock raised by the Kirghiz are sheep, horses, cattle, goats and camels. The sheep represent their principal source of wealth. They are of great size, frequently weighing 8 to 12 cwts., and are very fat. The sheep in the extreme south cost twice as much as those in the north. In 1897 there were 6,500,000 head of cattle in the Akmolinsk and Semipalatinsk territories together.

Hunting and other forms of the chase are the only amusements the Kirghiz indulge in. They have so little respect for the wolf that they consider it bad form to shoot him, preferring to ride after him and kill him by striking him on the head with the butt end of a whip. A wolf's run is generally from 10 to 12 miles. The Kirghiz only resort to poison or the gun when the wolves become too numerous. They tame hawks and train them to hunt foxes. Bee-keeping yields about 50 tons of honey annually. There is, however, room for a skilled and enterprising fish-curer in the region, as the industry is spoiled for want of knowledge how to cure the fish properly. Butter is produced in increasing quantities in the district, and, in the more mountainous south, some very fine qualities are obtained, with a good, waxy body.

I welcomed the view of the bridge over the Irtish at Omsk, which is 2100 feet long. We reached the old fortress town of Omsk at last. It has a population of more than 50,000 and is situated at a distance of about two miles from the station of the same name, and 1870 miles from Moscow. The climate of Omsk is not all that could be desired. The air is very dry and the temperature uncertain, fluctuating between extreme cold and extreme heat. Winds and storms are frequent in the summer, raising clouds of dust on the unpaved thoroughfares. The forest zone begins two miles to the north of Omsk. Omsk itself is almost denuded of vegetation. Siberian troops are stationed here, but not in the same numbers as formerly when it was a most important Cossack centre. The ruins of the old fort serve as a reminder of the fact that Russia

COSSACK CHURCH, OMSK.

did not take possession of the land without considerable trouble with the native tribes, whom she is now gradually raising to the level of a civilised nation.

The town consists largely of wooden houses. The principal building is the cathedral, with its magnificent domes. There is also a smaller Cossack church, in which the banner of the pioneer Yermak is preserved. A number of the descendants of the hero live at Omsk and are proud of the history of the conqueror of Siberia.

Much has been written about the prison at Omsk

E

towards the end of the eighteenth century, when, from the number of deaths that took place there, it was named the "dead-house." At one time it accommodated, or was made to accommodate, as many as 800 prisoners at a time, and, when it is remembered that the intense cold of the Siberian winter rendered it almost impossible to ventilate the place without dangerously lowering the temperature, the extraordinary mortality will be understood. All over Siberia the ventilation is sadly inadequate, as it is impossible to introduce the cold air from outside and maintain the requisite temperature within the building. A contrivance which would admit of the air being thoroughly warmed before it is introduced into the houses would be an inestimable boon and the death-rate, which is now so high, would be reduced very appreciably. At present the traveller entering from the open air is almost overpowered by the thick, poison-laden air of the dwelling-houses in winter.

Omsk possesses twenty-nine educational establishments, one of which is a military training school. Among the scientific institutions the chief is the West Siberian branch of the Imperial Russian Geographical Society, which has done splendid work in exploring Siberia and other portions of the Asiatic continent. The town possesses three libraries. Owing to the favourable situation of the place as regards available water-ways, both for purposes of imports and of exports, the town promises to become a very important manufacturing centre. Butter is the most important article of export at present, raw hides and wool come next. Numerous butter merchants have their offices at Omsk and most of them do business in the sale of separators and other agricultural implements. Last year the leading firms, whose headquarters are in America, sold about £150,000 worth of harvesting machinery among them and made a good profit by selling to the butter merchants, who re-sell the machines to the peasants at a profit of from 25 per cent. to 30 per cent., or more if exchanged for butter.

Messrs Deering & Company sell to the Government, who send the machinery to Siberia at cheap rates and retail them in Government shops, acting as the sole buying agents and giving the peasants a three years' credit, which is quite twice as much as a private firm can afford to give. The firm referred to is reported to have sold £60,000 worth of machinery through the Government during 1903. The other two principal firms are also American and have an estimated trade of £40,000 each, while Messrs Marshall, Son & Company and Messrs Clayton & Shuttleworth—English firms—run them pretty closely in harvesting machines, thrashing machines and corn mills. There are, besides, several other English firms competing in the trade. These firms all find Omsk the best centre for their local office, and from here they send out their representatives to all parts of the country. The machines are well made and are frequently purchased by an artel, or by some merchant more wealthy than others who sets up a thrashing machine driven by a steam engine and fitted complete at a cost of £300 to £600. With this machine he does the thrashing for others as well as for himself. Three or four peasants also sometimes unite their forces to procure a machine costing £30 or £40, which is worked by four or six horses. Mowing machines are all imported from America, and cost about £20 each. The English harvesting machine is too expensive for the Russian peasant, while the Russian article is very clumsy. For this reason the American machine, which is light and inexpensive, easily holds the market. The ploughs made by the Russians themselves are best for their purposes. One of wood and iron costs from £1 to £1, 10s.; a steel plough can be obtained for from £2 to £3. Of these latter Siberia imported 4000 in 1903, which cost from £2, 10s. to £3 each.

Although the Government competition is keen, the butter merchants contrive to make a good profit on machinery, which they sell to the peasantry. There is no duty on machinery introduced into Siberia and, when the demand for good machinery throughout the country is supplied, there is every reason to believe that the results, especially where the production of grain is concerned, will be very satisfactory. The trade in machinery at Omsk is of quite recent growth, having sprung up in consequence of the construction of the railway, and the importance of the town as a distributing centre will be readily recognised

CAMEL AND SLEDGE WITH TEA FROM CHINA, AT OMSK.

when it is remembered that it is situated in the heart of a region of 2000 square miles of the finest pasture land in the world.

A long caravan of sledges, drawn by camels and laden with tea from China, lent the town a distinctly Asiatic appearance. The camel and its driver looked very tired after the long journey, as they trudged slowly into the town.

The hotel at Omsk is a very good one, but, as in all Siberian hotels, the proprietor stared at me when I asked for pillows and bedclothes, it being customary for travellers in Siberia to carry these articles about with them. After a good rest I paid a visit to the leading butter merchants, who were very numerous. Most of them are buying agents for English and Danish firms, and they told me that they make more by selling machinery than by buying butter. Their commission on butter varies from 1s. 6d. to 2s. per cask.

The quality of the butter from this district requires to be carefully watched, as it is, on the average, much inferior to that of Kourgan. In 1902 most of the merchants of Omsk lost heavily on consignments of butter to English firms, but they had not then learnt the art of making consignments, which has since been evolved, and which now allows the English merchant to lose instead. Some of these butter merchants are very smart men, with plenty of energy and good business qualities; their example of hard work should be of benefit to the Siberian natives.

As several writers about Siberia have stated that English firms are behind the times in supplying agricultural implements, I made inquiries from several Omsk merchants as to the reason. One agent for a large American firm of agricultural implement makers said : " English firms will only give six months' credit; they want to send the goods in spring and to be paid for them at the end of the summer, while American firms will send a consignment of machinery and, if they are unsold at the end of the year, will wait until the end of the following season, and in many cases even two years, during which time the farmer pays by instalments." To obtain confirmation of this statement I spoke to a large English firm at the London Agricultural Show last year and was told that " Siberia wants about two years' more credit than we can give. We get better terms for our goods elsewhere; and, besides, what guarantee have we that we shall ever get our money ? " I informed him that the passport system was one that keeps the whereabouts of the peasants well known to the police, and that it would be easy to stop the peasant from leaving the district if he owed money. It is, however, very clear that it is not so much that English firms are behind Americans in enterprise, but that the conditions of trade are such as the Englishman does not like.

The town itself is much more advanced than I expected to find. Besides the electric light and good hotels I noticed a bill announcing a biograph exhibition in colour

MAIN STREET, OMSK.

and relief which was to represent bull-fighting in Spain, the Spanish-American war, and a religious procession in Tunis.

The town is in a very important centre near the junction of the Om and Irtish rivers. The latter is the chief tributary of the Obi, taking its rise within the confines of China on the south-western slopes of the southern Altai. All the tributaries which enter the Obi on the right take their rise in the Altai Mountains, which are clad with a rich vegetation of larch, cedar, fir and pine.

These forests will afford enormous quantities of timber
for future use in exploration by means of rafts, and the
same chain of mountains contains deposits of black and
brown coal, which, being near the surface, are easy to work.
The Irtish abounds in fish, and fishing is largely carried
on between Tobolsk and the estuary of the river, and
between Omsk and Lake Zaisan. The principal fish are
sterlet, sturgeon and nelma. The river is 2666 miles
long, and its system comprises 1250 large and small
streams. This river is the most important in Siberia, and,
with its tributaries, allows of navigation in four directions—northwards to the ocean; eastwards to Eastern
Siberia; southwards to the western border of China and
the Central Asiatic dominions of Russia, and westward
to European Russia. It is either ice-bound or free of ice
according to the latitude it traverses, a circumstance which
gives a clear idea of the wide divergencies of climate. At
Tomsk the ice breaks between the 14th and 24th April, and
the water freezes again between the 20th October and the
15th November. In Semipalatinsk the river is free from
ice for 215 days, at Tara for 190 days, and at Tobolsk for
189 days.

The Irtish is divided into two separate systems, of
very different importance for trade. The middle reaches
of the river, from the town of Tobolsk to the settlement of Samarovo, with the rivers Tura, Tobol and
Obi, form an uninterrupted transit waterway between
the towns of Bysk and Barnaoul in the south, and
Tomsk in the east, and Tumen and Irbit in the west.
Steam navigation was introduced on the river in 1884.
The Irtish has no specially-organised fleet, all the
steamers and other craft plying within its basin belonging
to the fleet of the whole of the vast Obi basin. There are
232 steamers of from 20 to 7750 horse power, and 380
vessels of other kinds, with a total tonnage of 250,000
tons, besided 373 barges, four of which are convict barges.
There are several passenger steamers, which take thirteen

days to run from Tumen to Tomsk and from seven to ten days for the return journey. It is a pleasant means of getting to the western side of the Altai Mountains or the Tan Shan range, and should be used by future explorers. It is also a cheap way, if one has plenty of time, taking a drosky or sledge from Semipalatinsk. Mongolian sheep hunters could come this way to Kobdo over the Siberian line and take steamer from the Omsk landing-stages. The river transit, owing to want of competition, is dear and badly regulated. Moreover, the water in the rivers is very low in the summer, and the currents too strong in spring, and this renders navigation difficult and affects the rates charged. A steamer takes from eighteen to twenty-two days to go from Tomsk to Tumen. The steamers of the Obi-Irtish line make about three trips during the season. It is safe to prophesy, however, that an intelligent use of the marvellous water system will make Omsk a very important centre.

Our next settlement of importance was Karachi, 20 miles from the station of that name and the centre of thirteen settlements, having a total population of 25,000. The inhabitants export flour, meat, fish, poultry and butter. Thirty miles south-west of the station lies Lake Chany, which is the largest lake in the Tomsk Government, and occupies an area of 1916 square miles. It contains pike up to 30 lbs. and carp up to 10 lbs. in weight. The lake is leased to a private firm, and yields about 1500 tons of fish annually, part of which is exported from this station. The water of Lake Karachi, 10 miles from the station, is said to possess medicinal properties. The slime from the bottom has a sulphurous smell, and bathing in the lake water and slime is prescribed for rheumatism and diseases of the skin.

From Omsk to Kainsk we took the post train, which was not as comfortable as the Siberian express. It was necessary to look after one's own food at the stations during the long stops. A plentiful supply of hot water from the hot-water house or a *samovar* * enabled me to make my own tea in a kettle I had bought. At every station, nearly all the passengers and guards rushed away for hot water and cheap, ready-cooked refreshments from the peasant stalls. I went into the buffets, which were sometimes very small but always clean, the tables being laid with

THE SMALLEST STATION ON THE SIBERIAN LINE.

spotless white cloths and serviettes and set with white and black bread ready for the wholesome, ready-cooked food to be served by well-dressed waiters, who would do a London high-class hotel credit. Everything is bright and neat, even to the plants on the table. I walked along the corridor and mixed with the Russians, in order to learn as much Russian as possible, and was invited to tea and

* A self-heating urn for hot water.

other refreshments. The Russian traveller has only one meal a day, but it lasts all day, except for intervals in which he takes breath. Although I travelled first-class our compartment was full of second-class passengers, who had evidently arranged with the guard, and, as they insisted on closed windows and doors, there was no fresh air.

I was glad when we reached Kainsk station at last. A business friend had promised to show an English companion and myself round the town, which is eight miles from the station. He had been waiting four hours for our train and told us that it very often happened that the post trains were late, sometimes by as much as eight to ten hours. On our way to the town we passed through a village which has sprung up quite recently near the station. It contains a parish school of brick, in which a lecture illustrated by a magic-lantern is occasionally given. The population of Kainsk numbers about 6000, and consists for the most part of exiled Jews and their descendants. The town contains 525 houses, mainly of wood, two orthodox churches, a cathedral, a smaller wooden church, a Jewish synagogue, a meteorological observatory, a hospital with fifty-five beds and dispensary, a military hospital, a public club, a library, and a society for elementary education. All of which go to show that this out-of-the-way spot is well provided for.

We travelled at the rate of 12 miles an hour, the bells tinkling merrily, while one horse trotted in the shafts of the sledge and the other galloped by its side, throwing up the snow into our faces and slowly filling the sledge. This was my first experience of a winter sledge-ride on a dark moonless night across the lonely steppes. We pulled up at Kainsk Hotel, which, except in the matter of size, was not an imposing edifice. On approaching the bedroom stairs a huge, ferocious dog started up barking loud enough to shake its head off. Nobody took any notice, however, so we mounted the creaky stairs to our bedroom, which, by the way, had no paper on the walls.

We made an attempt to wash in the usual cupful of water, and then had dinner, after which we accompanied our friend through the town to his house. He warned us before leaving to lock up all our luggage against the probability of some other traveller taking a bag or part of its contents by mistake and perhaps leaving before the mistake was discovered. He also warned us to have a revolver handy in the breast pocket, after which we left for the dark streets.

The first thing that attracted my attention was the noise of the watchman's rattle. I examined the instrument. It is a hollow block of wood, not unlike a pulley block in shape, having a round piece of wood attached by string, which when shaken strikes the sides, producing a most unearthly noise, calculated to give the thief or burglar warning fully a mile away. The watchman makes this slumber-disturbing noise in order to inform the people that he is making his tour round the village. From his replies to some questions we put to him he led us to understand that he would have been highly offended with any burglar who failed to complete his little job before he came upon the scene; and I really believe he would have apologised to any burglar whom he had chanced accidentally to disturb in the act of carrying off the " swag."

My friend's wife, who is an English lady, was exceedingly pleased to see someone from England. Being the only Englishwoman in a district larger than the whole of Great Britain, she felt very lonely at times. She had accompanied her husband as an emigrant some time back, and they had been very successful. My friend, who has lived in Kainsk for two years, informed me that the people are born thieves, although they are supremely pious, and cross themselves fervently whenever they pass a church, an ikon, or any other holy picture.

Kainsk is very hot in the summer, the thermometer rising as high as 100 degrees Fahr. In winter it falls

to 110 degrees below freezing point. Being 320 feet above
sea level it is exposed to strong winds, which make it much
colder, and snow-drifts are deep and frequent in the
winter. In summer, dust storms make the place unendur-
able. It is certainly the most desolate place I visited in
Siberia. Besides the town, there are seventeen settlements,
having a total population of 8000, and engaged in agriculture, about 15,000 tons of various goods, including
large quantities of butter, grain, meat, tallow, poultry and
fish, being exported, in addition to spirits, wine and beer,
which are sold to the East. Fish are caught in the rivers
Om and Kainka. The town is situated principally on the
banks of the Kainka, at the junction of the two rivers, hence
its name of Kainsk. The letters *sk* at the end of the name
of a Russian town, always indicate that it is situated on a
river of the same name as itself. The exportation of game
from the numerous forests around Kainsk is increasing.
The most useful for export are black game, which weigh
from 2½ to 3 lbs. each, and can be bought at 6¼d. per pair
during the summer, or 1s. 0¾d. a pair in the autumn, when
they can be safely sent to England in special packing, and
including carriage, at 6d. per brace. A wholesale dealer
in London will pay from 2s. to 2s. 6d. each for these birds.
Ptarmigan cost 9d. to 10d. a brace. They are smaller
than black game, weighing only 1¾ to 2 lbs. each.
Adding 6d. per brace for packing and carriage to England,
they cost 1s. 3d. to 1s. 4d. per brace, and sell at 1s. each to
the wholesale dealer. If necessary they could be cold
stored at Riga at a cost of 4½d. for 26 lbs. for twenty-eight
days. They are usually packed in stiff brown paper. The
best time to buy is from October to November. White
hares can be bought at 2½d. to 4d. each, and cost 8½d. to
10d. for carriage, etc., to England, where they meet with
a ready sale at 1s. 3d. to 1s. 6d. It is a risky business, and
unless the English firm can thoroughly trust the shipper
it had better be left alone, as the latter can buy old birds
much cheaper, and these spoil as soon as they come out of

the refrigerator; on the other hand, young birds will keep
until the British public have time to buy and cook them.
The above prices were current in 1903 when I was at
Kainsk.

During the last three years birds have been exported
from Russia at an average rate of 2,500,000 head per
annum, and at an estimated value of £158,750. They
were sold chiefly in Germany and Great Britain, and about
500,000 head came from West Siberia. The feathers and
down are sold at the Siberian fairs. The quantity of
feathers exported every year for the last five years—1896-
1900—averaged 1935 tons, and is valued at £179,900, while
the quantity of down exported amounted to 129 tons,
valued at £31,760. It will be seen therefore that the
feathers and down are more valuable than the birds
themselves. These figures include the exports from
European Russia, as there are no separate customs returns
for Siberia.

Next day two dairy instructors drove us out in a
sledge to the Kainsk Dairy School, which is situated about
four miles from Kainsk. The dairy school was like a small
village, and I was surprised to find myself confronted by
a group of well-laid-out buildings. The Agronom's house
adjoined the creamery, so that he could always be on the
spot. The creamery itself was very clean, and the butter
of the finest quality. The next building we inspected was
the cattle department. The cows are scientifically stall-
fed and bred from certain well-known breeds, while the
pigs are crossed by our famous Berkshire breed, which I
found is well known even in the most remote parts of
Siberia. All the buildings are of brick, and their appearance reflects the utmost credit upon the Government.

Before this dairy school was established cows were
always kept in the open, although the temperature in
November and December frequently falls below 110 degrees
of frost. This not only froze some of the poor beasts to
death, but, owing to the excessive cold, all the food they

could procure was used up in creating warmth to keep them alive instead of being converted into milk, and in consequence they gave less milk. This state of things has improved since, but I saw several cows with the half of their tails frozen off wandering about the streets in a most neglected fashion.

There are many drawbacks to living at Kainsk. The

A SIBERIAN COW WITH THE HALF OF ITS TAIL FROZEN OFF.

drainage is very bad and small-pox is prevalent, owing to the drinking water being taken from the river, which receives the town refuse. This could be prevented by sinking wells, at a cost of £3 each, to a depth of 24 to 28 feet, where there is plenty of good water. This water, which is kept at a low temperature by the frozen earth, being only a shade above freezing-point, is cold enough to save ice at the creamery and would be excellent for the cattle. Fever is also prevalent near the lakes. One great

loss to the country is through the burning of manure for
fuel, which appears to be general. This custom is a very
serious matter and should be discouraged.

We enjoyed a cup of tea and a long chat with the
English lady and her German husband. My friend made
several serious charges against the Jews of Kainsk and
Siberia generally. He said, "Kainsk is called the 'Jews'

An Escaped Exile and Kainsk Hotel.

Paradise,'" and that the Jews were the curse of Siberia.
His complaints, however, like the complaints of others I
have met in Siberia, summed up, mean that the Jew is a
very keen business man, and as such is too keen for the
easy-going Russian.

On my return to the hotel I was approached by a
beggar in rags. I gave him a rouble and took a photograph
of him. The hotel people informed me that he was an
escaped exile and would not dare to show his face anywhere else but in Kainsk. Passports are not examined at

the hotel in Kainsk. This hotel is the meeting-place for the officials and peasants of the town and its environs and gambling is engaged in at night. At every other hotel I stopped at in Russia and Siberia they demanded my passport, which was sent to the police, and was handed back to me on the day of my departure endorsed with a stamp to the value of 5 to 20 kopecks, which I had to pay. I was glad to settle my bill and feel I was going away from the place, which was worse than Kourgan. We ordered the sledge in plenty of time to drive us to the station, but the man came late and it was an open question whether we could catch the express or not. The fine Kirghiz horses can go very fast when put to it, so we promised tea-money to our driver if he caught the train. I left my English friend at Kainsk. He was trying to induce the merchants to use his firm's cold store at Riga, offering to advance them 75 per cent. of the value of the goods at current bank-rates. The butter merchant proposed to accompany me to the train. Telling me to hold my revolver in readiness in my breast pocket, he jumped into the sledge and we were soon in the midst of the dark Siberian steppes. The sledge never carries lamps. We passed by one or two forests on the way that were pitch black in the darkness. Near the station we saw a beautiful meteor shoot from east to south. On my friend making inquiries I was glad to find the train had not gone. Thawing ourselves after the cold journey we sat down to lunch. One bell rang, which he thought was the signal for the approach of the train; but the second bell rang, and when I asked my friend what it was he informed me that the train had just come in. When a third bell rang it occurred to me all at once that it was my train. I rushed out of the waiting-room on to the platform just as the train started, and waved my hands for the station-master to stop the train. This he did, or I should have been left in that place of desolation for two more days, waiting for the next train. I was glad to feel myself once more in the clean and luxurious first-class carriage of the International Wagonlits: it was like stepping back into civilisation. Kainsk may be pleasant enough in summer, but it is a very rough place in winter.

Once in my compartment I could not help thinking of the rough life these emigrants—man and wife—were living. They had leased 1000 acres of land for twelve years with the intention of placing 200 cows on it, which, my friend said, would show a profit, even in bad times, of £2, 12s. each cow per year. He was paying 1d. per acre rent, and intended to begin making butter, which is very profitable, if he could only get his own cows. I inquired about the possibility of procuring milk from the peasants, and was told that the supply was unreliable, as the peasant will very often offer to bind himself for two or three years to a certain creamery if the manager consents to give 8 or 10 roubles a year to the church, and he mentioned a village, four miles away from Kainsk, which offered a creamery all the milk of the village if the proprietor would give 20 roubles a month to the village church. Of course the supposed market price is paid to the creamery for the milk, but it interferes with competition.

There are one or two banks in each of the twenty-seven towns in Siberia, but there was no bank at Kainsk, and, as it takes seven or eight days to get the money from Omsk, it was necessary to go to the Jews, who, not knowing anything about butter, took heavy risks and charged a high percentage accordingly; but, as the merchants only made use of them when it paid them to do so, I do not think there was any need for them to complain. The Government should attend to the banking arrangements, besides seeing to it that merchants get the right weight and quality of butter, which the bank pays for on behalf of the foreigner. A little illustration of how backward banking is in Siberia may be of interest. A banker's draft, drawn by a Bristol man on a London bank,

F

was sent to Kainsk, and was forwarded in a registered letter on the 3rd of February 1903 to Tomsk. No answer was received from Tomsk until the receivers wrote from Kainsk on the 1st March to inquire about it. They were informed that the draft had been sent to St Petersburg for exchange and sold at a heavy loss. This is, of course, not the way to send money to Siberia, but it serves as an illustration of the expense of sending a banker's draft.

The best way to work business there is with your own employee. He is trusted with enough money to enable him to buy the goods, which he then puts on the rail against the railway receipts; he deposits these, together with an invoice, with the bank, and receives whatever advance the bank may be instructed to give him. He can then repeat the operation. The agent is trusted with the amount necessary to buy the goods and the responsibility of seeing to the weights and quality of the goods, which the banks do not guarantee to check. The goods are then forwarded to the shippers, who make out a bill of lading, and this is sent to the bank. When the goods arrive at their destination the business ends, the merchant taking up the bills as the ship arrives in dock. It is astonishing that the enormous volume of business works so well.

I met two Danish butter merchants in the train on the way to Tomsk who spoke English very well, and with draughts and dominoes the time slipped along very pleasantly in the evenings. The scenery during the day was of the same vast steppe-like character, and the train passed through nothing more interesting until we reached the last station before the Obi, called Krivostichekovo, a name which even the Russians did not trouble to pronounce.

Within the range of this station there are eighteen agricultural settlements, with 28,000 people. Here, as everywhere else in Siberia, the peasants refuse to live apart on their own farms, preferring to cluster together in settlements. Over 12,000 tons of grain are exported annually to the Baltic ports, including 11,000 tons of Siberian wheat, which is of excellent quality.

There was a general awakening of interest one morning when our conductor informed us that we were approaching the famous Obi Bridge, one of the longest and finest bridges on the line. All cameras were out, and the passengers crowded to the windows, while I betook myself to the back of the train. This bridge is 2262 miles beyond Moscow and is nearly half a mile long. It consists of seven steel spans across the largest river in Western Siberia. The River Obi, with its wide, stretching tributaries, drains a basin 10,000 miles in extent, and supplies Western Siberia with a cheap means of communication and traffic with Europe. The importance of this waterway, the largest of the tributaries of which is the Irtish, may be perceived from the following facts. From 1870 to 1884, a period of fourteen years, the total quantity of goods transported by the West Siberian rivers of the Obi basin totalled 40,302 tons, whereas in 1894, at the time of the opening of traffic on the Omsk-Cheliabinsk line of the Great Siberian railway, 250,000 tons of various goods were carried. But the influence of the railway is seen still better in the fact that in 1897 over 980,266 tons of private goods were transported over the Perm-Tumen line.

The navigation of the Obi commences at the town of Bysk, at the point of junction of the Bia and Katun, whence the goods are carried for a distance of 1000 to 2000 miles. Notwithstanding the competition existing among the shipowners, the rates of transport are much higher than on the Volga, which is due to the uncertainty of navigation and the risks run by the steamers on their passage. The irregularity of the freezing and opening of the rivers and the absence of means of obtaining information on the subject by telegraph; the scarcity of the population along the chief rivers, especially the Obi, and the low level of the waters of the Tobol and Tura, are the cause of many accidents, which involve damage or destruction of goods and loss to the shipowners. The connection of the rivers Ket, a tributary of the Obi, and Kass, a tributary of the Yenisei, by a canal, has created another immense waterway, 2350 miles long, from Tumen in the west to Irkutsk in the east.' At present this canal can only be used by steamers from the opening of the navigation on the rivers until June, as, after this season,

BRIDGE OVER THE RIVER OBI.

the water falls so low that only barges with a cargo of 8 tons can use it. The Government are paying special attention to this. Siberia has such a marvellous waterway that if better steamers are built and the low water difficulty can be surmounted there will be no necessity to send anything but perishable goods, such as dairy produce, over the Siberian line.

Half-way across the bridge we became aware of a number of sledges on the river below us. The ice on the river forms a much better winter highway than the road, which soon gets very rough. I took a snap-shot of the verstman at the end when the train left the bridge, and before I could regain my compartment and get my luggage ready the train had pulled up at the Obi station. Here I was met by Mr Oswald Cattley, F.R.G.S., who was waiting with a sledge, drawn by two handsome Kirghiz horses, to drive me to his residence, about two miles from the station, at the settlement of Novo-Nicolaëvsk. I received a hearty English welcome from his family and was introduced to his son, Mr P. Cattley, who had arranged to take me round to see the business men of the place and was prepared to accompany me on my expedition to the unknown part of the Altai Mountains. That night I put up at the only hotel in the settlement, the accommodation of which was fairly satisfactory, except for the usual deficiency of water and bedclothes.

CHAPTER IV

NOVO-NICOLAËVSK—TOMSK—ALTAI

A stroll through Novo-Nicolaëvsk—A Siberian tool-smith—Travelling and
travellers in Russia—A "Taiga"—A convict train—Railway construction
extraordinary—We visit Professor Sapozhnikoff—He discourages my intention to climb Belukha—Further particulars of the Altai range—A visit
to the Governor of Tomsk—Tomsk University—Other educational and
scientific institutions—Commercial establishments—An interview with
an American gold miner—Importing machinery—Siberia and Klondyke—
Gold in Siberia—Silver—Coal production and coal-fields in the Altai—
Methods of working Siberian gold deposits—Criminal and political convicts
—The student riots at Tomsk—Siberians and the Government.

I HAD hitherto been favoured with glorious skies and in
every respect delightful weather, and the morning
following my arrival at Novo-Nicolaëvsk was no exception to the rule. Being desirous of seeing something
of the settlement, I took an early stroll through the
broad streets, which I noticed were laid out in squares
like those of St Petersburg. At convenient corners there
were sentry-boxes painted with diagonal bands of black
and white, the Government colour. In one of them the
watchman was asleep, which is scarcely surprising as his
duties last from nine o'clock till twelve each night and from
four to six in the morning — provided he does not over-
sleep himself. I presently emerged on the frozen river
near the Great Bridge, and from there I had a magnificent bird's-eye view of the whole of the settlement,
which is rapidly becoming a very important centre.

The proximity of the river and the railway give the
town a decided advantage over Tomsk, the capital of
Siberia. Being the terminus of the mid-Siberian railway,
and the most central town in the whole Government of
Tomsk, where enormous quantities of goods are tran-

shipped for export, it is bound to have a great future, and has, in fact, been found to be more central than the capital, and therefore better adapted for purposes of trade. The development of the majority of the Siberian towns situated along the great waterways or in the vicinity of the railway lines, is favoured by circumstances in every way similar to those which have created the monster cities of America. Prior to the construction of the railway, Novo-Nicolaëvsk was a village of twenty-four households and about 104 " souls." In six years the population had increased to 800, and to-day it numbers about 35,000. An area of upwards of 32,000 acres of land and 2,682 sites for building were granted to the population by the Administration of the land belonging to His Imperial Majesty's Cabinet. These can be obtained for a term of thirty years, at an annual rental of from 5s. 6d. to 22s., according to the location, the Administration reserving the right to raise the rent 10 per cent. after the expiration of six years. The building sites may be rented by anyone, irrespective of rank or class. Each building allotment is 105 feet in length and 119 feet wide, which accounts for the symmetrical plan of the town as a whole. A fine brick church has been erected in the centre of the settlement, and is dedicated to the warrior saint, Alexander Nevsky, the cost of erection having been borne by His Majesty and some private individuals. The town contains 113 shops and stores, some of them of brick. Of these four are beer-houses, two wine-cellars, two restaurants, and seven bakeries, while one is a confectioner's shop, owned by a criminal exile, who, by the way, makes first-class confectionery. This man was banished for the murder of his own mother.

A fair amount of business in agricultural produce is done at the market; the goods are brought from distances of 150 to 200 miles, and the annual turnover amounts to about a quarter of a million.

The fireman's watch tower is a very prominent land-
mark. A fireman is in attendance day and night on the
look - out for fires. One hundred common hackney
coaches, without springs, ply for hire, the fares being
20 kopecks a drive (5d.), or 30 kopecks per hour (6½d.).
One of the most important and most completely-equipped
stations at which settlers bound for Tomsk, the Altai
Mining District, and the lands of the Cabinet of His
Majesty are able to obtain food and medical treatment is
situated near this railway station.

My friend expressed great faith in the future of the
town. He had brought his wife and family from St
Petersburg and had been settled there for about two
years. He owns several factories and a tool shop.
He told me that great difficulty was experienced in
procuring from English firms the particular description
of tools which the peasantry needed; he therefore
made many in his own workshop. The ice-axe which
I had brought with me was copied by his Russian
smith, but he failed to harden the steel sufficiently.
In other respects the workmanship was splendid. My
friend's was the only tool shop in the town, with
the exception of that in connection with the railway
station, attached to which there were also a carriage-
building shop, a blacksmith's shop, and a foundry, employ-
ing a total of 450 workmen.

After a visit to the local butter merchants, there being
no time to lose, Mr P. Cattley and myself booked by night
mail-train for Tomsk, where I proposed to make an
exhaustive study of the conditions of Eastern trade. At
the same time I intended to avail myself of letters of
introduction, which had been very kindly given to me by
the President of the Imperial Geographical Society, to the
Governor of Tomsk and to Professor Sapozhnikoff of the
university of that town.

With a view to making ourselves acquainted with
Russian travelling and Russian travellers we booked second

class. It was dark when we boarded the train and the carriages were lighted by candles, but the light was not good and reading was out of the question. We partook of tea and refreshments in company with our fellow-passengers, who hospitably regaled us with whatever they had brought with them, including nuts of which they appeared to keep an inexhaustible stock. Next to cigarette-smoking, which is indulged in by both men and women alike in Russia, the eating of cedar nuts seems to be the most prevalent habit. The floors of the railway carriages were literally carpeted with the shells. The Siberians are as dexterous as monkeys in cracking the shells and extracting the kernels. I tried to emulate their efforts, but with no extraordinary success. The nuts are very small, and, although the kernel, when captured, is agreeable enough to the taste, I managed so frequently to lose it that the result was scarcely proportionate to the labour involved. The late Charles Darwin would, perhaps, have been able to build up his theory without any reference to a missing link if it had been his good fortune to travel with a train-load of Russians plentifully supplied with the native delicacy. The people in our carriage ate nuts for three and four hours at a stretch, and the quantities consumed in this manner must be enormous.

The nuts are obtained in the northern parts of the Governments of Tomsk and Mariinsk, and in the mountainous localities of the Kuznetsk districts, Tomsk being the principal market for their sale. From five to six thousand tons are collected in a good season, the nuts being sold wholesale at 10s. to 15s. a cwt. The harvest in the forest begins about the 10th of August and ends about the middle of September. The cones are obtained by climbing, or by shaking the trees, while, in remote spots, huge trees, centuries old, are ruthlessly felled by greedy collectors. One family will gather as much as 10 cwts. of nuts in one day during the season. The tree from which the nut is obtained, and which is called the Siberian cedar, is really a species of pine. It attains a height of over 100 feet, with a diameter of 12 inches at the top.

The greater part of the nuts are sent by way of the rivers Chulym and Obi to Tumen, and thence to European Russia, while a portion is consigned *via* the Siberian railway. The price is regulated by the crop and the trade is rather precarious, on account of the fluctuations in the quantities. For this reason more than one Siberian merchant has lost severely through unlucky speculations in the article.

Our route lay through a long stretch of almost virgin forest. At ten minutes past mid-day, local time, on the following day, we were informed that we would have to make a change for Tomsk, and shortly afterwards we stopped at the station of Taiga, an isolated spot in the heart of a virgin forest or "taiga." A year or two before, the only inhabitants of the place were the wolves and bears, but a settlement has since sprung up, and, for the growl of the latter and the howl of the former, the inhabitants have substituted the more welcome sound of the village church bells. We had two hours to wait before we could start on our last stretch of 54½ miles along the branch line which has been laid to the Siberian capital, and these two hours we utilised by taking a light lunch, which was excellently cooked.

I had left my camera in the train by mistake. It was brought to me by the Cossack in charge of the station while I was at lunch. I followed him out of the buffet, thinking to show my appreciation of his honesty in the approved and orthodox manner, the more so as a careful study of accepted authorities had primed me with the knowledge that honesty is almost a negligible quantity in Russia. I was more than surprised, therefore, when my proffered "backsheesh" was firmly but politely declined. However, this was not the first occasion on which my rouble had been refused. Twice previously the guards, once on the St Petersburg-Moscow train and once on the

Siberian line, had refused to be tipped. Obviously, therefore, the accepted authorities already referred to require some revision. It is scarcely just to label a whole nation as venal and dishonest because one or two individuals are found to be so.

I was, of course, very pleased indeed not to have lost my camera, the Goetz lens of which alone had cost me six guineas.

I may point out incidentally that, so far as Siberia is concerned, the authorities do not seem to be at all afraid of the camera and never interfere with anyone who uses it.

The greater part of the journey from Taiga Junction to Tomsk is through a drear, uninteresting country covered with swampy "taiga." Beyond the first important station, however, the outlook improves; the flat "taiga" is replaced by undulating hills, and the scenery for that part of Siberia is quite picturesque. Mazheninovka, the last station before reaching Tomsk, is an important exporting centre, from which 3500 tons of wheat are despatched annually. On arriving at Tomsk our train was delayed for a short time, as a convict train which had come in before us was in process of discharging its living freight. We did not mind the delay as it gave us a chance of observing the style in which these involuntary pilgrims travel. The carriages had small windows, each covered with a grating, and wooden seats " upholstered with wood." Beyond this there was no furniture, with the exception of a stove, similar to those on the emigrant trains, which stood in the centre of the carriage. I had already seen the train at Omsk and had taken a photograph of it at the time. I now availed myself of the opportunity to photograph the warders, and sturdy-looking fellows they were.

We had a drive of some two miles, over rough ground, before we came to Tomsk. The engineers who built the branch line have adhered to the tradition, according to which towns situated near the line are studiously avoided

It is said of the Emperor Nicholas I. that when the plans
for the railway which was to connect the two capitals was
submitted to him, with suggestions as to suitable stations
at various towns more or less on the way, His Majesty
took a ruler and connected St Petersburg and Moscow with
one straight line. " That is how the line is to be built," he
said. How far similar circumstances exist in respect to
the Great Siberian railway I am unable to say, but for

EXILE TRAIN, TOMSK.

a distance of 15 miles between Tomsk and the Siberian
railroad there is a continuous swampy "taiga," which
may well have prevented the laying of the line through
that part.

As regards the bribery and corruption alleged to have
been practised during the building of the line I am unable
to give any reliable information; but, in a conversation
last winter with an English merchant, who had been visiting Russia and Siberia annually for the last twenty years,
I was told to be sure to mention in my book, when I came

to write it, the bribery and corruption that was resorted to
by the engineers, and their attempts to extort money from
the municipal authorities of the towns near the line; it
being asserted that there are records at certain places,
which are now far away from the line, of the amounts the
authorities of these towns had refused to give for the
privilege of having the line carried through them.
Whether these stories be true or not I was unable to verify,
and give them just for what they are worth; moreover, as
I visited Siberia for other reasons than to find fault, I did
not make very careful inquiries about things of that kind.
We can indeed find a sufficient number of cases of bribery
in connection with Government contracts in England, as
was revealed during the South African War, without
making special search for them amongst other nations.

The Siberian Hotel at Tomsk, where we stayed, is well
built, but as usual the supply of water is scanty. There
were no bedclothes. The tarakaus, which I found await-
ing our arrival in the bedroom, were, on the other hand,
sufficiently plentiful. The tarakan is not so common as
that other member of the creeping fraternity for which it
has sometimes been mistaken. It is a small and fragile
variety of cockroach. It has three legs on each side of the
body and two feelers. I was quite impressed with the
tickling capacity of the latter. Its legs are long and
enable it to run at great speed; two or three hundred will
race across the floor together at a terrific rate and vanish
under the wall paper or down a chink in the wood. I
should think them the swiftest insects alive. I concluded
that they were too brusque and abrupt in their manners
for it to be worth my while to try to shoot them, but
assumed that they might be amenable to reason in the
form of insect powder, so I spread a tin of Keating's round
the bed to form a frontier and retired to rest with a piece
of muslin over my mouth. Perhaps it was just as well
that the company were too restless to allow me to sleep,
for I had to be up early on the morrow for a long day's

work. As soon as it was light I complained of the nuisance to the night porter, but he only laughed. They do not think very much of tarakans in Siberia. It sometimes happens, in fact, that a peasant will take a handful of these insects from an old house when removing to a new one, for luck. Englishmen are obviously too particular.

After breakfast our first visit was to Professor Sapozh-

TOMSK UNIVERSITY.

nikoff. We drove through the massive gates of the magnificent university in a sledge. The snow piled up at each side of the roadway at the entrance gave evidence of a snowy winter. After driving through several avenues of fir trees, and obtaining at the same time a splendid view of part of the university and the grounds, we pulled up at last before the door of a very fine house, which constituted the Professor's quarters. We were not surprised to be shown into a massive drawing-room full of mountaineering pictures. The professor is a fine specimen of humanity. Beneath his friendly smile the lines about his mouth are a good indication of the determination of character necessary for a successful explorer. He was very pleased to see me, as indeed I was to see him, but from the commencement of our conversation he discouraged and laughed at the idea of a winter exploration of the Katunskië Belki range. He even went so far as to say that it was an altogether impossible feat, and advised me to take snow shoes, which would enable me to get as far as the last village; Katunda, where he advised me to climb the Saptam Mountain and obtain a view of the Belukha, 40 miles away. He was rather taken aback when I told him I had come determined to climb the highest mountain in Siberia, which at that time was thought to be Belukha (14,800 feet), and that I was resolved to accomplish my object.

He insisted that it could not be done in winter, and informed me further, that on his Belukha expedition he had started on the 18th of June from a camp at the south side of Belukha and, at two o'clock in the afternoon, had reached the saddle of the mountain, from which he could see the glacier to the north. The temperature being two degrees below zero he was forced to beat a retreat. Nobody had ever attained that height before him and the only previous estimation of the altitude of the mountain was by Gebler, who, in 1835, looking at the mountain from a distance, had concluded it to be 11,000 feet above sea level. From several angular measurements which the professor had made he found, however, that the eastern peak is 14,800 feet, and the western peak 14,500 feet, high. The height of the saddle, measured with the aid of two aneroids, proved to be 13,300 feet.

By saying that the journey was impossible the professor sadly damped the ardour of my interpreter, who was quite unwilling to proceed until I talked him over. Knowing that nobody had been there in the winter I concluded that the conditions were merely guessed at.

The professor gave me exhaustive directions as to the best means of getting from the last village, Katunda, round to the south side of Belukha, a distance of 106 miles. He was of opinion that the north side of Belukha would be extremely difficult to climb in summer, and was quite sure that it would be impossible in winter, even if we succeeded in reaching the mountain at all, which was doubtful. The east side of Belukha and the Toplifka Valley, he told us, had never been visited by anyone, and numbers of glaciers and peaks awaited the explorer and discoverer. He also informed me that a deep pass was supposed to lead from the south of Belukha to the east, but it had never been explored. He gave me permission to use his maps, and to add any peaks or glaciers to them that I might discover, and, as I am much more of a merchant than a maker of maps, I thanked him and accepted his offer.

On his journey to the Altai in 1899 Professor Sapozhnikoff had explored the upper valley of the Kotchurla, a tributary of the Katun until then unknown. Twenty-three miles from the mouth of the Kotchurla is a lake 3 miles long, with a maximum breadth of 700 yards and a depth of 175 feet. The water is muddy and its temperature in summer, when Mr Sapozhnikoff visited it, varied from 48 to 54 degrees Fahr. Its surface lies 5700 feet above sea level. The lake is now marked in rough outline on the map of the Omsk staff, but no information is given about the valley beyond it, which is narrow, hemmed in by rocky cliffs, and strewn with old moraine and wood. The Mush-tu-Aire river was traced by Mr Sapozhnikoff to the glacier from which it takes its rise. The route he recommended after Belukha was that of the Argout Valley, which leads to the sources of the rivers Ungour and Toplifka. He believed that there were glaciers there which had never been explored. He would have been quite willing to join me if I had only come to visit the mountain in June or July, but he refused to go in winter.

He drove over to lunch with me at my hotel and, in the course of further conversation, told me that he had been amongst the mountains of Turkestan, some of which were over 16,000 feet in height with magnificent glaciers, which he intended visiting again. From exploration the conversation drifted to the Siberian conference of butter merchants which had taken place a few days before I arrived. Mr Sapozhnikoff presided over the conference, acting as the representative of the Government. Butter merchants from England, Germany, France and Denmark, and the Chinese Railway Legation, were represented there. The trade was discussed, particularly with reference to the East. Freights to Kharbin, Dalney, and thence to Japanese and Chinese ports, were considered, and through rates quoted. From the special cheap rates and the number of refrigerator waggons and other encouragements supplied by the Government it was clearly shown that the latter had but one aim in building the commercial towns of Dalney and Vladivostock. This will be the more readily understood if we consider that for butter alone, by being able to ship it through Japan and China, the merchants can get two to three times the price that it will fetch on the West European markets. Prices were studied, but these details cover too much ground to be mentioned here. Over 1116 tons of butter were shipped to the Far East in 1902, and it was expected that three times that quantity would be shipped in 1903. Six years ago only about 4000 tons were shipped to Great Britain, whereas to-day we import nine times as much. The markets of the East have previously been supplied from Europe with very dear butter, preserved in tins. Since the commencement of the Russo-Japanese War the importation of this latter article from Europe has increased, and the exportation of Siberian butter to the East has ceased, except to the Russian troops in Manchuria and the East.

With a view to making the most of the time at my disposal, I decided to call upon the Governor of Tomsk

G

with a letter of introduction from a member of the Government Council at St Petersburg. The Governor's house was one storey high and was entered through a large hall or vestibule, in which I kicked off my goloshes and hung up my furs and cap. I gave my card to the servant and was announced without delay. I had to pass through a large room in which five " Ispravniks "—chiefs of police—were waiting their turns to be received by the Governor. They eyed me and my companion very inquiringly as we passed into the Governor's room. The latter, worthy man, appeared in a very sombre mood, and, without shaking hands, sternly demanded to see my passport. His manner towards me was not unnatural in view of the student riots which had recently taken place and of the fact that a Minister had been assassinated by one of them only a few days before. After reading my passport and my letters of introduction his manner relaxed and he became smilingly anxious to make me comfortable and at home. He procured a map and repeated the professor's warning that we should find it impossible to accomplish our undertaking, as the road might break up at any moment and imprison us in some remote village for five or six weeks. I mentioned my plan of coming back another way, but, owing to my interpreter giving his own ideas about the scheme, the Governor strongly deprecated my tempting Providence in the winter. He promised to send me a letter which would help us through, but up to the time of my leaving the hotel I had not received it.

After taking leave of the Governor we paid a visit to the shops of Tomsk in order to complete our outfit. We were able to buy apples newly arrived from the Caucasus, tea from China—only 400 miles away and brought by a sledge or drosky by the overland trade routes first opened by Peter the Great—and many kinds of goods from Germany, such as kodaks, photographic material, and all kinds of up-to-date articles. We also paid a visit to a barber, who could compare favourably with one of the first-class barbers in the West End of London and was quite as dear, charging us 1s. for a shave and hair cut. I was in every way very favourably impressed by the town, which is built upon hilly ground. With a population of about 60,000, it is as rich in churches and public buildings as any English or American town with five times the number of inhabitants. The university is a most imposing building and contains two faculties : those of medicine (232 students) and law (159 students). There are in all about 2000 students, the remainder being engaged in a general course of study. There are, besides, 6000 students in the other fifty-six educational institutions in Tomsk. This capital, in fact, takes the third place as regards educational importance in the Empire. During a period of ten years, over 1000 students have qualified. Of these 239 have taken degrees with them to their desert homes in Siberia, and, together with the numerous lawyers sent out by the university, will, in the near future, introduce a new element of civilisation in Siberia.

In addition to a mineralogical and geographical museum there is a library, which contains 100,000 volumes. A substantial aid to the students is furnished by privately-endowed scholarships, which, at the present time, amount to over £500,000. The town contains a handsome cathedral, built at great cost, as well as other buildings too numerous to mention. There are, moreover, six local publications and a commercial Exchange for ascertaining the general conditions of Siberian trade. Tomsk is, besides, the chief manufacturing town in Siberia. There are 210 factories, while four banks testify to its extensive commercial operations. The latter are, the branch of the Imperial Bank, the Siberian Trade Bank, the Russian Bank for Foreign Trade, and the Siberian Public Bank. Tomsk possesses three hotels—the "Russia," the "Europe" and the "Siberian Hotel." There is not very much to choose among them, and the traveller is strongly recommended to be generous with Keating's.

I was introduced here to the chief partner of an American Gold Mining Company, and I thought I should like to get his experience in gold mining, so I asked him a few questions. "What do you think of the future of Siberian gold mining?" I asked. He replied, "Siberia will in the future be a tremendous mining country, and although in the best days of California you might have been lucky enough to strike an occasionally very rich mine, the Siberian gold is finer and more widely distributed. The working of vein ore is not frequent, the system commonly worked being known as the 'placer' system. The Siberians are very primitive in their methods and machinery, and the Russians cannot work under 2s. 11d. per cubic yard to get an appreciable profit; but with the machinery my company are placing down they will be able to work as cheaply as any other mining district in the world. If you get a permit from the Governor at Tomsk, or the district where you are working, you can bring machinery into the country free of duty. This is a privilege not allowed in any other gold mining country, but there is a string tied to that arrangement, for you have to pay the duty at the frontier and your bill of lading specifies what you have brought in. The Government engineer inspects the mine and makes sure you put the machinery down in working order; he then gives you a certificate to get the rebate, which it takes about a year to accomplish."

"How does Siberia compare with Klondyke?"

"There are no difficulties here to compare with those of Klondyke. The regulation claim is 5 versts long and 700 feet broad. By the new law of 1902 we pay 50 kopecks (1s. 0¾d.) per dessiatine (over two acres), but the tax in other places is one rouble (2s. 1½d.), according to the quality of the mine. We own 21 miles of mine and water rights. Before 1902 the Government tax on gold was 3 per cent. in the south Yeniseisk district, and 4 to 15 per cent. in other places, but this has been abolished and we

Томск Cathedral.

now pay an industrial tax according to the profit made. In addition to the cost of the convict labour you hire, you pay a police tax for each of the men. We are paying 500 roubles for 160 men, which is 6s. 7½d. per week each. In Western Siberia there are about 10,000 miners employed, and in Eastern Siberia they number over 30,000."

" Where do you sell your gold ? "

" The Government was the only legal purchaser until 1902, since when a free circulation of gold is permitted, except in the case of the Czar's mines and some districts in Trans-Baikal. We used to receive a certificate of weight from the district engineer and then brought the gold to Tomsk. A six-months' bill was given us on the Treasury, after deducting the cost of transport to the mint in St Petersburg, and a tax of 3 to 15 per cent. was imposed on the raw material. The State also levied a tax of one rouble (2s. 1½d.) per dessiatine on land conceded, but this has been abolished since 1902, because the miners escaped a lot of taxation by filling up incorrect returns, through which the Government lost heavily. We found that there was competition for labour, and that if our mining competitors were to fill up proper returns they could not pay the wages they were then paying. The price of labour has risen recently ; the building of the Siberian line helped to raise it temporarily, and afterwards, when the railway was completed, the butter industry helped it to keep its level. It is my opinion that gold-mining in Siberia is only played with and that the earth is scratched or skimmed rather than worked, as a result of which the mine soon becomes unprofitable and is abandoned, whereas with good machinery it would work out very profitably. Many of the mines which were once closed down have since been re-opened and are working at a profit. There are a number of mines in several places where gold is known to exist, but there is no capital in the country to work them. As soon as American capitalists get to know that the Government is specially favourable to them there is sure to be a rush."

I asked: "But how about English capitalists?"

"Well, you see the Russian Government gives a decided preference to us Americans as compared with Englishmen, the reason for which is that we understand the Russian Government and its policy better than the English people seem to do and we have no papers that systematically run down everything that is Russian. If I judge the British aright they seem to be trained from youth to regard the Russians with detestation and to lend ready belief to all the exaggerated exile stories that may be invented for them."

"But," I said, "how about the American people and exile stories?"

"Well," he replied, "there is a small percentage of people in America who really would not think much of Siberia were it not for the imaginary convict horrors which are sometimes so graphically described; but the majority of American people are far too enlightened to encourage such stories."

I said: "Probably the American people are so used to hearing tall yarns of home manufacture that they are suspicious of reports from other countries."

"I guess you have just hit the right nail on the head," he said; "anyway, we Americans have the pull everywhere in Siberia. I have noticed it repeatedly when travelling with Englishmen through the country. Can you expect anything different?" he added.

"No," I replied, "I am quite convinced that we are making one of the biggest political and commercial blunders possible by not cultivating the friendship of the Russian Empire, whose people cover one-sixth of the Continental surface of the globe and have such splendid resources, and I quite believe you when you say that American capitalists enjoy the preference in the matter of gold mining."

That very large quantities of gold exist in Siberia is no recent discovery, it was announced by the early Voyevodes; but no systematic mining was undertaken until about 1830. At present Russia is the fourth gold-producing country in the world and, although the methods employed are most primitive and the long winter interferes very much with the working of the mines, she holds that position easily. As soon as capital and improved machinery appear in sufficiency in the country she will become of much greater importance. I hold that there is more gold to be obtained in Siberia at present than in any other country in the world, principally because the resources have as yet been scarcely touched. Two-thirds of Russia's output comes from Siberia. The annual yield of gold for the Russian Empire from all sources is 518 cwts., 70 per cent. of which come from Eastern Siberia, but only 9000 cwts. have been taken out of that part of the Empire up to the present. Assuming, therefore, that Siberia is as rich as South Africa was in its virgin state, there is a greater future in store for the former. Five per cent. of the total production of gold comes from Western Siberia, and 25 per cent. from the Ural district. The railway is likely to have a very important effect upon Siberian gold development, more especially in the Altai Mountains. The word Altai means gold, but if it denoted silver it would more accurately represent the actual metallurgical value of the mountains, as the output of silver in the Altai districts is greatly in excess of that of gold. At one time the works in the Altai used to turn out an average of about 320 cwts. of silver per annum—more than ten times the production of gold—but from the end of the 'Sixties to the twentieth century the quantity began to fall off, not because the silver was getting exhausted, but on account of the conditions governing the supply of fuel, the forests within convenient distances of the works having been very much thinned or completely exhausted. Following the railway development which is anticipated, and which will tap the extensive coalfields of Kusnetski and Chulim, which occupy an area of 19,323 square miles, this deficiency will no doubt be supplied. The districts in question represent two of the largest coalfields in the world, containing deep layers of coal of excellent quality. Researches at various times have revealed layers from 21 to 42 feet and sometimes up to 175 feet in thickness, while the reserve of coal seems to be enormous. Besides the Kusnetski basin, about 50,000 tons per annum are extracted in the Government of Tomsk.

It will pay the United States to place their overplus of silver on the market and introduce a gold standard before these coal beds can be utilised to develop the Siberian silver mines. If this is not done the position of America will become worse than it is at present, for there is no doubt that Siberian silver in the past has played an important part in lowering the American silver standard and raising England's gold one. The Russian nation were evidently aware of the prospects of silver mining and were prompted by that knowledge to adopt a gold standard in 1876, which action will bring its reward when the silver in Siberia is developed to its fullest extent.

The words of Mr Andrew Carnegie on page 40 of his book, *The Empire of Business*, should be remembered by the citizens of the United States of America, because the 482 millions of dollars in depreciated silver—which he mentions as being held by his country—will very quickly fall lower in value still. France is also bound to lose heavily on her reserve of 650 millions of dollars. Such a condition of affairs enables us to appreciate the foresight of English statesmen in adopting the gold basis. Having in view the many good reforms which have been introduced into India during the last few years, I hope she will also be put on a gold basis at once and before the crisis comes, even though it be at a serious immediate loss. It is difficult to say what the actual possibilities in Russian silver mining are, but with cheap fuel the production is sure to become enormous, the earth up to the present having, as it were, only been scratched with very primitive machinery.

The district producing the most gold at present is the Yakutsk Territory, which lies between 54 degrees and 73 degrees north latitude, and 73 degrees and 141 degrees east longitude, covering an area of about 2,300,000 square miles and having a population of 521,000 inhabitants. This is a rough and desolate district, scarcely fit for colonisation, owing to the absence of fertile land. It is a favourite haunt of the nomadic tribes from the Central Asiatic steppes, and may be described as the Klondyke of Siberia. It is, moreover, part of the coldest district of that country, and therefore of the world.

Gold is obtained by two different processes: either by working the deposit after first removing the covering of turf to the depth of from 3 to 20 feet, or by washing the gold from auriferous gravel taken from the bottom of rivers, which are first diverted into new channels with the aid of dams and other contrivances. The metal is also obtained by underground mining, sometimes at considerable depths. The gravel is brought to the surface by shafts with the aid of a horse winch. The work in the mines is carried on notwithstanding that the soil is perpetually frozen, wood fuel being employed to melt it. In these mines the underground works are usually conducted on the pillar system, the spaces worked out being faced with stone. The mines that are now being worked are situated at a distance of 1150 miles north-east of Irkutsk, in the Olekminsk district, and are divided into the Olekminsk and Vitim groups, under the management of the Irkutsk mining department. The working of these mines dates from 1851, the annual output of gold during thirty years having been from 136 to 313 cwts. The best yield is sometimes half a pound to every ton and a half of ore, an ounce to a ton and a half being considered good. The richest mines in Siberia, or for that matter in the Russian Empire, are worked by the Vitim Company, and

produce from 56 to 76 cwts. per annum. It is not remarkable that English, French and American syndicates have
sent out engineers to prospect. A prospecting party
consists of a leader and from six to eight workmen, with
ten or fifteen horses, which are hired at the nearest village
and loaded with the necessary saddle-bags to contain the
provisions, tools and so forth. The cost of a prospecting
expedition averages about £500. If the examination of
the pyrites or quartz gives favourable results, trees are
felled and a hut is built, the peasants using no other
instrument in the construction than the axe, and not a
single nail being employed. The claim is afterwards
marked out, two posts being erected at each end of the
plot decided upon, and is registered with the Commis-
sioner of Police or the Director of Mines. A Government
surveyor then inspects the claim and draws up a map.
The preliminaries being thus completed, the prospector
may borrow money on the security of his mine at the rate
of 20 or 30 per cent. A mine that is once registered must
be worked. If the finder has not the means to work it
himself he is at liberty either to sell or transfer it by some
other process to another party. If the claim is not
worked it becomes forfeit to the original owner of the land.
The Nertchinsk mines are the only ones in which convict
labour is employed, the village of Gorni-Zerentui being
reserved for the residence of convicts deported for criminal
offences and that of Akatui for political offenders. It is
generally believed in England that the criminals thus
employed in the mines are treated with barbarous cruelty
—that they are, in fact, frequently compelled to work
while in a dying condition, or heavily fettered, and that they
are often obliged to sleep while attached by chains to heavy
wheel-barrows. I recollect reading a story, which was
supposed to be authentic, of miners keeping the dead body of
a fellow-prisoner down in the mine for several days in order
that they could get his portion of food in addition to their
own, and I have met Englishmen who believed this tale to

be true. As a matter of fact, however, each convict has his own quarters, to which he can return after his day's work is done, and no miner is ever kept under ground at night. Women prisoners, on the other hand, are only employed above the surface, in much the same way as women work in connection with the coal mines in England. Deducting holidays, the convict works for eight months in the year, his hours of labour being from six o'clock in the morning to midday and from two o'clock in the afternoon to seven during the summer, and from seven o'clock in the morning to four o'clock in the afternoon during the winter. There are more severe conditions of labour than these to be met with in England, particularly if what is said and written about the notorious sweating system is correct. It is possible for a prisoner, by good conduct, to become " a free command," that is to say, he is obliged to wear the convict dress, but is only under police supervision and is at liberty to make any money he can by practising a trade or engaging in business. He may marry, and if he has any private money he is entitled to retain it. He is also at liberty to receive his friends.

The climatic conditions render it impossible to work the mines all the year round, so that the prisoners are employed at other trades. There is not sufficient work to keep the whole of the convicts in constant employment; they therefore, as a body, do not work as hard as a similar body of British labourers. Sunday is a holiday and so is the day dedicated to the patron saint of the mine. There are, besides, so many holidays which the nation has grown accustomed to keep, that they have a tendency to interfere with the commercial development of the nation, and these holidays could, with advantage, be considerably reduced in frequency.

I had read before leaving England of the riots of the students at Tomsk, so that when I arrived at Novo-Nicolaëvsk, I was prompted to satisfy my curiosity on the subject by sounding everyone from whom I thought I would be likely to obtain trustworthy information as to the cause and probable effect of those disturbances. The riots had been said to have been of so serious a character that the faith of the Central Authorities in the Governor of Tomsk had been severely shaken, and it was rumoured that he was about to be removed from his post. The following version of the occurrence was given to me by a member of the Russian nobility who was living in banishment at Novo-Nicolaëvsk, and was substantiated by several members of an English family also residing there. It was afterwards confirmed by the owner of a gold mine at Tomsk, himself an American, some three weeks after it was given to me. I feel confident therefore that it is substantially correct.

A student of Tomsk University was suspected by some of his fellow-students of being a spy in the pay of the Government. They reported to the Director of the university and demanded an investigation. The Director complied with their demand and, having convinced himself that there was no foundation for the charge, called the students together and told them the conclusion at which he had arrived. The matter might have ended here, but the student against whom the accusation had been brought complained to the chief magistrate and, in the result, brought an action for defamation of character against several of his fellow-students. On the 18th February 1903, the day of the trial, 100 students assembled at the court. The police wished to expel them from the court, a course of action against which the magistrate very rightly protested, and they were allowed to remain. After the proceedings were over and the students left the court, the police followed, keeping close to them. There appears to have been some hustling and the police, not being represented in sufficient force, called upon the riff-raff of the streets to support them, as a result of which the students were badly mauled and some of them had to be treated in the local hospital. On the following day

1000 students assembled in the neighbourhood of the university to make a public protest against the treatment they had received on the 18th. A strong force of police arrived on the scene, but not being considered sufficient the military were called out, and the Vice-Governor came down and urged the students to break up. This they refused to do except on the condition that the police were withdrawn. Their request was acceded to and the students dispersed without making any disturbance. Again the trouble appeared to be at an end and no disturbance would have occurred if the mistake had not been made of prosecuting a number of the students who were concerned in the demonstration, the late Minister of the Interior having arrived on the scene to investigate the case.

A banished nobleman — with whom I engaged in several passages-of-arms, as he was particularly critical of the Government, which he blamed for many things, from " men having no work to others having too much money "— condemned the action of the police. Some of my English friends were of the same opinion, but others upheld the action of the authorities.

It is, of course, difficult to arrive at a just decision in a case of this kind, especially as, on the one hand, we have to deal with hot-headed university youths, running over with exaggerated conceptions of their rights and obligations to society, and, on the other, with an administrative force perpetually in readiness to crush disturbances of the public peace.

English people are prone to believe that because the people of Siberia have no voice in the settlement of national questions they are of necessity opposed to the Government. I, too, went to Siberia with that idea, but soon discovered my error, and found that there were more people in favour of the existing system of government than against it, and that it is a very general opinion that if a census could be taken of the views of the people the majority would be found to have voted for the Government.

To the American already referred to I made the following remarks with regard to the rioting I have dealt with above. I said : "In the first place it is not likely that the police would have picked a quarrel with the students, as they must have known that they were in the minority, especially as they were obliged to call the mob to their assistance; secondly, it is not likely that the mob would have helped the police if the students had been molested first; thirdly, to fight the police at all was a defiance of the law which would have been put down with a strong hand in England or any other civilised country, and, lastly, the very fact that the students had assembled to the number of 1000 showed their intention to defy the law, which prohibits such gatherings." But proof that justice is tempered with mercy in Siberia may be found in the fact that when the students refused to disperse unless the police and the soldiers were withdrawn, the demand was immediately complied with, the authorities being plainly desirous to deal as leniently as possible with the young people. My American friend, who was an eye-witness of the disturbance, endorsed my reasoning on all points. Had the same thing occurred in England and 1000 students collected in any part to defy the law, refusing to disperse at the request of the authorities, there is no doubt that very strong measures would have been taken against them.

The demonstration against the Government spy was the culminating episode of a curious history which was told me by the same informant. The students had for some time been under the influence of a nihilist agitator, a Jew, named Rabinovich—the name means son of a Rabbi. This man was banished, shortly before my visit to Tomsk, as a result of the investigations made into the affair after the riots. He was a returned emigrant who had spent many years in America. He contributed articles to a paper published in Tomsk called *Siberian Life*. He had taught English to several of the students, who were subsequently the ringleaders of the disturbance. His articles were always strongly antagonistic to the Government. He had always a grievance, did no work except teach the students English and photography and write articles, which were frequently censored and very often entirely suppressed.

One day, I was told, the police desired to have the use of his telephone to summon the fire brigade, as his was the nearest telephone, but he swore at them and refused to allow them to enter his place, afterwards making a boast of it. He went about the town proclaiming that as he had been in the States a number of years and was a naturalised American subject, although born in Russia, he was " no common moujik " and the authorities dared not touch him. He poisoned the minds of the students and incited them against the Government by his defiant manner and abusive language. He had a number of friends among the students and spent much of his time with them, so that when, on the occasion of the disturbances, he was seen in company with the ringleaders, one of the officials ordered him to go home. One morning, some time afterwards, the American was sitting in the hotel near some of this man's student friends, when he came in and asked them to lend him the money with which to get out of the country as the police had taken his passport. My American friend told me that he looked very crest-fallen and despondent. The next that was heard of him was that the police had taken him away in irons, and he is now under police supervision in some Siberian village, probably the one in which he was born. This my friend told me was only one of many cases he had witnessed, and was typical of the manner in which the Government deals with agitators. This man had filled the heads of the students with insane ideas of self-government and brought serious trouble upon them and those related to them. My

H

friend referred to the removal of Rabinovich as a good riddance. "He was a fanatic," he said, "or, as we say in America, a 'nutty pole'—one of the same type of men as the madman who shot M'Kinley."

In another case I was told that the governor had been assaulted and his life threatened.

It was perhaps a mistake on the part of the Minister of the Interior to take so much notice of the riot, thereby giving the students an exaggerated idea of their own importance. Probably he may have been misled by incorrect versions of the disturbances, similar to those which were circulated in England at the time, and which stated that the military had shot down the students. This is not the only case of false reports respecting the terrible slaughter of Russian students, that has appeared in the columns of our Press. One of my merchant friends, who has been visiting Russia and Siberia for the last twenty years, informed me that he was in St Petersburg at the time when a serious riot was said to have taken place. On inquiry it proved to have been nothing more than an act of insubordination against the university authorities and, although the police were called in, there was no serious trouble. The headlines of the English papers read: "Military called out; serious student troubles."

The tolerance shown in the case I have mentioned proves that the Government will not banish the students if they can deal with them otherwise, even although to send them to prison at Tomsk is impracticable, owing to their outnumbering the police. The Emperor has since pardoned many of the students banished to the province of Yakutsk, but, by the irony of fate, as one train brought back a number of students another train was proceeding in the opposite direction with\ a fresh batch to take their place. A Government is obviously in a difficult position when it has to deal with men who use bomb-shells and pistols as arguments. It is a great pity that the energy so harmfully expended cannot be diverted into some practical channel, say mining or agriculture. Let us hope that this will some day be done and, in the meantime, let us refrain from judging the Russian Government by the standard of the civilisations of England or America. The telegraph, moreover, plays atrocious pranks with messages from Russia, as I know only too well from my own experience. This, of course, is due to ignorance of the language on the part of the operators, and sometimes even of those drawing up the messages.

Driving past the theatre at Tomsk we met three sledges containing exiles. I left my own sledge and took a snapshot of the party from the rear. I would much have preferred a full-face photograph, but was afraid that the soldiers, who were marching with fixed bayonets on each side of the sledges, would take possession of my camera. There are so many convicts in Tomsk that these exiles passed quite unnoticed by anyone except ourselves. The histories of some of the residents of this town would fill volumes. There are here some of the most intelligent and enlightened men in the world—men who have studied and attempted to bring about numbers of reforms, and have been involved in numerous conspiracies against the Government. The presence of so large a number of offenders against the laws of the Empire is a great obstacle in the way of peaceful Government.

A story was told to me which I give for what it is worth. It is said that the Czar Alexander the First, disgusted with the failure of his plans to better the conditions of the people, abdicated the throne. While on a journey to the Crimea for the benefit of his health, he caused a report to be spread about that he had died at Taganrog. With the consent of his successor, Nicholas the First, a corpse was taken to St Petersburg and there buried in state. Alexander disappeared and nothing was heard of him until he turned up as a wanderer in Tomsk, where he is said to have been recognised by a merchant who had seen him under other circumstances. The secret was well kept, and it was not till long after his death that it leaked out that the old man who had lived at Tomsk in very humble circumstances, and was known as Theodore, was the great Czar. I should myself not be at all surprised if this story were true, as the task of governing an enormous empire like that of Russia, with its hundred different races, must be a very trying one for any man.

CHAPTER V

A WINTER EXPEDITION TO THE ALTAI

We leave Novo-Nicolaëvsk—Sledging in Siberia—Shooting "ryabchiks"—
Barnaoul—Immigration—Cattle-breeding and other local industries—Influence of the railway—Exports—Waterways—The hotel at Barnaoul—We
leave for Bysk—Butter-caravans—Wolves and dogs—Kharlipko—A night
at a post-station—Bysk—We attend a reception—I am supplied with a
"shuba"—Krasnobaisk—A journey through the dark to Altaiskoë—
Shimelovskaya Pass—Barancha—Tavourack—A Russian bath—We are
upset—Siberian horses—Chorni-Anni—A dust storm—Kalmuck settlement—Abbi—A difficult journey—The Koksa River—Ouemon—We are
advised to abandon our undertaking—Katunda.

SHORTLY after we arrived at Novo-Nicolaëvsk the weather
changed and we began to fear lest the roads should be
spoilt by the thaw. We therefore hastened our preparations in order to be able to make a start after a day's rest.
We had decided to take a large, heavy, covered sledge, as
we would require to sleep in it at night. Mr O. Cattley
and his family assembled outside to have their photographs taken and to bid us farewell. They made a very fine
group round the sledge. At four o'clock in the afternoon
of March the 28th we started. We were drawn by a
"troika," * but the pace was very slow at first. We had
been warned that the roads were impassable owing to an
unusually heavy fall of snow. Moreover, the sledges that
had passed along before us had worn deep holes in the
road.

The general idea of sledging is of a swift, easy motion
over the firm surface of the snow at an average pace of
from 12 to 14 miles an hour, to the "tintinnabulation
of the bells." In our case the bells were present, it is true,

* "Troika," three horses; one trotting between the shafts and the two
outside horses cantering.

117

but the speed was not exhilarating and the jolting of the vehicle, as it alternately subsided into a hole or rose on the edge of one, soon persuaded us that we were entering upon a journey of a rather difficult and not too agreeable

ROUGH SLEDGE ROAD, ALTAI.

description. Our luggage, with hay piled upon it, served us for seats, and it was not very long before we were shaken down into positions which cramped our limbs and impeded the circulation of the blood in our legs, causing us to feel the cold very acutely. The speed soon settled down to about five miles an hour, and our road took us along the trade route on the River Obi, by which all the traffic is done with the Wonderland of the Altai mountain group; but the winter was nearly at an end and the traffic had worn the road very badly. In places, owing to the weight of the sledge, the horses were brought to a standstill, so that when we reached the first village, that of Bersk, we decided to change our cumbrous vehicle for one of lighter make. Travellers often buy their own sledge to avoid changing, but this is not always wise, as it is frequently impossible to decide beforehand upon the most suitable conveyance for the different stages of the journey. Our first driver only charged us 7s. for a 12-mile stage; but we discovered, on attempting to make a bargain with his successor, that we would have to pay the same amount for the next one of not more than 8 miles. To prevent collusion, therefore, between this man and the one who took his place, we stopped him outside the yard and went inside to make our bargain. We arranged for the next man to take us 12 miles for 3s., and although after he had spoken to our driver he tried very hard to induce us to pay more, we carried the day. I advise all future travellers to adopt this plan, as we found it worked admirably. The moujiks, knowing we were helpless in their hands, did not scruple to take every advantage of us, and it was only by forestalling them in the manner described that we obtained fair play at their hands. We travelled the greater part of the night, although the cold was very severe, the thermometer registering between 16 and 20 degrees below zero. On the next day the sky was again cloudless. We changed our sledge at nine post stations, and found that the 15 miles between stages were quite long enough, on account of the cramped position we were obliged to observe while seated on our belongings exposed to the cutting wind caused by the motion of the sledge. At one stage of the journey, while travelling through rich pine forests, a distance of about 28 miles, we varied the monotony by

shooting several ryabchiks * and other game birds.   There
was no occasion for us to leave the track as the birds came
on the roads to pick. up stray morsels of food, the prolonged cold of the winter having rendered their supply of
food in the forest sufficiently precarious.

At Barnaoul we made a short stay.   This town is one
of the most prosperous in the Altai region.   It is situated

SHOOTING ON SLEDGE TRACK.

about 180 miles from the Siberian railway, contains
70 factories of various kinds, and 1200 workpeople,
out of a total population of 30,000.   It is a pretty
town of wooden houses and contains five churches, but
the streets are unpaved.

Barnaoul is the centre of the most thickly-populated
district in Siberia, which contains 580,344 inhabitants,
or an average of ten to the square mile.   The original
inhabitants of the country belong to various tribes of

* Hazel grouse.

the Ural Altai races, with an admixture of $4\frac{1}{2}$ per cent. of outlanders. The former belong to four principal branches: Finns, Turks, Mongolians and Samoyeds. The number of professing Christians is small, the predominant religion being Shamanism. Within the last ten years 17,659 exiles, with their voluntary companions, have been sent to the Tomsk Government, besides 300,000 voluntary settlers. The allotment of new grants of land has been temporarily suspended to allow the settlers to establish themselves. Only one-twentieth part of the total quantity of arable land is under cultivation, yet there is a surplus of 300,000 tons of grain per annum in the Government of Tomsk, which is practically the Altai region. Before the outbreak of hostilities with the Japanese, moreover, the district possessed over two million head of cattle, about two million sheep, and the same number of horses. Apiculture is a source of considerable wealth to the inhabitants. Model apiaries, with grand hives on a new and improved system, are in use in the Barnaoul district, and a bee-keeper residing at Barnaoul edits a journal called *Northern Apiculture*, which is subsidised by the Government and the object of which is to instruct the population and to introduce the most approved methods in the industry. Other industries are sure to spring up as soon as the proposed new railway is laid through the fertile regions at the foot of the Altai Mountains. The most important of these new lines is the one which will connect Tashkent with one of the stations of the mid-Siberian line, taking Barnaoul on its way.

The enormous increase in the trade of this district is directly due to the presence of the New Siberian railway. Although agriculture is by far the most important industry, apiculture, cattle-rearing, hunting, trapping and forestry, are not unimportant. The growth of the dairy industry and particularly of the production of butter, has been wonderful, although the existing creameries are only small concerns, and much inferior to those situated nearer the railway line. This state of affairs will soon be remedied, however, as an agricultural school is about to be established at Barnaoul, at a cost of £10,300, at which the dairy man will be taught the essentials of the business, so that Barnaoul bids fair to become the leading centre for the collection of butter and other dairy produce in Siberia. By way of encouragement, further, the Government has awarded gold medals to dairy owners in competition, for the best butter.

It would be difficult to parallel the enormous growth in the exports of the town since it was brought into comparatively easy connection with the West. In 1899 the total quantity of butter sent out did not exceed 36 tons; but in 1902 it had reached the respectable figure of 8050 tons, no less than 233 times as much. What the future can produce is left to the imagination. The war demanded one man in every five and, as many of them are dairymen, the industry was seriously affected. About one-fifth of the butter comes through Barnaoul from Bysk direct to Europe; but most of it is sold at Barnaoul, being brought from Bÿsk by sledge in winter and by boat in summer. The butter is accompanied by a salesman, who is required to bring the purchase-money back with him. For this reason it is usually disposed of for any price that offers; much of it changes hands, is weighed, and sent forward immediately. Sometimes the Barnaoul merchants, acting for British firms, store the butter in ice-cellars, greatly to the detriment of the quality, as the temperature of the cellars is very irregular. In addition to the dairy school already referred to, the Government would be well advised to erect cold-air stores at the principal centres, in which the butter could be stored between the times of shipment without danger of its quality deteriorating. Such cold-air stores could be built at Barnaoul and Omsk. The one at Barnaoul would be of immense value, as it would prevent the very heavy losses which are now suffered by the peasants and

merchants every year, owing to the impossibility of
dispatching goods to the railway during the spring
thaws, which last three or four weeks. Another serious
disadvantage consists in the circumstance that the
steamers plying on the River Obi are not fitted with
refrigerators, owing to which large quantities of butter
are exposed to excessive heat in summer and are consequently spoiled. This means a very serious loss to the
traders. A permanent cold store could supply the boats
with cold air which would keep at a low temperature for
three days, if they were fitted to hold it. It would be
a splendid speculation for a British firm to construct three
fairly powerful, flat-bottomed boats, fitted with refrigerators, and run them on the Obi. They would be independent of competition, as the existing boats, owing to
their not being provided with cold storage, could not run
against them, and the traders would never risk their butter
in any other conveyance once the refrigerator boats were
running. The charges on the existing boats vary with
the season, and according to the difficulties and dangers
of navigation. They are highest in July and August,
when the water in the river is low. The bed of the
river being broad, an extensive surface is exposed to the
fierce glare of the summer sun, as it meanders through the
level steppeland, while the water evaporated in this way
is only inadequately replaced by that from the mountain
sources of the river and its tributaries; but little snow falls
on the mountains in summer, and the hard, frozen glaciers
contribute very little towards filling the streams during the
short summer months. It is for this reason that the boats
plying on the Obi must be flat-bottomed, and fitted with
sufficiently powerful engines to enable them to make head
against the swollen floods in spring. When proceeding
down stream the boat could drift with the current
and reserve her fuel. The refrigerator plant and engine
could be taken into the country free of duty, and cheap
labour can be obtained on the Obi for their erection. The

existing boats carry passengers at much cheaper rates than those which obtain on the road, and, as they are not too strict in the matter of passenger luggage, it is far the best and cheapest, and most comfortable way of travelling.

The hotel at Barnaoul is a good one for Siberia, and not expensive. There was a large organ in one of the

MARKET-PLACE, BARNAOUL.

rooms, driven by steam, which was a passable substitute for a band of wind instruments. When started it was powerful enough almost to blow the roof off. I paid a visit of inspection to the market and was very much interested. The shops sold a very complete assortment of articles, from a needle to a sledge. The motor-car does not seem to have penetrated so far as Siberia, which is to be regretted, as a good machine would sell well among the rich merchants, while one or two cheap motor vans or carts would be invaluable on the flat steppes.

After a stay of two days we left Barnaoul for Bysk.
The weather had been warmer and very fine; it now became colder. The roads were very rough and travelling
increasingly difficult. The holes worn by the sledges in
the snow were from three to five feet deep. In some places
the snow was very deep, while in others it had been blown
away altogether, and all along our route the track was so
narrow that there was never room for more than one
horse upon it at a time. The forests were not so thick as
those we had passed through on the way to Barnaoul.
The country east of the River Obi was hilly and covered
with forests, while that on the west was uniformly flat
and destitute of vegetation. The forests were largely
composed of birch and aspen trees, with a sprinkling of
pine and dark firs. The oak grows very small. The
distance between Barnaoul and Bysk is 150¼ versts, or
100½ miles, not 120 miles as I had been led to believe from
the writings of previous travellers. Soon after leaving
Barnaoul we had to cross the River Obi. As the ice was
breaking up we made the crossing in a drosky. I was
impressed by the prosperous appearance of the villages
and the size of the houses of which they are composed.
Most of the peasants about here are the descendants of
early Russian colonists who migrated hither and were
granted large portions of land, upon which they have pros-
pered exceedingly ever since. Many of them collected
around our sledge when we stopped, and plied us
with questions. When we told them we came from
England they appeared mystified—they had never heard
of such a place. They appeared to be a free, bold
peasantry, very superior to the humble and rather timid
native of European Russia. We changed our entire turn-
out six times before reaching Bysk. During one half of
the journey the country was very hilly, while the track
being too narrow to allow two horses running abreast, the
second one of our team very often slipped up to the collar
into the soft snow at the side of the road. Once or twice

we were obliged to pull to one side to allow caravans of sledges loaded with butter and other produce to pass. These caravans were often very long, consisting of 50 to 60 sledges. One man in charge of about five horses took it in turn to lead the caravan, while the rest followed very slowly behind, the drivers taking their sleep in turn on the sledges. The butter is wrapped in mats and covered with hay to keep the sun off. It is during these journeys across the steppes that butter is occasionally exchanged for snow and rubbish, which finds its way to the English market. Very unfairly, the blame has been laid upon the Russian merchant, although he is nearly always quite ignorant of any fraud having been perpetrated. It is true that cases have occurred of bricks being neatly wrapped in parchment and placed in the centre of casks of butter, but tricks of this kind are easily traced to the particular dairy. The Government should provide the vehicles for the conveyance of butter through the steppes. Some form of mechanical traction with a locked-up refrigerator van would meet the requirements of the case, and the vans could be replenished with cold air at certain stations. An arrangement of the kind suggested is imperative, in order to render the efficiency of the railway more complete, while its introduction will increase the confidence of everyone connected with the butter trade.

We enjoyed some excellent shooting by the way. There were numerous white hares in the district, and these afforded first-rate sport. One wolf was seen by us at a distance of about 100 yards and accommodated with a shot, but he only howled his dissatisfaction at the treatment he had received and vanished round the corner of a farmhouse, near which he was evidently on the lookout for a stray meal. A little later the driver called out " Volki ! " which meant wolves, and pointed across the snow to a mound, We looked, and sure enough there were two impudent-looking heads just showing above the elevated ground. I jumped out of the sledge and my companion followed with

the gun. Being knee-deep in the snow, and in a stooping
position, they did not see us until we were about ten yards
off. I was just about to shoot when they became aware
of my presence and made off barking. I did not shoot, as
they were dogs and not wolves; but they were very like
them in appearance, sufficiently so, in fact, to suggest the
explanation that they were a cross between the domestic
animal and his disreputable relation. I was rather disappointed, as I would particularly have liked to take a
wolf-skin back to England with me, but the annoyance
did not last very long. We had been looking for wolves
all the way from Barnaoul, having been told that owing
to the winter having lasted six weeks longer than usual,
with severe cold, there were large numbers prowling about
in the neighbourhood of the villages looking for food;
but although we frequently heard of exciting wolf-hunts
during our travels we were never lucky enough to meet
a pack ourselves.

Travelling by night is not a very desirable thing at
any time; it is still less pleasant in the middle of winter
and through a Siberian steppe. We narrowly escaped an
upset which would doubtlessly have deposited us at the
bottom of a steep gully. It was half-past eleven when we
reached Kharlipko, our next stopping-place. We drove
throught the silent village and into the skeleton gateway
of the post-house at full gallop and pulled up abruptly in
front of the entrance. Here we knocked. A head appeared
at a window, and presently a lamp was carried into the
travellers' room. We shook the snow from our clothes and
entered. The room was stuffy and close from the heat of
the stove and the presence of eight or ten weary way-
farers, who, with their boots removed but still wearing the
rest of their clothing, lay huddled together in an adjoining
room. I took a peep at them in the interests of science,
but immediately withdrew. The landlady brought us a
" samovar," and shortly afterwards we were enjoying a
cup of coffee and a good square meal. We instructed our

driver to be in readiness at 4 a.m., as we wished to reach Bysk as early as possible. This allowed us four hours in which to get what sleep we could. At 4.30 we started. The thermometer registered 15 degrees below freezing point. We had evidently started without consulting the convenience of a number of white hares, whom our progress disturbed very considerably, but they were very quick in their movements and difficult to shoot, besides which we had very little time to spare in following them over the snow. They are good sport and adepts in the art of vanishing. We obtained our first view of Bysk at one o'clock on the following day. From the brow of a hill we had an excellent view of the two rivers, Bye and Katun, where, by their confluence below Bysk, they form the Obi. The Bye flows out of Lake Teletskoë, the largest in the Altai district, while the Katun is swelled by a number of tributary streams rising in the Katunskië Belki range, and has its source in the Belukha glacier, south of the mountain of that name. A descent of 250 feet brought us to Bysk on the banks of the River Bye. The domes of two pretty churches, burning in the sun, lent additional attractiveness to the pretty wooden buildings which constitute the town. The weather was spring-like, notwithstanding the fact that the thermometer stood at 16 degrees below zero. We noticed, when we had crossed the River Katun, that one half of the vehicles were droskies and the other half sledges, proving that the surrounding country, like that we had traversed, was still frozen, while the town, being sheltered from the wind, was relatively free of snow. .

We had been invited to stay at the house of the only Englishman resident in that district, so we immediately drove to our quarters.

The following morning I paid visits to the various butter merchants of the town, who are at the same time dairy owners and who collect from other dairies within a 300-mile radius. Two of them showed me gold medals which they had received for their produce at the Agricultural Exhibition held some short time previously at Barnaoul.

BYSK FROM A HILL.

Bysk appears to be a coming centre for the butter trade. As at other centres, the peasant who brings his butter to Bysk takes the opportunity at the same time of pur-

I

chasing whatever he may be in need of and, as the town
contains the only market within a very wide radius, an
extensive trade is done in a number of various articles.
The practice, already referred to, of selling separators to
the dairy farmers, with a guarantee to pay the best prices
for the butter supplied by them, is common at Bysk, and
has the inevitable effect of maintaining a low standard
quality of the butter. Until the practice is stopped the
peasant, who has no incentive to improve the quality of
his product, will make no effort in that direction. Other
articles are sold by the butter merchants, such as agricultural machinery, casks, wrappers, parchment and salt,
but the latter is of poor quality and frequently spoils the
butter. The farmers of Bysk are forming associations
similar to those which exist in other centres.

On the following night we attended a reception, several
prominent citizens, including the judge for the district,
being profoundly interested in what they were pleased to
call my venturesome winter expedition. One or two of
my hosts had been as far as Altaiskoë, which is about 50
miles from Bysk, in the direction of the mountains; they
were therefore interested in them. One man present
proposed to let me see some photographs of the glaciers
which Professor Sapozhnikoff had discovered, and accordingly I called upon him. The worthies of Bysk were
careful to draw my attention to the dangers which
awaited me in the mountains and, by describing crevasses
such as they thought I had never met before, they
evidently expected to terrify me very much, and, in fact,
actually succeeded in doing so with my companion. He
was particularly depressed when we left to come home, and
went out again soon after to a card-party at the local
club, from which he did not return until the early hours
of the morning. We had arranged to start at eight o'clock,
but when, at ten, I knocked at the door of his room, he
declared that it was his intention to turn back, as he had
serious objections to being killed on a mountain, and, as

he happened to be the eldest of the family, his father could ill afford to lose him. This, though reasonable enough in itself, was rather disconcerting to me, as it meant that I would be left to my own resources with only a smattering of the language at my disposal—by no means a pleasant prospect. We discussed the matter for three hours and, as he saw that whatever turn events might take it was not my intention to return, he began to show signs of giving way. I took care to point out to him that the Russians would have the laugh of the Englishman who was afraid. To this he retorted by reminding me that everyone at Bysk believed that we would be risking almost certain death, either from cold, or from the wolves or bears with which the district was only too well supplied. We finally compromised matters on the understanding that he would be at liberty to stop at the last village and engage a huntsman and horses and spend his time hunting, while I went to the mountains. At four o'clock that afternoon we resumed our journey, and I was truly delighted that I had not been compelled to proceed alone.

Mr N. A. Sitcheff, a wealthy merchant of the place, was good enough to lend me a "shuba," which is a heavy coat made entirely of fur. It was so thick and heavy that I thought it quite a joke to put it on, feeling that no cold, not even that of Siberia, would be intense enough to penetrate it. I was mistaken. It is impossible for anyone who has not experienced it to realise what the cold in Siberia is like, or to calculate the thickness of the clothing necessary for comfort in that country.

As there is little or no difficulty in making the journey as far as Bysk, I have not given the intermediate stations or their distances. Beyond Bysk, however, the country is so little known, and there are so many different post routes, that I propose to describe the country more minutely, in order that my description may serve as a guide to any future travellers.

The first stage was one of 16 miles to Krasnobaisk.

We spent about two hours on the way shooting white hares; meanwhile the sun set behind the distant Altai Mountains. It was half-past seven when we reached Krasnobaisk. We directed our yamshtchik to drive us to the post station, but instead of doing so he took us to his friends. The domestic arrangements at this place left much to be desired. The house was very small and stuffy, the interior being illuminated by a solitary candle, while a family of eight lay huddled in sleep upon the floor. While the baggage was being shifted I did my best to fraternise with the inmates. The linguistic difficulty being practically insurmountable I endeavoured to allay any suspicions which might be lurking in some recess of their unsophisticated intelligences by adroitly balancing a paper funnel on my nose and applying a lighted match to it. This impressed them very much. They said that they had never seen anything like it before. The eight recumbent forms assumed an erect position and a general expansive grin, and when, at half-past eight, we resumed our journey, some fifteen polite and amicably-disposed peasants raised their caps and wished us " God-speed," or its equivalent in Russian. The church was the most attractive building in each village.

The journey to Altaiskoë, our next station, was one of 34 miles. The post road is marked out by square verst posts about 8 feet high and one foot square, painted black and white, the official colours, and showing the number of versts from the nearest station ; that is to say that half-way between two stations the numbers begin to reduce, showing the distance to the next one. These posts are one verst, or about two-thirds of a mile, apart, and are the only solace to the traveller in the bitter winter night as he shakes along in the sledge, jolted up into a corner, cramped, nearly frozen, and seated on the sharpest edge of some article of his baggage. On this occasion the darkness was so intense that the verst posts were altogether invisible, while a thick haze seemed to accompany us all the way, making it appear as if we were continually driving into a wall of snow-hills. We passed quite close to a leader of a pack of wolves, but when we turned back he was not to be seen. Presumably he had no desire to sample the contents of an English-made cartridge, or that his skin should be taken to England as a trophy. In addition to wolves there are large numbers of wild dogs roaming about the

THE CHURCH WAS THE MOST ATTRACTIVE BUILDING IN EACH VILLAGE.

country, of which the peasants say that they are more dangerous even than the wolves. At one part of the journey we noticed a horse running in front of our sledge. It had evidently strayed from the last village, which was some ten miles behind us. It would probably wander till it was exhausted and then lie down to die, when it would provide a welcome meal for a pack of wolves. Our driver experienced considerable difficulty in keeping to the track, as the only signs that the moujik goes by, sledge ruts, were not to be seen. The drivers are not remarkable for intelligence, they have no landmarks, and cannot tell you, with anything like certainty, whether they are on the right track or not. If you display any unseemly anxiety on the subject the driver will endeavour to reassure you with some pregnant remark like "nichevo" (no matter) or "seychas" (presently). We were not at all surprised, therefore, when our man suddenly pulled up and went ahead to look for the track. He came back delighted and drove us up an incline, the snow on which proved so soft that the sledge sank deep and the horses went in up to their collars. There was nothing for it but to get out of the sledge and extricate the horses. He then continued on the level for some distance and made an attempt to ascertain his whereabouts from the inmates of an isolated farmhouse; but although we could hear that there were people inside they were evidently too frightened to answer, and the only response to our knocking was the weary and monotonous barking of the dogs. We decided to continue our journey. We tried another hill, and were once more compelled to alight and disinter the sledge from a deep drift. We called a halt, and while we were resting became aware of the sound of running water not far away and of voices raised high in conversation. We shouted, and discharged our revolvers, but failed to attract attention, although the speakers seemed to be quite near us. The sound of the water was disquieting, as there was the danger of driving into it, although hitherto all the streams we had crossed were frozen hard. Eventually we crossed the hill, and, after twice losing our way and several times sticking fast in a drift, did the rest of the distance with but little to complain of, except the intense cold and the want of something to eat.

It was two o'clock in the morning when we reached Altaiskoë. The people in charge of the post stations are always very willing to get up and accommodate a traveller, whatever the hour of the night, if only he is endowed with the muscular strength necessary to rouse them out of their sleep. Then the "samovar" is lighted and soon boils, and the weary traveller can dispose himself among the tarakans and enjoy his tea and collaterals. The peasants are a serious people, but they are friendly and do their best to make a stranger feel at home. We would gladly have stayed longer, had it not been for the excessive heat in the house, which, to an Englishman, was almost unbearable.

Our peasant host asked us what he could do with asbestos, as he had discovered a large deposit. My companion advised him to state his claim to the Government and endeavour to obtain assistance to work it. There is, however, very little likelihood of the discovery being worked to a profit, owing to the lack of available capital. It is for this reason that many similar discoveries are profitless to the persons who make them.

The road to Onguadi and Mongolia, the route which one or two expeditions in quest of the wild goat have taken, branches away to the south-east from Altaiskoë, while our road lay to the south-west. We experienced some difficulty in securing the services of a driver and sledge, and, when we succeeded, it was by agreeing to pay double fare to the next stage at Baranchu, a distance of 27 miles. The moujik assured us that he could earn more by bringing trees into the village from the forest, an occupation in which large numbers of the peasantry engage during the winter months. We had not proceeded very far from the village when we came to a number of trees that had been cut down and brought out of the forest quite recently, and further on we met numbers of sledges laden with tree trunks coming out of the forest in all directions, the depth and softness of the snow having prevented all access to the forests until about a week previously. We drove along at a very good pace. The horses were fresh and spirited and the driver an exceptionally good one. The call which the Russian driver emits when encouraging his horses was louder from this particular driver than I ever heard it, and the team appeared to respond to it with something very much like intelligence. We stopped occasionally on the way to engage in a few minutes' shooting, the white hare and the ryabchik falling to our guns.

Presently we emerged into more hilly country, covered for the most part by what appeared to be practic-

BEYOND ALTAISKOË, NEARING SHIMELOVSKAYA PASS.

ally virgin forest. Some of the cedar trees we passed were exceptionally fine specimens, the most numerous, however, were aspen and birch, with a sprinkling of a species of fir with a dark brown bark. We rested for a brief spell at the summit of the Shimelovskaya Pass, 3500 feet above sea-level. The distance from Altaiskoë to the base of the pass is two miles, while the summit is two miles further. We halted near a verst post, which stood a few yards off the road, and arranged a shooting match, the verst post serving as target. My revolver shot left a hole quite half an inch in depth. The summit of the pass is consecrated by a small chapel containing a sacred ikon, but I did not notice that our driver paid it any special reverence   From this point we obtained our first good view of the Altai Mountains. The descent from the highest point of the pass was a very gradual one, and shortly before reaching Barancha we came upon a small creamery situated on the slope of a mountain in a truly ideal spot for the purpose; but the drainage is very bad and the separator and other implements used are cheap and primitive. Unlike the dairies in the vicinity of the Siberian line, however, this one had been erected near a running stream of pure water, invaluable for washing purposes. It only needed about 20 feet of drain pipes to render the sanitation of the place exemplary, but the idea had evidently never occurred to the proprietor, and the creamery was too remote for the supervision of the Government Inspector to be exercised over it. We obtained from the people in charge about five pounds of butter of very fine quality, and were told that the weekly output of the place is about 5 cwts. The butter was purchased by the representatives at Bysk of a Moscow firm, and judging by the prices the peasant told us he was receiving for it they must have been making a very fair profit on the business. The separator, although inexpensive, was a new one, the old one having been destroyed during the popular demonstrations against these machines, which the superstitious peasantry denominated " devils." We reached Barancha at about noon, having enjoyed the journey immensely. Our way had been through warm, sheltered valleys, and we would certainly have journeyed in a more leisurely manner had such a course not been sternly vetoed by our driver, who threatened to turn back if we did not proceed, as he wanted to get back to his business of carting trees. As we had paid his fare in advance we were at his mercy. He was a curiosity in more ways than one, and recalled a hot-headed Irish " jarvey " in charge of a jaunting car, rather than a

sluggish Russian peasant. It was a curiosity, moreover, to
see a moujik in a hurry. The fact that it was Lent troubled
him very little. We had not met with a single case of
breach of the Lenten observances, but our friend did
excellent execution with our five pounds of butter, remark-
ing, that it was not his intention to starve himself to death
as the peasants of his village had been doing during the
fast. While we were having lunch we were introduced to
another curiosity in the shape of a local policeman. This
was an exceedingly harmless and timid individual. He
informed us, with captivating modesty, that he was the
village policeman, and that he was waiting for the Ispravnik
of Bysk, whom he had expected to arrive the previous
evening. He also told us that he had known we were
coming. I could not conceive at the time how the news
had got ahead of us, but I learned afterwards that ·the
chief of the police had received instructions from the
Governor of Tomsk to keep an eye on us and follow us to
Katunda if we went so far. Owing to my interpreter
having let everyone at the club at Bysk know that we had
abandoned the idea, the chief evidently concluded that my
projected expedition had failed, and that it would be no
longer necessary for him to make the dreaded journey.
This accounted, too, for the fact that the Ispravnik at Bysk
had refused to give us any assistance whatever, and had
insisted upon it that the task was impossible of accom-
plishment. The policeman sat near us in that room of the
post station with much of the air of a person who was
about to be led to execution, or of a boy looking forward to
a thrashing. The expression, " the strong arm of the law,"
was certainly not applicable to this particular limb of the
executive. I expect it is his business to keep an attentive
eye on whatever transpires in the village and report to the
chief of police when he makes his annual visit. I am
certain he was not good for anything else. Probably if a
disturbance were to arise he would be missing, as it is
currently maintained the English policeman, to whom he

presented so marked a contrast, is on such occasions. My
interpreter and myself owe this police-officer a hearty
laugh, for I never saw a better caricature of a policeman
on the stage. Our lunch over, we presented him with half
a small tin of jam, which he gratefully accepted. We
made a careful examination of our luggage, as I felt certain
that our last driver would repay watching to make sure
that he had loaded our sledge with all our belongings.
Turning over the hay at the bottom of his sledge I found
a gun-case in one corner, which may have been left there
by accident. However, it is wise to watch your luggage
carefully.

The next stage to Tavourack was a short one of 14
miles. The owner of the sledge asserted that the road
was in a very bad condition and refused to take us except
for double the ordinary money. This we consented to
pay and were rather thankful that we had been able to
persuade him to take us at all. The journey was exceedingly difficult. In one narrow valley particularly, the
horses had a very severe struggle. At another place the
moujik, pointing to a hole in the snow, informed us that a
peasant from the next station had started with a load of
hay for Barancha, and that horse, sledge and load had
capsized in the snow and been lost, the peasant himself
escaping with great difficulty. By the time he could
procure help to extricate the horse the poor animal was
dead. Shortly afterwards our own man upset us into a
stream that was just breaking up and my interpreter got
wet through, while the driver was treated to some heated
Russian language that I had never heard before. To
add insult to injury he said "nichevo" (no matter), at
which my interpreter absolutely lost control of himself
and threatened to knock him off the sledge, but the
moujik did not appear to be discomposed by the threat.
My interpreter found, on referring to his note-book, that
we had paid our last driver to take us a distance of 60
versts, which meant that he should have brought us to the

next station, and that although we had watched him carefully he had got the best of us at the finish. It is well,
therefore, in order to avoid extra expense, to see that
your driver does not drop you half way, as they all
insist on being paid before they start. We reached
Tavourack at 5 p.m. The man at the post station had to
send for the owner of the sledge and team, an operation
which occupied half an hour. However, when he did
arrive he refused to take us that night, as one half the
journey was uphill and there was a very dangerous
mountaiu ridge with heavy snow-drifts to be crossed. A
doctor, he told us, had been out all night the previous
week owing to the sledge sticking fast in the snow, while
he had returned for fresh horses. He promised faithfully
to be in readiness at four o'clock next morning, so we
dismissed him. The post house at Tavourack actually
contained a bed, but as I thought it would be too much
trouble to use the insect powder to the extent that would
be necessary, I decided in favour of the accustomed hard
boards of the floor, only removing my boots.

We started at five o'clock the next morning for Chorni-
Anni, a distance of 24 miles, with a preliminary ascent of
6 miles up the valley. It was along this road that I
made my first inspection of a Russian bath. This was a
small hut erected at some distance from the dwelling-
house. It contained a roughly-constructed stove in
which wood is burnt until the stones of which it is composed are nearly red hot. Water is then thrown on the
stones, the steam thus generated filling the room. In
some baths a raised platform is erected, which is reached
by a series of steps and is flanked by wooden benches.
This is called the "polka," and, owing to the superheated
steam ascending to the top of the room, is a very hot corner.
The method of using the bath is to raise some soap-suds
in a bucket of hot water. A bundle of birch twigs with
the leaves still on, called a "veynik," is dipped in the hot
soap and water and the body soundly thrashed with it.

The heat of the "polka" is so intense that the Russian peasant frequently thinks nothing of coming outside *in*

WE WALKED UP YEDTOGOL PASS.

SUMMIT OF YEDTOGOL PASS.

nudibus and rolling in the snow. We walked some distance up the Yedtogol Pass. The weather was warm, the thermometer only registering 38 degrees Fahr. (2 degrees above zero). The trees on the summit were all bent over in a southerly direction, giving evidence of heavy northerly winds. The River Chagran takes its source near this point. Although in the valleys we had passed through the ice in the rivers was all breaking up, the Chagran, owing to the valley being more exposed towards the north, was still frozen over. The river grew visibly in expanse as we followed its current. Almost the whole of the way down the mountain slopes our sledge reposed gracefully on one side, a most uncomfortable way of travelling. Finally it upset altogether, depositing us by the way and, as we were practically smothered in mud, we decided to walk. The snow had melted away and the road was exceedingly heavy for the horses. It very often happens that the sledge will run for half a mile or so on one side, the wings, if the driver is skilful, preventing its turning over, while the horses are drawing it along at a very fair speed. The Russian driver is an adept in the art of righting the sledge by alternately jumping on and off while it is going at full speed. He is also very skilful in shifting his seat so as to balance the vehicle, and his method of encouraging the horses, by shouting expletives at them, enables him to extract an effort of 30 or 40 miles out of them on nothing more substantial than an unstinted supply of Siberian air. It is currently reported that the Siberian moujik regards it as an absurdity to give the horse food when the air is so good, and that he maintains, moreover, that a horse runs lighter without a good meal than with one. However this may be it is quite certain that the natives contrive to get an astonishing amount of good work and speed out of the scraggy little animals.

The mountains in this neighbourhood, if the appearance of hundreds of cattle passed by us on the way can be taken as evidence, furnish ideal grazing, although they are awkward for travellers.

We reached Chorni-Anni at one o'clock. The village is rather pretty and contains a church. It appeared to be fairly prosperous. It is situated in a basin at the junction of four valleys, and is subject to severe dust-storms. We were unfortunate enough to witness one of these storms, which broke over us without the slightest warning. The four valleys were swept by strong winds which met and raised the loose, black soil in dense clouds. Sometimes the winds swell into a hurricane, causing danger to life and

KALMUCK BOY IN CHARGE OF BULLOCKS AND WAGGONS.

property. We were told that, owing to the frequency and strength of the storms, the snow could not rest in the village.

We started on our next stage in a drosky. Melia, our destination, is about 10 miles distant from Chorni-Anni, and the first part of the journey led us along the banks of the river, which were as flat as a billiard-table, until we reached the junction of the Beli-Anni with Chorni-Anni. Two miles out of the village we passed the first Kalmuck settlements. Away to the right a boy was tending three large bullocks, attached to waggons very similar in their appearance to the familiar bullock-waggons of South

Africa. Further on we passed a party of Kalmucks on
their way to market to purchase flour, carrying hides
with them to pay for it. Chorni-Anni appears to be the
centre for the exchange of commodities between Siberians
and Kalmucks. Our next encounter was with a moujik,
with whom we entered into conversation. He informed
us that he was about to be expelled from his village,
although he had built a house for himself. He asked our
opinion as to the ethics of the question, and we, being
only posted in one version of the dispute, unhesitatingly
gave our verdict in his favour. After he had gone on his
way rejoicing our driver told us that the reason he had
been expelled from the village was that he refused to pay
any taxes, and that the house he spoke of had been
erected by him on land that had been occupied by the
Kalmucks for many years. In answer to my question as
to what the Kalmucks did to protect themselves, he
replied, that it very often happened that a Siberian
colonist built his house on land that had been squatted on
by the nomad Kalmucks for ages and simply told the
Kalmucks to move off. This they usually did, as they
were under the impression that the land belonged to the
colonist. We had been told at Bysk that the Kalmuck
was shy and retiring, a description which turned out to
be correct. They are a very mild and inoffensive race,
unselfish and not quarrelsome, but brave and enduring.
Sometimes they lose patience, as in a case we were told
about, in which the Kalmucks had compelled the chief of
police to take refuge in a boat and row out into the
middle of a lake, as they threatened to kill him for
raising their taxes. I have seen the Cossacks and the
Kalmucks, and I think that the latter are better horsemen,
better huntsmen and better men all round. They deserve
all the encouragement the Russian Government can give
them and would make excellent soldiers if the Russian
nation would allow them to enlist. They are excellent
judges of grazing land, and their cattle, which are never

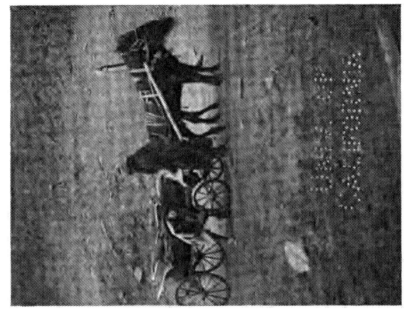

A TRIFLING MISHAP TO THE DROSKY.

KALMUCKS ON THEIR WAY TO MARKET.

K

looked after, increase in numbers and find abundant food
for themselves all the year round. As a consequence, the
Kalmucks own enormous numbers of heads of sheep and
cattle, which are sold very cheaply : sheep selling at 5s. and
6s. a head, and other cattle and horses in proportion. The
horse is the Kalmuck's companion and friend ; he keeps it
as long as he possibly can and, when it is too old to work,
he kills it and eats the flesh. The bark huts of these
people are found in all the prettiest spots in the mountains
and wherever the grazing is good.

The scenery through which we passed was most beautiful. The valleys are level and the mountains rise abruptly
from the level and protect the lowland from the winds.
We had some trouble with our drosky, the tyre of one of
the wheels coming off repeatedly, and the 10 miles took
some considerable time to traverse. We completed the
stage at last, however, and started on the next one to Ouskam, a distance of 20 miles. The road was over level land
and travelling was sufficiently easy. We stopped occasionally to do some shooting, bagging some ducks among other
game. At one spot we passed some hills that looked as
if they consisted of gold and copper, and we photographed
a Kalmuck shrine near a settlement of these interesting
people. The rites appear to consist in lighting a fire and
walking round it with lighted faggots in their hands,
offering prayers. Their religion is said to be Shamanism,
but from the part that fire plays in the rites it would
appear rather to be a form of Zoroastrianism.

We arrived at Ouskam at seven o'clock. Most of the
villagers had gone after a pack of wolves that had, very
inconsiderately, eaten two horses the previous night, so we
experienced some difficulty in procuring a sledge and team
to take us further. We got these in instalments at last,
the horses coming from one peasant and the sledge from
another, and at eight o'clock in the evening we started on
a 40-mile stage to Abbi.

The first part of the journey was through very fine

scenery and over level ground. Some of the valleys were
about a mile and a half across, and their extent was about
20 miles. The rest of the journey escaped my observation
as it was my turn to sleep. When I awoke, the temperature had fallen and the thermometer now registered 7
degrees below freezing point ; my feet were slightly
frozen.

KALMUCK SHRINE, ALTAI.

We were very glad when we reached Abbi. We had
travelled for thirty-two and a half hours, with three halts
of an hour each, from Tavourack to Abbi, a total distance
of 76 miles, 20 miles of which were over mountain
passes.

A peasant who had just arrived from Koksa, 40 miles
further on, offered to take us the whole journey for three
roubles, or about 6s. 4½d. This was too good an offer to
miss, so we arranged to start at half-past six the next
morning. It was four o'clock when we arrived, but we

were anxious to get away again, as the moujiks were
pretty generally of the opinion that we would not be able
to get anyone to take us any further. For the first 10
miles the road was level and the scenery very fine. At the
end of that section of the road we turned away to the left
from the River Koksa and began to ascend the Korgomskië
Mountains, 5000 feet above the level of the sea. At one
place the track ran for a distance of about 200 yards along

PASS OVER THE KORGOMSKIË MOUNTAINS—5000 FEET.

the edge of a sheer precipice overhanging the River Koksa.
The track, moreover, had a deep hole running along in the
centre, and, as we drove along that ledge, one runner of the
sledge kept in the hole, causing it to lean over in a
dangerous and exciting position. We did not dare to tell
the driver to stop, as, had we done so, he would probably
have jumped off the sledge, a very dangerous thing to do
with the vehicle in so precarious a position. We were
going at a very good rate, however, and soon had the ledge
behind us, emerging into one of the most beautiful valleys

I have ever seen. The mountains around were clad with pines, firs and birches, but there was a scarcity of trees in the valleys. Everything was as still and quiet as the grave. When we stopped to arrange the harness on the horses we heard no sound except the murmuring of the river. All the birds seemed to have migrated and to be waiting for the return of the spring weather. The air had become much warmer after we crossed the Korgomskië Mountains, but the snow became more troublesome for the horses. In spite of this drawback, however, our team on this section was a very hardy and enduring one, and gave an excellent exhibition of what a Siberian horse can do. The driver stopped at his farm, which was on the way, to change horses, and while waiting we had some refreshments. The moujik showed us an old wooden house which he had abandoned for the winter. The place was infested with tarakans to such an extent that it was no longer possible to live in it. He intended, therefore, to see what exposure to the frost of a Siberian winter would do towards killing off the pests. He told us some astonishing stories of the havoc these insects work with food stores in a house, which represented the tarakan as the most formidable insect in the world; but as I have only this man's authority for their truth, I refrain from inflicting them on the reader. A little further along the road we passed five Kalmucks, on horseback and armed with very primitive guns. They were also provided with "lyzhy" (skis). Our driver, who spoke their language, asked them what they were going to shoot, to which they piously replied, "Whatever God may send us."

Bears and game of all kinds are plentiful in this neighbourhood, but to our disgust the bears were hibernating when we paid our visit to the country.

We had to take to the river presently, as the snow became too deep for the horses. In many places we drove through water, fervently trusting that the ice underneath would prove strong enough to support us. The climax

JUNCTION OF THE RIVERS KOKSA AND ABBI.
BROKEN ICE.

CONSULTING KALMUCK ABOUT ROAD NEAR RIVER KOKSA.

came when we reached the River Abbi, a tributary of the
Koksa, where the river flows between steep mountain
slopes. Here the ice was so broken up that we had to
take it in turns to go in front of the sledge and test it

KOKSA RIVER.

before we ventured upon it. Judging from the speed of
the water, as seen in holes in the ice, the current of the
Koksa is very swift. At this part the river is about 20
feet deep and beautifully clear. We left the river shortly
afterwards and took a road to the left to Koksa. In the
afternoon we were informed that Belukha could be seen,

but found that such was not the case. The peasants were supremely interested in our guns, and we had to discharge them once or twice to show them how they worked, as their own weapons are very primitive.

We left Koksa in the afternoon for Ouemon, a distance of 16 miles, travelling mostly downhill and over very rough ground, and reached that village in the evening. There was a doctor stopping at the post station and we were informed that he was the only one within a radius of 100 miles; but there is very little sickness in this Siberian Switzerland.

We were bearers of a letter of introduction to Mr Oshlikoff, a wealthy merchant of Ouemon, but we found, on arrival, that one half of the village was situated on one side of the river and the other half on the other, and that the man we wanted was on the wrong side, so we decided to defer our visit to him until the following morning and to retire to rest in the meantime. The following morning was very warm, the thermometer registering 98 degrees Fahr. in the sun and 40 degrees in the shade. This too in the middle of April. We walked through mud for a quarter of a mile to the River Katun, and were ferried across to pay a visit to our friend. He lived in an uncommonly fine house, for Siberia, in which there were two splendid bedrooms, with beautifully clean beds in them, so that considering that we had not taken our clothes off for about ten days, and had not seen such luxury anywhere else in Siberia, we were very sorry we had not come across the river the previous night. Mr Oshlikoff gave us some fatherly advice, and among the rest he strongly urged us not to attempt the mountains. He assured us that we would, in all probability, get lost, as no one had ever been there in the winter. My interpreter was duly impressed, and told me, that our friend's opinion confirming what so many others had said went to prove that our expedition was hopeless; to which I replied by pointing

CROSSING THE RIVER KATUN ON A PLANK.

CYTHEREAN
OF
SMITH

out that as no one had ever been there in winter, not
even the natives, nobody could possibly know whether the
mountains were accessible or not, and that the sooner
someone settled the question the better, as the inhabitants
live mainly upon the chase, and, that part being un-
inhabited, the probability was that it would be very
plentifully supplied with game and would therefore be a

BRIDGE OVER KATUN RIVER.

magnificent hunting-ground for them if it was once opened
out. This altruistic treatment of the problem clinched
the argument. Our friend proposed to assist us to
procure rusks and bread for the journey, which we could
not have done without him, as the winter supplies had
been exhausted through the cold lasting two months
longer than in previous years. The spring is three weeks
earlier in this part than near the settlement of Novo-
Nicolaëvsk on the Siberian railway, and the previous

year the ice had all thawed before the 25th of March. The winter begins in October—December being the coldest month. The cold is not so excessive as in Central Siberia, the thermometer rarely falling lower than 62 degrees below zero, Fahr.

The village of Ouemon has a population of 1000.

We left Ouemon at midday and drove up the mountain slopes to the Katunda saddle, which I measured to be 4850 feet above the level of the sea. We had a fine view of Katunda to the right, with the Saptam Mountains on our left and the Katunskië-Belki range in the distance ; but we could not see Ouemon, as it was hidden from our view by a dense forest through which we had just passed. We descended into the flat valley of Katunda, 3000 feet below, the mountains forming a circle round it.

We reached Katunda late in the afternoon, having completed the journey from Bysk in three days and three nights. During the journey we had changed our horses and sledge nine times, making eleven stages, of which the shortest was 8 and the longest 40 miles. We had started at Bysk at an elevation of 600 feet and had attained the highest pass over the Korgomskië Mountains, 5000 feet above the level of the sea. We had driven through eight valleys, enclosed on all sides by mountains, which I have called circles, the smallest of which was about 4 miles across and the largest about 40, the breadth varying from 1 to 8 miles. The temperature of the air depended on the direction of the wind and the situation and height of the valley.

Rivers and lakes in Siberia freeze to the bottom about October. They break up at different times, and, in the late winter, as on the occasion when I visited the country, will always be uncertain, difficult, and even dangerous to the traveller. They remain frozen to the bottom during six months of the year. An undercurrent begins to form about the end of March, and in April they break

up—to freeze again in November. There is much uncertainty as to the condition of the rivers in the spring, as
they do not all break up simultaneously, and the peasants
in the different villages cannot tell you much about the
river beyond their own village, or even, for that matter,
about the state of the roads further than the next post
station. Some system of communication which would
enable the men in charge of the post stations to supply

KATUNDA SADDLE—4850 FEET.

the traveller with prompt and reliable information as to
the state of the roads and the ice on the rivers would be
of the greatest value.

The rivers near the Arctic Ocean are the first to
freeze and the last to thaw. The Katun, which is the
principal tributary of the Obi, is a fast-flowing river,
which takes its rise in the southern portion of the Belukha
glacier. It follows a semi-circular course, passing the
valley to the north of the Katunskië-Belki. The numerous
tributaries from the same range, which flow north for a
distance of from forty to fifty miles, are indebted for their

tortuous courses to the peculiar shape of the mountains, which resemble a partially-opened fan. In consequence of the flatness of the valleys, a canoe could be used by huntsmen to bring their trophies down the river. In summer, and particularly in July, the waters are very low, and safely navigable by any small craft. In early spring, however, the rivers are much more dangerous for navigation, owing to the speed of the currents, which are nowhere broken by waterfalls. The River Katun, for instance, has an unbroken fall of 3700 feet in 200 miles, and some of its tributaries falling into the river from the mountains have a gradient of from 2000 to 4000 feet in a similar distance.

The post-house of Katunda has two stories, double windows, and is well-built. Two forms, one table and a stove constituted the dining and bedroom furniture. The peasant in charge of the house and his wife lived below.

It was not long before lunch was ready, and, while we were enjoying that meal, quite a little crowd of peasants came round the door and gazed at us curiously. They asked all sorts of questions which at home one would have considered very impertinent.

We found that of the two hunters recommended by Professor Sapozhnikov, one would not go because it was winter, and the other wanted double pay. He told us that as the ice had just broken he could earn more by fishing; a good catch that day had made him independent. As he was the only man at Katunda who had been the way we wished to go, we were compelled to take him, but we managed to engage another Siberian at the correct price. We gave them a day in which to get ready.

That evening we were visited by candle-light by at least forty very inquisitive, well-meaning peasants, who stood about inside our room and in the passage, supported, to judge by the murmuring of voices, by many more outside the house. The priest and our Ouemon friend, Mr Oshlikoff, took dinner with us.

All the conversation was about the mountains. When

I told them we intended climbing Belukha, Mr Oshlikoff
was shocked, while the priest nearly fainted and pleaded
with us not to run so grave a risk, as though he were
trying to save our lives. All hope of persuading my
interpreter to climb with me soon vanished, but I convinced the gentlemen that, at least, nothing would stop
me, and repeated the argument, that as no one had ever been
through the gorges and the passes in winter, it could not
possibly be known if it were practicable to do so or not.

While the hunters were making preparations on the
following day, we arranged for the post-house keeper to
provide us with horses and accompany us to the Saptam.
It was necessary to learn to use the skis, so we took two
pairs with us, starting at ten o'clock in the morning.

We went through about 18 inches of snow over the flat
valley, and had not been more than two hours away before
we gained the mountain slope. We dismounted a little
way up the mountain to have a shot at a few kourapatki
(white pheasants), but owing either to the horses being in
motion or to bad marksmanship, we missed. We came across
what appeared to be the skeleton of a bear, and were
informed that this was a good place for shooting. In fact,
the inhabitants rely upon hunting for the great part of
their living. Besides bears, there are gluttons, lynxes,
foxes, badgers, klonkas, squirrels, sables, ermine, otters,
hares, and a large variety of game birds. The chief attrac-
tion, however, are the ibex and the real *Ovis Ammon*,
both having exceptionally large horns. It is stated in the
Great Siberian Railway Guide that the Altai is as rich in
animals to-day as Europe was at the time of Julius Cæsar,
2000 years ago. These mountain slopes are the very best
places in the Altai, so as the information was calculated to
lend attractions to even the most ordinary mountain, we
kept a bright look-out. As we neared the summit the
wind changed to the north, and the temperature dropped
very suddenly. I had some good ski practice on the slopes
of the mountain where the snow was deep, and on more

L

than one occasion descended into a basin-like dip head fore-most into the snow. After a few tumbles I became fairly proficient—allowing for occasions when one leg would

SAPTAM MOUNTAIN, NEAR KATUNDA.

persist in going in the wrong direction, compelling me to lie down in very inconvenient positions.

When we gained the summit of the Saptam, 9750 feet above the sea level, we were in a splendid position to see the mountains. I took a few photographs, and then, leaving my friend and the hunter, advanced towards several higher peaks of the Saptam ridge.

I enjoyed six hours of very interesting and difficult climbing, which was rendered the more difficult from the fact that, thinking only of ski practice, I had left my nailed-boots behind. The most difficult bit of climbing was on the third pinnacle, where the rocks of the summit were split in two and it was necessary to climb about 30 feet down a wall and then drop to the rocks opposite across a ravine, about 4 feet wide and 80 feet deep. One of the highest peaks looked as though it had been split in two, forming a wall of rock about 400 feet and as smooth as glass. The rock of these summits was very soft—a kind of shale—and easily broken with the fingers. On the north side the slopes were all of loose rock, and, being covered with snow, afforded very insecure footing.

The second summit was 10,000 feet in height, the third 10,050 feet, the fourth 10,020 feet, the fifth and sixth 10,000 feet each. I named the third, fourth and fifth peaks Faith, Hope and Charity, in the order as I came to them.

I was informed by the priest, who had lived in Katunda about thirty years, that no one had ever climbed those pinnacles, although hunters had frequently ascended the Saptam mountain in quest of game.

When I returned to the Saptam summit the moon was out and it was with difficulty I found the hunter with my horses, my friend having gone back to Katunda four hours earlier. The descent was very difficult and even dangerous on horseback, because with sunset the slopes had commenced to freeze, and the mountain is steep enough to ride down under the most favourable circumstances. We slipped and tumbled about merrily before we reached the the valley. The moon made the snow-clad mountains look quite near, and lit up the valleys like daylight.

We arrived at the post-house about midnight. The journey was a splendid one, and I saw enough snow-capped virgin peaks from the Saptam summit to keep the members of the Alpine club climbing for the next few years. If they care to take the journey, they will find the mountains quite formidable enough for expert climbers. There will be the uncertainty of ever gaining the summit, and the possibility of meeting bears and other wild animals on the way. With these attractions, the climber will require to add another to the many qualifications necessary for a successful mountaineer and be able to shoot well, both for protection and food.

CHAPTER VI

PEAK-BAGGING IN THE ALTAI

KATUNDA is situated in 86° 10′ east longitude, and Belukha is 86° 30′ east of Greenwich.

From information I had received from Professor Sapozhnikoff I learned that Belukha, which was believed to be the highest mountain in Siberia, somewhat resembles Mont Blanc, in that it consists largely (on the south side) of a slope and a glacier. I had made inquiries about the most suitable route and had learned that the southern approach is about three times longer than that from the north. The passes, moreover, were choked with snow, and therefore inaccessible to horses. On the other hand, we could not have succeeded in dragging the sledges containing our instruments and provisions for fourteen days in the mountains ourselves, even if we had been desirous of doing so, while dogs that could be used as draught animals were not procurable. After carefully weighing all the pros and cons we decided to take the road to the north, although we had not the vaguest idea as to what it would be like. The bracing air and the pleasure of the unknown helped to keep alive the spirit of adventure, and rendered us sufficiently indifferent to obstacles. We even decided that, if further progress were at any time to become impossible by any other means, we would attempt the journey on snow-shoes, and accordingly added a pair to each man's outfit.

SOUTH SLOPES OF BELUKHA, 14,800 FEET.

We made our first halt, after leaving the village of Katunda, at the house of a peasant recommended by Professor Sapozhnikoff as a suitable guide; but he refused to accompany us, as he considered the journey too dangerous. We had some lunch at his house, a small wooden building which accommodated three families. The families

were sufficiently prolific.   While seated in the heated room
which had been set apart for our use, a little girl,
about three years old, peeped through the open door at me.
I beckoned her to me and presented her with 20 kopecks.
She went away and returned presently at the head of a

AUTHOR AND HUNTER LEAVING KATUNDA FOR KATUNSKIE BELKI.

flying column of youngsters, whose ages ranged from two
to twelve, and who were quite plainly of opinion that they
were entitled to the same consideration.   There were
fourteen of them, but I ceded the point with as good a
grace as possible.   How the three families contrived to
live in that one small house was a mystery to me.   The

huntsman made us a parting present of half a sheep, as he did not think we would be able to shoot anything until we were nearer the mountains. A very small flour-mill, driven by water power, stood opposite the house.

Half an hour's ride from the place brought us to the River Katun, which we crossed, although the ice was breaking up. Arrived at the other side we entered a dense, trackless forest, through which we groped our way in complete darkness; it was wonderful how the leading horse found his way through it. Our rate of travelling was not more than about three miles an hour, the state of the ground rendering more rapid progression out of the question. We had intended to follow the course of the river, but this was impossible as the ice was breaking. We very nearly had an accident with one of the pack horses, which became frightened and restless because of the holes in the ice. At one time it seemed as though it would tumble through a hole, in which case it would have been washed under the ice by the fast-flowing river, which at that place was deep.

A second forest was entered and left behind us, and then we entered a mountain pass which led us up to a height of 6100 feet. A Kalmuck followed closely behind us and seemed to think it a great privilege, as, like all Kalmucks, he seemed to be afraid of high passes. He had not been over the pass in the winter before and, as many of the Kalmucks were starving for want of food, he took the opportunity of following us over to visit a friend in the Akkem valley to see if he could spare any stores. It was about halfway up the pass that he joined us, and seemed to bring bad luck, because we were immediately greeted by a snowstorm. We were not long in reaching the summit of the pass, however, where we noticed the pieces of coloured ribbon which the Kalmucks tie to the branches of trees by way of thanks-offerings for their safe arrival. After a brief rest we made a rapid descent, still accompanied by the storm, into the Akkem valley. The

road down the pass zig-zags for two or three miles,
ending in a steep dip to the right into the Akkem
valley, which at this place is quite flat, with the River
Akkem flowing down it. It was snowing hard when we
reached this spot. We were undecided whether to pitch

On the March through the Akkem Forests.

our tent, when I noticed a Kalmuck bark hut, which made
the valley seem quite civilised. Night was setting in, so
we called a halt and prepared our camp by scraping away
the snow and erecting a tent.

The Kalmuck who occupied the bark hut was quite
pleased and excited at seeing us and, while he scraped
away the snow, his children brought some dry sticks from
the hut; he then lit us a fire, while we unpacked the luggage,
putting the guns and everything we wished to keep dry in

his hut. We gave him our kettle, and he soon had it filled
with water from the river. Pushing a stout branch of
a tree into the ground, so that one end leaned over the
fire, he placed the kettle on it. Before we had unpacked
the tea and provisions the water was boiling.

My interpreter prepared dinner, one of the hunters and
myself pitched the tent, and the other hunter looked after
the horses. We sat round the fire in the thick snowstorm.
The thermometer registered 20 degrees below freezing
point and snow was falling fast, but we did not permit
either the snow or the cold to interfere with our dinner,
which consisted of tinned ox-tail soup, Army and Navy
rations, rusks, black bread, jam and tea. There seemed
little likelihood of the snow abating, so we did not sit very
long by the fire. My companion proposed to retire to the
tent. He was 5 feet 10 inches in height, while the tent
was only 6 feet 6 inches long, stood 3 feet from the ground,
and weighed 12 lbs. I had not contemplated using it
except on the ledges of precipices while climbing the
mountains. However, we succeeded in collecting sufficient
clothes to spread ou the ground inside the tent, and
presently retired. When 1 crawled in it seemed to me
that the inside was rather damp, and I had not been
asleep very long when I was awakened by a small stream
of water running down my neck. It came from the small
hole in the tent, through which the cord is inserted which
is used to tighten it up, so I had to change my position.
This was not as easy as it sounds. There were only a few
inches of room left, and any sudden movement might have
brought the tent down. We slept fairly well and comfortably afterwards. The water down my back soon dried,
but it seemed to soak into our articles of bedding, making
the soil underneath nice and soft, and allowing the body
to settle down into a mould, thus preventing my interpreter from rolling on me, or me on him. In the
morning, as we had expected, we found the ground on
which we had been lying afloat, and the ancient sheep-

skin coats, which had served us as rugs, saturated with water.

The Akkem valley in which we camped is 4325 feet above sea-level, and the spot at which we had stopped was the last Kalmuck settlement along the Akkem river. Our little tent was pitched quite close to one of the Kalmuck huts, which was of the usual pattern, being made of long

FIRST CAMP, AKKEM VALLEY, AND KALMUCK.

poles or selected saplings, stripped of their branches, ingeniously disposed and covered with strips of bark from neighbouring trees. Each hut has a heavy wooden door 2 feet from the bottom, measuring about 4 feet by 5 feet and opening outwards. The Kalmucks were very amicably disposed towards us. One of them, who helped us to pack our tent, was exceedingly doubtful as to the success of our undertaking and pressed us very much to stay awhile with them on our return journey. He informed my huntsman, who spoke the language of the tribe, that no one else had ever thought of making the journey in winter, on account of the severe cold and the quantity of snow. He was quite sure no horse could stand on the ice-glazed slopes of the mountains, and that it was quite possible the horses would slip down and fall upon the River Akkem, and be killed with their riders.

The river winds its way through the mountains. One bank is precipitous, while the other is a gentle slope of 45 degrees clothed with a forest growth as dense as an Indian jungle. The sound of our voices was re-echoed as in some vast cavern, and the scenery was wild and impressive. At first we had a rough road and one or two frozen streams to cross, but afterwards we came to the ice-glazed slopes. The pack horses managed to shake their burdens into such a position that it was necessary to dismount and re-adjust the luggage about every half mile.

We found the forest slopes frozen for about 20 miles. Before we had travelled half the distance we had been through all the antics and positions possible on horseback, from sliding down the slope on the horse's back to dragging the helpless animal up some very steep slope. It is surprising what one can grow accustomed to, even to tumbling and getting the horse up again without losing the stirrups, by merely jerking him up by the aid of the bridle, with one leg pushing against the slope ; and scraping between thin trees by using all one's strength to push them apart.

The snow was usually deep and soft at the bottom of the slope, with ice-glazed ground underneath, but on the higher slopes it had all slipped down, leaving the ice-glazed slope, and making it much more difficult for a horse to stand. With the exceptions of halts to extricate a fallen horse or to re-arrange the baggage, we were in our saddles for nine hours, there being no convenient spot at which to call a halt. There was no track, and our horses had frequently to pick their way among the fallen trees

KALMUCKS, AKKEM VALLEY.

scattered over the frozen slopes, making riding an increasingly difficult task.

The trees in this part of the country, which are

WE HAD TO RE-ADJUST THE LUGGAGE ABOUT EVERY
HALF-MILE.

principally firs, are very tall and graceful, tapering to a fine point at the crown and almost devoid of branches. Their shape at the base is rather peculiar and different from that of any trees of the same species that I have ever seen. The first 8 or 10 feet are relatively much thicker than the rest of the tree. These trees do not grow in the valleys, but only on the mountain slopes and down to the water's edge. Our hunters were constantly on the lookout for bears, *Ovis Ammon*, ibex or other big game, and we saw by my Zeiss binocular several herds of what appeared to be ibex or *Ovis Ammon*, too far away to stalk, so we had to let them go. I watched one herd while the hunters were dragging a pack horse out of a snow heap and, although we did not seem to be making much noise, considering the distance, they raised their heads and vanished among trees.

Descending the slope and crossing the Akkem river at an altitude of 5650 feet, we obtained our first good view of the Katunskië-Belki range. We watered our horses at a place where the ice had broken. On reaching the opposite bank we found that the horses could not get up it, and were, therefore, obliged to unload the pack horses and help them up the slope, dragging the baggage after us. The bed of the forest is composed of rock, with a layer of sand, which no doubt accounts for the slender roots of the trees. Several of them fell during our progress through the forest, making a dull, crashing noise. A large number of trees on the side we were now on appeared to have been uprooted by a recent hurricane. They were lying in all directions against one another and on the ground. We had constantly to push the branches out of our faces, and sometimes the man following would get a slash across the face if he did not keep his hand up to catch the branch.

After rounding the slopes of a mountain we emerged out of the forest to the left, and eventually reached the banks of the River Yarlow, a tributary of the Akkem. We selected a suitable elevated spot at the base of a mountain, and in close proximity to a forest, where we thought we would be protected from the wind and find a sufficiency of dry wood to enable us to maintain a good fire, on which our lives depended, as the tent would only hold two of us

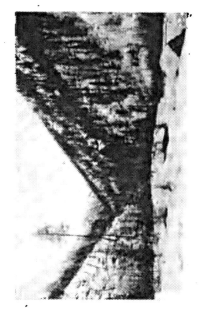
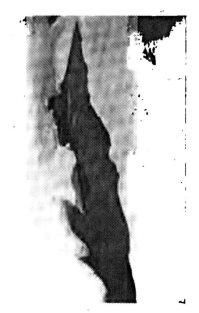

FIRST NEAR VIEW OF KATUNSKIE-BELKI RANGE FROM
AKKEM RIVER.

WE WERE OBLIGED TO UNLOAD THE PACK-HORSE.

M

and the hunters or ourselves would have to sleep in the open.

On Professor Sapozhnikoff's map, which is the only one of this district, there is a River Yarlow. We found

MOUNT BRONYAR, OPPOSITE "WINDY CAMP."

where this river evidently flowed in the summer, but it was quite dry, and, judging by the stones forming the bed, it is only a fairly large mountain stream, which had evidently been dry·a long time, as there was no frozen water in any part of it. This appears to me to prove that the mountain tops and glaciers must freeze suddenly, or that it is very much colder there than in the valleys, or the whole stream would have frozen; as it was, we found the river quite dry, owing to the intense frost. This river takes its source in the east of the Katunskië-Belki range, and, in the summer time, is, according to Professor Sapozhnikoff, a fast-flowing stream. By all appearances there is a glacier near the source, which remains to be explored.

We had been on the road two days since leaving Katunda, fourteen hours of which had been spent in travelling through dense forests. It was on the second evening that we encamped, at 5.30 p.m., 8150 feet above sea-level. Snow commenced to fall at eight o'clock, the temperature in the open being 15 degrees below freezing point. We could see Belukha mountain rising before us, in a direct line, about eight miles away, and we were practically in the circle of the Katunskië-Belki range.

Opposite our camp was a bank, covered to a great depth with snow, evidently a lateral moraine of the Belukha glacier. It must have been a very old moraine, as small trees were growing on it, but the trees were much younger than the forest trees around. Everywhere was ice and snow and perfect stillness; a more rugged spot could not be imagined. I pitched the tent, while the huntsmen went in search of wood. Having finished my task I joined in the search, and found that I was able to break several of the young trees quite easily, owing to their extraordinary dryness. When the fire was lighted they burnt like matchwood, giving out a good heat. The kettle was boiled and soup prepared, after which we roasted the half sheep and two ryabchiks, which had fallen to our guns on the way. These birds are vastly superior to partridges. Dinner over, we felt quite satisfied with ourselves and our surroundings and reconciled to the complete loneliness and silence. One striking thing I noticed while sitting at the fire was the sudden shifting of the wind. No sooner did we move

KATUNSKIË-BELKI AND LATERAL MORAINE, FROM "WINDY CAMP."

round to prevent the smoke of the fire blowing in our
faces than the wind followed us round. It shifted so
often, filling our eyes with smoke, that I christened this
spot "Windy Camp."

We were near the junction of three valleys, and no
doubt the next explorer who reaches this spot will know it
by the Nestle's milk tins, Army and Navy ration and soup

"WINDY CAMP," RIVER YARLOW.

tins, and the general clearance of the trees. I advise him
not to pitch camp near this spot, if he wants comfort.

Despite the wind, we chatted pleasantly for a short
while, making plans for the morrow, and then decided to
retire to the tent. Just as we were on the point of falling
asleep a terrific hurricane sprang up, which scattered the
fire and threatened to tear up the tent. In the deafening
turmoil I peeped from the door of the tent. The moon was
shining brightly. Belukha, although eight miles away,

appeared to be quite close to me, and the whole scene was wrapped in a death-like mantle of snow and ice. The intense cold of the wind caused me to shut the door of the tent very quickly and to wrap my fur coat more closely around me. My neighbour was snoring vociferously, as if challenging the storm, but I soon fell asleep notwithstanding.

We were up at five o'clock the next morning and I spent this, our first day in the mountains, in an exploration of the Belukha glacier, obtaining as close a view of the mountain itself as was possible from one side of the glacier. One circumstance struck me as being rather peculiar, and that was the absence of crevasses. The ice also was uncommonly hard. I made one or two experiments to see how much the glacier would move, and, as far as I can judge, the glacier does not move more than at the rate of about 1 foot in twelve months. I am sure the ice is as stationary as any glacier in the world.

I soon discovered it was impossible for the nails in my boots to make any impression on the ice, for, although I stamped my feet, I was unable to make the nails stick enough to walk up the slightest incline. We discovered a large number of boulders which had been scratched and grooved on the side nearest the glaciers. These were situated about two miles from the glacier itself, and showed how far it had receded. Some of the grooves, of which I took photographs, were half an inch broad and a quarter of an inch deep. There were no marks of the progress of the glacier on the other side of the stones. The mountains on both sides are composed of granite, and are entirely without vegetation above the level of the glaciers. From these, huge blocks of rock had fallen. The only crystallised granite mountain is Belukha, yet thousands of enormous boulders were scattered abroad six miles from that mountain. Judging from the character of the glacier and the boulders I should assume that the mountain was at one time quite twice its present

HUNTER ON GLACIER-SCRAPED BOULDER.

height. Most of these mountains appear to have been split in half quite recently by some powerful natural agency. One proof of this was the extreme softness of the rock, which had tumbled from the peaks and had

BELUKHA MOUNTAIN AND MORAINE.

sharp edges which did not show the slightest wear by ordinary denudation. Some of the rocks were so soft that I could break them by dropping them a yard.

The Katunskië-Belki group forms a circle, the principal peaks of which have an average height of 14,000 feet. In

the centre of this circle, there are three mountain ridges,
branching north and south, which, at a distance, have the
appearance of three enormous fins. It was these fin-shaped
mountains which appeared to be split in two. A Swiss
Alpine climber soon learns that even the mountains crumble
and in some cases are just like a pile of loose stones, and
this is still more apparent in these Siberian mountains.
The highest point of the glacier on the north side of the
Belukha is at an elevation of 12,000 feet, and the rocks
which shed their boulders upon it tower some 2000
to 3000 feet above, barren and desolate almost beyond
conception.

   There had been the heaviest fall of rock from a peak
on the right side of the glacier, which appeared to have
occurred very recently, and we were fortunate enough to
see several falls of rock in the course of our journey, the
only objection to which was, that they added materially to
the perils of climbing the mountains. Instead of the
Siberian climber looking out for single stones, as he
would in the Swiss Alps, he runs the risk of a few
thousand tons of the mountain falling his way.

   The moraine is composed of two ridges, which are from
200 to 250 feet higher than the glacier itself, and there
appeared to be rather more moraine than glacier. Speaking from my own experience, I had never seen so large a
moraine. I have visited and stumbled over many of those
in the Alps, but none of them can be compared in size to
this one. Its present length is 5 miles, but there are
indications that it cannot at one time have been less than
8 miles long. In two places lakes have formed,
dammed in by the moraine, which were buried deep in
snow. There is very little vegetation near the lakes, and
what there is, is of the wildest description. Professor
Sapozhnikoff's map of the same locality only shows one large
lake and one small one, but his visit was made in the
summer. A Kalmuck who had accompanied us from the
last settlement told us that large quantities of animals of

KATUNSKIÉ-BELKI WITH BELUKHA WEST PEAK ON EXTREME LEFT, FROM HEIGHT OF 11,000 FEET.

all kinds came down to drink at the lake during the summer, and that it is a splendid place for shooting, but that with the exception of one other Kalmuck Nimrod and himself no one knew of its existence. There are high passes on both sides of the glacier. My interest being aroused by another glacier and one or two very high

HUNTER ON SKIS—FROZEN LAKE.

passes, I decided to explore one of the valleys, arranging to start on my expedition at three o'clock on the morning after our arrival at our camping-place, but I could not persuade the huntsman to accompany me, on account of the thick haze which hung around us and completely obscured our view of the peaks and glaciers. At four o'clock, however, we made a start on skis, crossing the frozen moraine and the lake. It was my third experience of skis, and one leg persisted in going the wrong way, laying me low on the soft snow. Once over the deep snow that covered the actual moraine we went over lumpy earth for about 300 yards to the frozen lake. Continuing over the lake we went too far to climb the glacier that we had intended to climb, so we decided to go to the end of the frozen lake and follow the course of the stream which flowed into it to its source. We left our skis at a spot on the bank by a clump of trees, and proceeded without them, but were soon obliged to desist, owing to the steepness and hardness of the ice. My companion had crampons on, while my boots were only furnished with ordinary Alpine nails. We could not stand, or make any impression on the ice, so we abandoned the stream and took to the steep slopes which flanked it. Here we had some formidable loose earth to negotiate at an angle of about 70 degrees. Once at the summit, however, the ground was fairly level, although buried in snow.

The skis, which we had left behind us, were bound with fur, the object of which was to take a firm grip of the snow and prevent our sliding backwards. We lived to regret not having taken them with us, as we sank deep into the snow at every step. Leaving the snow at last we climbed some steep rocks, only to find ourselves on a snow slope, the surface of which only was frozen over. We presently reached the lower end of the glacier, and again found the ice too hard and smooth for our boots. We were, therefore, compelled to take to the loose rocks once more. Following these by a zig-zag course, which introduced us to frequent snow slopes and isolated square blocks of rock, also covered with snow, we at last reached the top of the glacier, which we found to be as flat as a billiard-table, and nearly as hard as rock. The altitude was 13,000 feet. We found it impossible to retain our footing without striking our feet hard against the glassy surface, and even with this precaution and the additional one of roping ourselves together, we frequently slipped. At the upper end of this glacier, which was only about 200 yards across, there

GLACIER NEAR WILLERS' PEAK.

END OF FROZEN LAKF.

N

VALLEY, LOOKING TOWARDS WILLER'S PEAK.

was a hanging glacier, which presented a very pretty sight. The ice here was buried a foot deep in snow, and snow lay also on a steep slope to the left, which was exposed to the north. I made the hunter photograph me,

AUTHOR ON THE TOP OF A GLACIER.

and then I took another photograph of the top of the glacier, afterwards picking out, with my Zeiss binocular, the way which I intended ascending the first slope. There were an ice-glazed slope and some steep rocks, and it looked as though I was in for some good climbing.

I looked at the rocks very carefully to see if there was any possible route, and all the time the hunter was evidently taking in the situation. He pointed to the rocks and wished to know if it was my intention to attempt to ascend them. When I told him that such was my modest desire he demurred with considerable vehemence, so I left him and took a course up a steep slope to the left. Fearing an avalanche, I changed my course a little farther on and selected a more difficult ascent over a shoulder of steep rocks, not unlike the shoulder of the Matterhorn in character, but with an outward dip and descending slope. Once on top of this I proceeded along an easy ridge— 13,300 feet high—which led to the summit. I took my own photograph, and afterwards proceeded up the ridge. I encountered several very steep gullies, which demanded respectful treatment, owing to the presence of a quantity of loose rock. Great caution was necessary in stepping from one piece to another in order to avoid being precipitated on to the ice below. The general impression produced by the mountain at this part was that it had at one time been considerably higher, but had been shattered by some powerful agency. I was now on the south side of the ridge. The north side was a sheer precipice with semicircular gullies varying in width and depth. The last of these gullies was about 150 yards from the northern extremity, making an almost complete semi-circle of the ridge and nearly cutting off the summit, which required some very good climbing to attain. On reaching the summit I found that no snow had accumulated on the steep northern slopes, which were composed of loose rock, while the north-eastern face of the mountain was cased in hard ice, and was quite impossible to climb. It was completely free of snow and reflected the sun's rays like a looking-glass. I had never before seen ice adhering to a mountain peak at an angle of 70 degrees. The Matterhorn glacier breaks and falls on the Swiss side at an angle of 53 degrees.

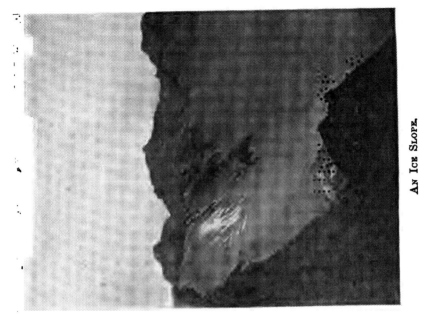

An Ice Slope.

" I selected a more Difficult Ascent over a
Shoulder of Steep Rocks."

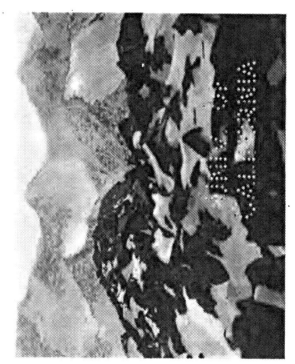

ICE-GLAZED PEAKS FROM WILLERS' PEAK.

PHOTOGRAPH OF THE AUTHOR TAKEN BY HIMSELF ON
THE TOP OF SOME STEEP ROCKS.

These peaks are apparently too much exposed to the strong winds and blizzards to retain any snow on their summits. The intense cold of the blizzards plasters the side of the mountain with snow, which is speedily converted into the hardest ice. The hardness of the ice is difficult to realise, and is due principally to the fact that the mountains are fanned by the bitterly cold winds which sweep across the Siberian steppes from the Arctic regions, freezing everything they come in contact with and expending their dying fury on these remote peaks, which they clothe in a translucent armour of sky-blue ice of indescribable beauty and purity. There is a wealth of beauty in the snow-clad summits of the Alps when the sun is upon them, as seen from some neighbouring peak. I have gazed at Mont Blanc from the summit of the Matterhorn, and at the Matterhorn from Mont Blanc, and some of the grandest views in Switzerland, but the northern faces of the Katunskië-Belki range, with the crystal clear glaciers hanging in the sun and sparkling like diamonds, form a picture so striking and beautiful that my experience can offer no parallel to them. It is mere commonplace to say that it was the finest view I had ever beheld. The wind was intensely cold and the mountain seemed to draw nearer, the glory of the panorama before me making me wish for someone with whom to compare impressions. One peak in especial, of a shape reminiscent of the Matterhorn, but having an obelisk of rock about 2000 feet less than that of the famous Swiss mountain, particularly impressed me. It stood out among its comrades with such imposing grace that it was difficult for me to remove my eyes from it. This peak was draped in ice about 50 or 100 feet thick, forming a wall about 2000 feet in extent. I took several photographs and felt as if I could have taken hundreds more. The indescribable beauty of the view before me and the consciousness that I was gazing upon a scene that had never yet been desecrated by the camera, or described by any human being, was one of a lifetime, and amply repaid me for the difficulties and inconveniences I had experienced on my way. Here all was virgin ground. There were no passes known and labelled ; no well-trodden routes to be followed ; no Mark Twain had ever made the ascent of these peaks in imagination ; no telescope had scaled their heights before my Zeiss binocular ; no avalanche had hurled its hapless victims to an untimely death ; no Alpine hut vulgarised the slopes or ridges or obscured the view of the summit ; no Baedeker enumerated the guides or reduced the glories of the ascent to a matter of pounds, shillings and pence. I was in the home of the maral, the marmot, the ibex, the bear and the red Alpine wolf. When the summer came the mountain slopes would be alive with the song of countless myriads of birds and the hum of numerous insects, unmolested by civilisation and unhunted by man.

I found myself wondering whether, when the great Mogul race was predominant in Asia, some stray adventurer had ever visited these mountains, or whether they too had dreaded them as the Kalmuck and the moujik dread them to-day. It is certain that this particular cluster of mountains is altogether off the line of the caravan route from Omsk to China, or the Mongolian sheep-hunter's route *via* Onguadi ; and this fact, coupled with the comparative isolation of Siberia from the West of Europe, would account for my having had the great honour of leading the way to the exploration, a lead which I hope will soon be followed, of a land far excelling Switzerland in its wild Alpine beauty. I am confident, from what I saw, that the range contains mountains of even greater altitudes and magnificence than those I have described.

A host of thoughts crowded through my mind as I stood amid those rugged giants of the Altai. The word Altai means gold, and golden mountains they appeared to be as they reared their mighty crests in the rays of the slowly - descending sun ; and later, when the after-glow rested upon them, the scene was such as no Alpine

sunset can reproduce or emulate, beautiful though the
peaks, like the Matterhorn, are under like conditions.
Not a bird sounded its call, no rippling stream was to
be heard, no avalanche raised the echoes with the
thunder of its fall, no Alpine cow-bell sounded in the
distance; a silence that could be felt rested on all
around me. Yet, in the silence, the stately mountains
seemed to welcome me and to invite a closer acquaintance. The frozen river lay in its winter sleep beneath me,
the lakes in their ice-sheets slept peacefully beyond. In
the distance were the pure white snow-fields; around me
scores of glaciers clothed the slopes and precipices. The
summits dreamt in the glow of the closing day. The sky
was clear and of a beautiful blue tint. I felt that my
journey had not been in vain.

Ere long, I hope, others will visit those mountain
scenes and record their impressions of them, and who
knows but that some day, after the pioneers have broken
the ancient solitude of these mountain regions, organised
excursions will be led to them for the benefit of the
Kalmuck, and Kalmuck hotel proprietors will make their
little fortunes, as their Swiss precursors have done before
them. '

From the peak on which I was standing the Belukha
mountain was visible in its complete and majestic proportions. I placed my aneroid barometer on a sheltered
ledge of rock and estimated the altitude of the mountain to be 17,850 feet, or, after deducting 50 feet for the
known error, 17,800 feet. My aneroid had been officially
tested by the best authorities before I left England, and
found to be correct. Mr Edward Whymper has also very
kindly examined and tested it since my return to England,
and has declared it to be a very good and reliable instrument, and it was also tested by the Kew authorities.
I mention these facts merely because aneroid barometers
occasionally get out of order, and therefore require to be
very carefully tested both before and after use. I took a

number of photographs and several prismatic bearings. I also conceived the idea of photographing myself on the summit by attaching my camera to a screw on the head of my ice-axe and pushing the stock of the axe into the snow. An india-rubber ball attached to a long tube of the same

PHOTOGRAPH OF THE AUTHOR TAKEN BY HIMSELF NEAR SUMMIT OF WILLER'S PEAK, 17,800 FEET.

material served to take the snap-shot. This method was fairly successful, but the axe occasionally insisted on falling forward, distorting the picture and entirely spoiling the effect. The temperature by this time had fallen to 12½ degrees of frost, and it fell still lower after the sun went down.

I wrote my name on a stiff piece of paper, in English and Russian, and deposited it under a pile of stones. The rocks at the summit I found to consist mainly of schist, felspar and hornblende, and, somewhat to my surprise, to be so brittle that I could break pieces off them with my hand quite easily.

The Katunskië-Belki form a circle of peaks, of which Belukha appears to be the highest. To the north of Belukha there are three mountains, shaped like huge fins and parallel with the glacier. They are abruptly pointed at the summits and extend in a direction from north to south. The peak which I climbed had a position from east to west. These ridges were far too attenuated at the top to serve as a resting-place for the snow that fell upon them, and which the winds sweeping across them from the Akkem valley consistently carry away with them, but a prominent peak just beyond them was better adapted for the purpose, being dome-shaped.

With the mountaineering instinct still unsatisfied within me I commenced the descent of the peak, and, after a three hours' climb, reached the snow pass. I was too tired to walk down through the deep snow, so I decided to let myself slide, and, fortunately, succeeded in doing so without accident. Being too tired to walk down the glacier I lay down on my back, and, steering myself with my ice-axe, again glided gently to the bottom. Here I rejoined the Kalmuck hunter, who was waiting for me, and returned to the camp. I put on my snow-shoes to cross the lake and the snow-field that lay between me and the camp, and travelled across as far as the moraine, but being too tired to tie the skis on properly, I had two awkward tumbles while descending the moraine. I was thoroughly exhausted by this time and was heartily glad when I got to the tents.

I shall never forget dragging my weary limbs into camp and sitting down by the fire. I had been away for seventeen hours, two hours of which I had spent on the

summit of the peak, and had only eaten a few raisins and
a little chocolate which I had taken with me, as, when we
set out, I had not foreseen that by going up the valley we
would arrive so near the mountains. The temptation to
climb them had been so great, however, that I had given
way to it, and had made a much longer journey than I had
originally intended. At dinner-time I was so tired that it
was necessary for my interpreter to wait upon me, an
office which he performed with great kindness and
willingness.

One of the Kalmucks whom we had encountered at the
last Kalmuck hut was sitting at our fire when I returned.
My interpreter prepared supper, including a very welcome
cup of tea in the *menu*. The Kalmuck handed me a piece
of sugar to put into my tea. After I had drunk three cups
of tea without stirring it to dissolve the sugar, I took a
fourth one and was surprised to find that the most energetic
stirring failed to reduce the dimensions of that miraculous
piece. I took it in my mouth, to discover, amid the
laughter of the Kalmuck who had given it to me, my two
hunters and the interpreter, that what I had taken for
sugar was a small piece of marble, and that the Kalmuck
had scored upon me in a very decided manner, proving
himself a humourist.

As the tent had been taken down we all slept that
night in the open. The exposed situation, and the fact
that the tent only weighed 12 lbs., made it rather troublesome to fix it. It had been blown down during the day.
That night the horses became so frightened that they
would not leave us, and came quite close to the fire. The
hunters said there were wolves about, and the horses had
evidently seen them. Wolves or no wolves, it did not stop
me from rolling myself up in my fur coat and tumbling off
to sleep.

I slept until about 9 a.m., the following day being given
up to hunting the particularly wily ibex and the wild
sheep. Our hunt was fairly successful. The ibex is a

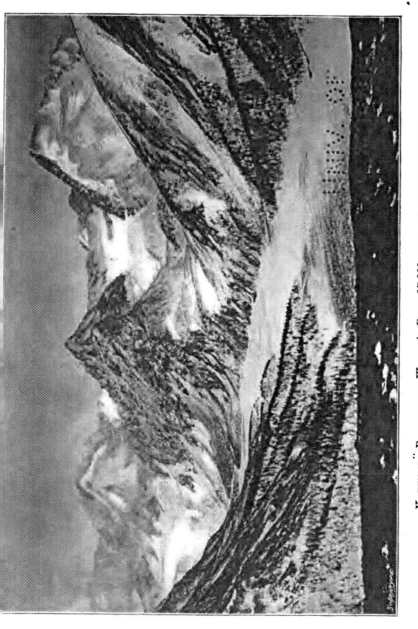

KATUNSKIR-BELKI, WITH WILLER'S PEAK 17,800 FEET, ON EXTREME RIGHT.

O

skilful climber, so that in order to stalk it the huntsman requires to be a fairly good mountaineer himself. These animals are exceedingly intelligent and wary. Our arrival in the vicinity of their haunts had caused them to withdraw fully two to three miles from the camp, and our party had a long and weary tramp before we got within stalking distance of one or two herds of them. Ultimately we discovered a small herd on a rocky ledge of one of the peaks. The Kalmuck detected their presence long before the rest of our party had the least idea of it, and, resting his gun on the two sticks which were attached to it for support, he fired, hitting one in the neck. It turned over and fell to the bottom of the precipice. The remainder of the herd made their escape, and, for an hour or two, our prospects of securing anything to take back with us appeared very doubtful. Shortly afterwards, however, my interpreter and the two hunters came across several large ibex, each of which received an ounce of lead too much. We returned to the camp with our trophies and made a meal off one of the ibex, which we enjoyed exceedingly. Our Kalmuck friend boiled the half of the animal for himself in a large black pan. I thought he would never finish eating. I have never seen a man eat one quarter of the quantity that Kalmuck could account for, and probably never shall again, unless it is my good fortune to revisit the place. Yet with all that he was thin and wiry.

We took a photograph of the horns of the ibex we had shot, and measured them. My own trophies were:—a large horn 42 inches long and 10 inches thick; another horn 25 inches long and 8 inches thick; and a third 23 inches long and 7 inches thick. This last is not so large as those of two others shot by my interpreter.

The horns of the ibex are sold by the Kalmucks to the Chinese, who grind them to powder and make medicine of them. For this reason the Chinese are their best customers. The southern and western slopes of the Altai range, which are hunted by the Mongolians, are becoming exhausted, the animals being steadily driven to the more remote valleys and secluded gorges, similar to the spot where we had made our bag. The Kalmuck informed us that the horns of some of the ibex he had shot were much larger than the largest secured by me. Evidently the hunter, like the fisherman, is the same all the world over. If that is not the case, however, the ibex in question must have been larger than any of which there is an authentic record, which were not more than three or four inches longer in the horns than the one secured by me. It is to be hoped that some English sportsman may be induced to visit the locality and find out for himself what those mountain valleys and ridges have to offer. I am convinced that the sport he will have will repay him for the trouble of the journey.

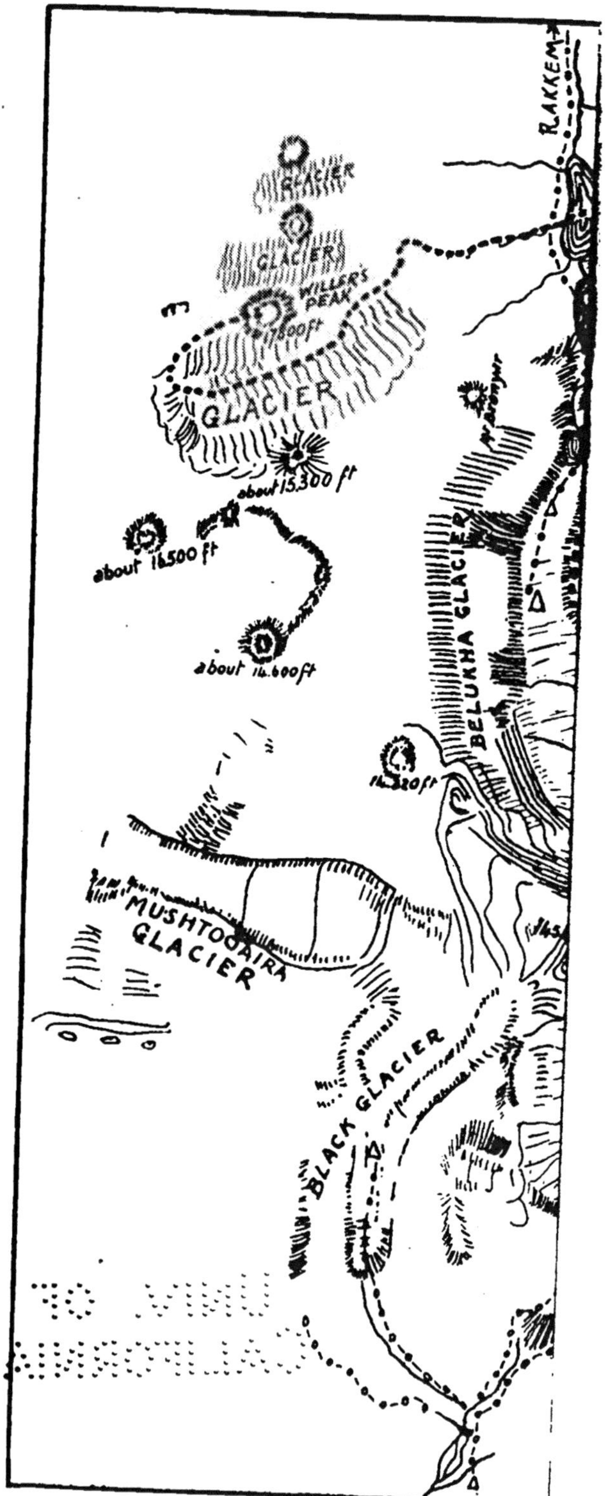
RAKKEM
GLACIER
GLACIER
WILLER'S PEAK
GLACIER
about 15.300 ft
about 16.500 ft
about 14.600 ft
BELUKHA GLACIER
MUSHTOOAIRA GLACIER
BLACK GLACIER

To face page 213.

CHAPTER VII

CLIMBING BELUKHA

THE weather on the following morning was calm and promising, so I decided to climb Belukha. The thermometer registered 45 degrees below freezing point, and there was every prospect of a good climb. It was my intention to move the main camp as near as possible to the mountain, but the hunters refused to go as far as I wished. I explained that the distance from our present camp to Belukha was eight miles, and, owing to the very difficult moraine, and the peak being quite unknown to me, it was quite necessary that we should move the main camp much nearer to Belukha. The hunters argued there was no wood procurable for a fire and that we should all be frozen to death. I told them of a large number of fir trees at the base of the glacier which I had noticed the day previously, and said I was quite sure that the spot was much better than " Windy Camp," as we should be protected by the peaks.

All my arguments were of no avail. My interpreter was very much against my climbing, and the hunters, seeing this, felt that they were right in refusing to go further. However, after a lot of talk, it was agreed that we should camp on the side of the lake about one mile nearer Belukha.

We packed our horses and had very great difficulty in getting them over the deep snow of the ancient lateral moraine, at which the hunters complained very much. We soon reached the lake. The water had evidently flooded the top of the lake and frozen again, because it broke and let the horses through it for about six inches at each step, but no deeper, as the ice underneath was very hard.

BELUKHA—FROZEN LAKE.

Just as I thought we were getting along splendidly the hunters made for the side of the lake, and, when I informed them that we must at least go to the end of the lake, they threatened to go home and leave me unless I allowed them to have their own way. They both argued that, even if I went to the end of the lake, I should not be able to reach the peak in one day, and they would proceed with my light tent as far as I wanted. This being the best I could do, as soon as we made the second camp I intimated that I wanted to sleep on the top of the glacier at the foot of the Belukha precipices that night. Continuing on our way, we rode the horses to the end of the lake and tied them up to the trees.

When we started from the camp at about 11 a.m. the hunters were quite willing to go to the spot where I wanted to sleep, but as we gained the moraine they got into difficulties on the ice-glazed boulders and constantly slipped off, sinking up to the hips in snow and getting their legs jammed between the boulders. They soon wore a look of disgust on their faces.

I had anticipated, that if I did not carry luggage myself, they would complain of their loads being too heavy, so I had taken as much as both of them together, and, when they began to complain, reminded them of that fact. I quickened my pace and left them some distance behind. When we left camp the weather was very cold, the wind blowing from the north. The sky was clear and blue.

An hour later, as we were making our way up the moraine on the left, snow began to fall and my companions became anxious to return; but I argued and cajoled, and finally prevailed on them to go on. We proceeded for another hour, when they finally struck, although it was next to impossible to camp on that moraine, and they had agreed only two hours previously to carry out my wish to sleep that night at the base of Belukha. We had, therefore, only covered two miles of the six which lay between us and the peak. My arguments were of no use, however, for, suiting their actions to their word, they both put down the luggage and were about to leave me, when I agreed that if they would help me to find a suitable place for the camp, they could come up at 4 a.m. in the morning and carry it to the base of Belukha, which they solemnly promised—a " Russian promise "—to do.

They took up the luggage again and we wandered on a little, but there was no place for a camp. I wanted to take them a little farther, when they insisted on my choosing a spot close to where they sat. The rest of the moraine was quite as desolate, so I turned over as many boulders as possible to get the dryer side. After scraping away the snow and levelling up the boulders, I found that there was no

" Desolate Camp," Tent on Moraine and Belukha West Peak.

possibility of driving pegs in between them, so I had to tie boulders to the cords of the tent and pile others round it to protect it in case of wind. I had pitched my tent by about 1 o'clock p.m., 11,000 feet above sea level. The hunters, who complained bitterly of the cold and snow, turned back hastily, refusing to wait for me to make them a cup of tea.

I was soon very stiff and cold with the bitter wind and snow driving against me, and was glad to crawl into my small tent, lay my big coat on the boulders, unpack my knapsack and make ready to light the spiritine lamp, in order to make some soup and obtain as much comfort as was possible under the circumstances. I was surprised, and not a little alarmed, to find that the spirit had all leaked out of the lamp. I was beginning to realise the awkwardness of the situation, when I recollected that I had taken a few small tin blocks of spiritine as a precaution, little thinking at the time that my very life was to depend upon them. My legs began to freeze in the big leather boots studded with heavy nails. I took them off in time to restore the circulation and put my "valenki" on instead. Then I lit two small blocks of spiritine, after thawing the tops. I reached out my hand and tied up the opening of the tent, in order to prevent the entrance of the bitterly cold air, and then boiled a tin of soup, drinking it eagerly to warm myself. Supper * over, I left one block of spiritine burning, and rolling myself carefully in the fur and putting on my warmest cap, turned over and tried to go to sleep, the fierce wind doing its best all the while to tear my little tent from its moorings. I congratulated myself on the manner in which I had piled the stones and boulders round for protection, and shortly after, amidst half-conscious reveries, in which I wondered whether I should survive the cold and get back to dear old England again, I fell asleep.

I awoke suddenly about midnight with an icy shiver, as though I were lying in a cold bath. The light had gone out, and in my sleep, dreaming of home, and mountains, and ibex, and wolves, and bears, and snowstorms, I had kicked off the coat. It took me half an hour to restore the circulation to my frozen limbs, and, concluding

---

* I call it supper because I was going to sleep on account of the storm. The time was about 5 p.m.

that it would be dangerous to go to sleep, I lay thinking,
wondering how I should ever succeed in making the
ascent through all that snow. Nature proved stronger
than my determination, and I presently dozed off to sleep
once more. I must have slept for three or four hours,
for when I awoke day was breaking; it was about three
o'clock in the morning. I reached for my boots and
found that they had frozen very hard and that I could
not get my feet into them. My feet were also swollen.
I thawed the boots by lighting a block of spiritine, and
managed to squeeze my feet into them. My body was very
stiff after sleeping upon those boulders. I consulted my
watch and found I had been in the tent thirteen hours,
during about ten of which I was asleep on the boulders.
I named that camp " Desolate Camp."

I opened the tent and crawled out, brushing the snow
away from the boulders as I did so. It had fallen to the
depth of about six inches during the night and was falling
still. The wind had dropped, however, so I decided to turn
in for another hour. Looking out of the tent some time
afterwards, and finding that the snow had ceased falling
and that it was lighter, I again crawled out, brushing
away the snow. The peaks were being lit up by the
first rays of the sun. I waited for some time for the
hunters, and, while doing so, took a round of photographs,
including myself and the tent. About two inches of very
hard snow, almost as hard as ice, was frozen on my tent,
and the boulders piled round the tent, which had been
turned over, were ice-glazed.

I decided that I would not sleep in that tent another
night. The hunters had made a faithful promise to be
up at the tent by four o'clock, but it was now nearly
five and there was no sign of them. I could see that it
was no use relying upon them to take my tent to the
base of the actual peaks above the glacier, so I decided
to make a bold bid, or rather a rush, for the summit. I
took as little baggage as possible, and proceeded over

SNOWBOUND TENT AND UNNAMED PEAK, AT 4 A.M.

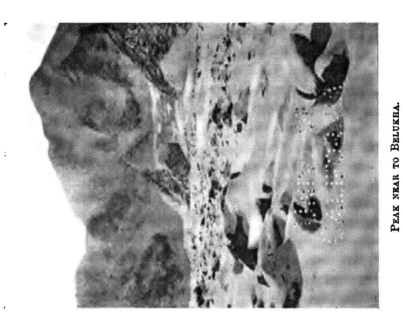

PEAK NEAR TO BELUKHA.

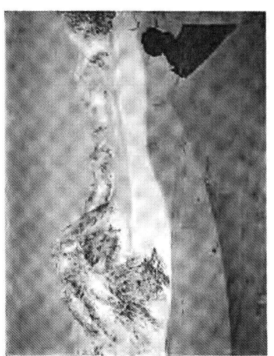

TENT ON MORAINE, AUTHOR, AND PEAK NEAR BELUKHA,
AT 4 A.M.

the ice-glazed boulders. I have had considerable experience in scrambling over Swiss boulders, but those which
formed the moraine of the Belukha were glazed from the
fresh snow that had frozen upon them. They were nearly
all covered in this manner, and I found it very difficult to
keep my feet upon them. To avoid sinking up to the hips
in the soft snow that lay between the boulders it was
necessary to jump from one to the other of them, and with
all my care I overbalanced myself repeatedly, and was
obliged to step down between two of them, severely jarring
my legs and narrowly escaping a broken limb. I have
never found climbing so difficult as on the moraine of the
Belukha glacier.

I then decided to try the glacier itself, but could
make no better progress. The ice was too hard to allow
the nails of my boots to grip, especially as I was not
sufficiently heavy, although my boots were shod with
Mummery steel Alpine nails. The weather had become
very warm and sultry. I changed my course once more
and took to the boulders. As I stepped from one to another
of them I loosened them, and it was rather interesting to
hear how boulder after boulder, as I stepped from them,
went tumbling down into unseen holes. Several times I
only succeeded in saving myself, by throwing my body
forward, from accompanying them on their downward
career. After many difficulties and troubles I sat down
to rest on a boulder as flat as a table, and round. It was
quite 3 feet across. I·unpacked my rucksack and made a
good meal, as I could see there would be no chance of
taking anything up the precipice with me. Whilst
resting on these boulders I heard a noise, and looking
down the glacier I saw the hunter Cherapanoff about 4
miles away, beckoning for me to go back.

I had heard quite enough from the hunters about the
dangers of the mountains, and, as the clouds seemed to be
drifting up towards me, I thought he was trying to warn
me of the coming storm. The clouds which were descend-

ing from the peaks all around me made me hurry. I took my aneroid and left the rest of the luggage on the slab of rock.

I first of all tried a gully up the precipice of Belukha, but the rocks were too ice-glazed and, after proper examination, I concluded that it was quite impossible to make the ascent that way. I turned back to some steep

A PEAK OF THE KATUNSKIE-BELKI RANGE NEAR BELUKHA.

rock which I concluded led to the ice ridge, and, for about an hour climbed up slabs, and wriggled up cracks of all sorts. The snow and ice gave me trouble and it presently began to snow. Whilst resting on the top of the ridge I measured it. It was 13,800 feet. I left my card under a piece of rock and proceeded through the mist towards the higher ridge.

On gaining this ridge I was reminded of the long ice ridge of Monte Rosa near the summit of Dufour Spitz. After proceeding over deep snow I came to a ridge of hard

WEST PEAK OF BELUKHA AND NEXT PEAK FROM TOP OF GLACIER.

P

WEST PEAK OF BELUKHA FROM GLACIER.

STEEP ROCKS LEADING TO ICE RIDGE, BELUKHA.

ice at an attitude of 14,300 feet.   I had attained a height
on this mountain that nobody had attained before me.
Professor Sapozhnikoff had gained 13,300 feet from the
south side in the summer time, but it was altogether
another matter in the winter, and the hurried climb up the
northern precipice of Belukha began to tell on me.

After the difficulty I had experienced, the sight of the
summit stimulated me ; I was so exhilarated that I felt
like making an attempt to run up the slope, although I
knew running would be impossible.   The summit could

NORTH FACE OF BELUKHA FROM GLACIER, TWIN PEAKS,
14,800 FEET.

not have been much more than 150 yards away.   The
first 30 yards were over deep snow, and afterwards
clear ice, which lay at an angle of 35 to 40 degrees;
but after that the ridge seemed to lie up an easy, if
somewhat narrow, slope, apparently covered with soft
snow, which I expected to be able to walk up without difficulty.   I laboured across the first stretch and
exhausted myself, the deep snow making the climb
exceedingly heavy.   I was ready to take a rest, so I stood
awhile and admired the view.   To the north was a circle
of mountains, and several avalanches fell, while I was looking, from the north-western peaks, near the glacier and

moraine along which I had come. The weather was
unsettled but the snow-fall had ceased. Turning to look
along the glacier, which was about 8 miles long on the
south side of the mountain, I could also see a large
number of snow-capped peaks. The glacier was covered
with fresh fallen snow. The ridge on which I stood
was rather dangerous, as the hard ice with which
it was coated would not allow the nails of my boots
to get a good grip. The view of the summit, however, filled me with an irresistible desire to climb it,
and although badly in need of a rest I began to cut at the
hard ice. I was disappointed to find that my hardest
blows only succeeded in chipping away small pieces of the
ice scarcely larger than a hazel nut, and it was nearly
half an hour before I succeeded in cutting one decent
step. This convinced me that it would be impossible for
me to reach the summit that day, especially as I had
nothing with me to shelter me while I slept upon
the ridge. The north face of the precipice, near
which I was standing, was glazed with ice, which
rendered the few cracks and hand holes that might
be there quite useless. On the other hand, even
had I been able to climb that part of the mountain, it
would not have been possible for me to get further than
to the west side of the ridge. The only way out of the
difficulty, was to gain the south side of the peak at the
base and make the attempt from the west. I had
noticed that the western ridge was not so long, and persuaded myself, that as it was sheltered from the Arctic
winds, the ice might be softer. So I determined to try it,
although I knew well enough that the snow was soft and
an avalanche exceedingly likely. I had come a long
way and was not inclined to give in without a struggle,
even if it involved some risk, so I started very carefully:
but after going on for about 6 yards, I suddenly became
aware that the snow was giving way beneath me, and the
next moment I was on the top of a billow of loose snow

that was gliding down the mountain side considerably
more swiftly than was either comfortable or safe. I had
concluded that it was all over with me and that an
obituary notice was perhaps the thing I should be requiring
next, when the motion stopped suddenly. I immediately
relinquished hold of my ice-axe and knocked the snow
away from about my head until I was able to breathe
freely, but my body was crushed down in a most uncomfortable manner. I pushed away the snow and secured
the head of my axe, and, using it as a lever, was presently
able to wriggle myself out of the snow. The snow had
gone down my neck, making me very wet and uncomfortable. I brushed as much of it away as was possible.
Then I began to crawl, the ice-axe serving to drag me
along, while with the disengaged hand I managed to
secure a hold of any protuberance that offered, however
small. In this manner I advanced slowly, foot by foot,
well aware all the time that if I was so unfortunate as to
start that avalanche on its downward career once more I
would most certainly be precipitated on to the ice below
and killed. In spite of every care, however, my knees
slipped on a smooth piece of ice and I felt myself gliding
again. To save myself I threw myself flat and lay for a
second, until I could get a better hold with the axe and
scramble to my knees again. I now remembered my knife,
so I got it out and opened the short blade which I used
for opening tins. This was a great help, and, with its
aid and that of the axe, I managed to regain the ridge;
but it seemed to take about two hours to accomplish the
distance, which seemed to be about 60 feet. It is probable,
however, that I was wrong both in my estimate of the
distance and of the time it took me to cover it. On re-
gaining the ridge, I scraped the snow as well as possible from
my neck, but it melted and gave me a cold bath. After my
pockets were cleared and clothes shaken out, I felt quite
thoroughly wet and very cold. To keep up the circulation, more than with any idea of climbing the ridge,

I decided to cut as many steps as possible and return the next day to complete the step-cutting. I had cut the second step much more quickly than the first one, at the risk of breaking my ice-axe, but while I was engaged in cutting a third one a strong wind sprang up from the north and forced me to abandon all further work for that day. Although cutting the step had restored the circulation to my limbs, the fierce northerly wind chilled me to the marrow and absolutely made me beat a retreat. My clothes seemed to stiffen upon me, and at one time I felt that I was going to lose the use of my hands. I began the descent, but the wind had glazed the rock with ice and I was a very long time climbing down, and had to exercise the greatest caution. The climax came when I found myself above a gully which required to be climbed down and appeared to project very considerably. I had not come up it, so I concluded that I had lost the route by which I had made the ascent. I stuck in that gully, carefully calculating whether I could let myself drop with safety onto a ledge, about two feet wide, covered with snow and slightly slanting outwards, some distance below me. I knew that if the slopes were ice-glazed I should almost certainly slip and fall down the mountain, but I was unable to get back. I argued that the ledge had been protected through being in a north-westerly position, and at last let myself drop. As luck would have it, I was able, just as I landed on the ledge, to grasp a projecting piece of rock which had been invisible to me from above, and clinging to it with my ice-axe, which hung on my arm fastened by the leather strap, I was quite safe. The remainder of the climb was fairly easy, because it was below the line where the fierce wind had frozen the snow into ice. In a little while I regained the moraine, where I had left my camera and several other things, and started on my return journey. The temperature on the moraine was 18 degrees below freezing point. I found it very difficult walking, as I was getting very tired and my body

was racked with internal pain. There was no fighting
the feeling that I was quite ill. I knew, however, that if
I gave up there I should probably never be found, so I
made another desperate effort. Progress over the moraine
became difficult in the extreme. It required all my will
power to cover the four miles, and each mile took me
about an hour. At times I was compelled to sit down
absolutely exhausted, with a feeling that I could not move
another yard. I had been tumbling from ice-glazed
boulders and sinking up to the hips in soft snow between
them so often that I began to think one of my legs was
broken. Still I struggled on. When I reached the tent
I found my hunter resting quite contentedly with his back
to the tent and with my overcoat over him to protect him
from the cold wind. He was very pleased when I told
him to pack up, and was not long in taking down the tent
and packing the remaining things together. He explained
that he had managed to get so far alone, but that the
other hunter had been afraid to come. He spoke as
though he thought he was very brave, and, as he had
never been on a mountain moraine or glacier before, no
doubt he was right. He pointed to a hole in the glacier
which he had narrowly escaped tumbling into. He also
expressed his opinion that he was sure that if he had tried
to follow me he would have been killed. He showed me
nasty bruises on both legs, the result of his tumbling on
the ice-glazed boulders. From inquiries I made, I found
that he had been four and a half hours in covering the two
and a half miles between the main camp and the tent, but
his interest had been attracted by a huge bear whom he
had encountered by the trees at the bottom of the moraine,
and whom he tried to kill with his large knife. He had
spent quite an hour and a half of his time in stalking him.
He explained that the bear ran when he got near to him,
and that he vanished in the mountain pass. I was not
inclined to believe his story, as it sounded too much like
an excuse, but he showed me what appeared to be the

track of a bear in the snow, together with his own, and I
was constrained to accept his explanation. Curiously
enough, the hunter was not at all afraid of the bear, and
explained that he had killed several with his large knife
alone, but he admitted that he was desperately afraid of
the mountains. I was feeling very ill by this time, so I
decided not to spend another night up there and in that
small tent. The hunter's assistance and companionship
were very welcome on the journey to the camp, which we
reached late the same evening. My interpreter remarked
that I looked very unwell, and I was very sick for about
an hour. I attributed it to my having swallowed some
solder from the tin which contained oxtail soup, which I
had drunk so hurriedly in the little tent. I have no doubt
also that the snow and ice water we had been drinking,
and the poor bread we were eating, together with the
tinned food, had something to do with my illness. I went
to sleep by the fire. During previous nights, sleeping in
our fur coats in front of a big fire kept us warm enough,
but this night the wind blew a hurricane and the thermometer was very far below freezing point.

I awoke very early in the morning to find that my
eyes were closed with inflammation and that I could only
bear to open them for a few seconds at a time. As soon
as daylight appeared I gave the order to pack up, which
was gladly obeyed, as my illness and the state of my eyes
made any further climbing out of the question; but I
determined to return and conquer the last few yards of
that mountain at some future date. We rode the first twenty
miles in a bitter cold wind and through a driving snowstorm, sheltered only by trees. My eyes were very painful
and I could not see for above five to ten seconds at a
time, consequently the branches of the trees swept across
my face, leaving severe scratches; the marks on my nose
will probably remain with me till I die. The faces of the
whole party were nearly frozen by the wind. The ibex
horns on the horse's back, and the leather bags on the side

Snow had obliterated all Traces of our
Former Track.

The Large Ibex Horns knocked
against the Trees.

of the horses, knocked against the trees and shook them as we passed, and the snow dropped upon our backs and down our necks. We tried to find our former track, but the snow had obliterated all traces, and we were very uncertain at times of the direction in which we were travelling. The horses fell frequently during this part of our journey

KALMUCK BARK HUT, AKKEM VALLEY.

and required a lot of pulling up, and every time this happened the luggage required to be repacked. It was a pleasant relief when we reached the Kalmuck's hut and were able to obtain shelter and to dry our clothes.

An iron slab in the centre of the floor of the hut held the boiling pan, and a Kalmuck girl was grinding rusks to powder to be boiled in milk. Her mother lay ill on the wooden bed at one side of the hut. Over her bed was the icon, and the pig-tail of the one man had been shaven off all of which denoted that the inmates had been converted to Christianity. I had an opportunity to study the character of these nomads of the Altai, and, from observations and inquiries which I made, I am led to believe that they are the most natural and unaffected people in the world. They are very calm and alert, and are particularly friendly in their relations with each other. They commanded the respect even of our fighting hunter, and it is quite astonishing how much the Russians think of them. They are so modest that your best feelings go out towards them, and so simple, unpretentious and happy, that it would be impossible to take advantage of them. They are born horsemen and hunters, and, as already stated, although the Russian Government will not allow them to serve as soldiers, they excel the Cossacks in many respects. . They are respectful, but brave and chivalrous. They wear a skin cap on their small round heads and a coat of bear or sheep skin tied round the middle, and their boyish faces and high cheek bones are eloquent of vigour and strength. The Kalmucks wear the same skin coat all the year round, summer and winter. They evidently think that what will keep out the cold will keep out the heat. If a man's happiness depends upon the fewness of his wants, the Akkem Kalmuck must be the happiest man alive.

I was delighted to be able to distribute some chocolate amongst the children, who had collected in the hut to welcome their mysterious white friends. Two of the Kalmucks had come ten miles to see us. They had never heard of England, Europe, St Petersburg, Moscow, or, in fact, of any place further than Bysk, yet they were as happy as mortal man can expect to be. There is plenty of fresh air in these huts, as they are open at the top. We were made very welcome and I had a chance to ask many questions. As for the hut itself, it seemed a little palace to us after sleeping so many nights in front of our camp fire. We slept comfortably that night rolled in our coats on the floor of the hut, the fire being kept up all night. I tried to draw the inflammation out of my eyes before the fire, but without success.

We were up early next morning, as we wished to reach Katunda as soon as possible. Before we went, I sold the rifle which I had bought at Bysk to one of the Kalmucks who had followed us to the mountains, and he was very pleased. He paid me in Russian money and appeared to be fairly well to do. He had made money out of cattle, and this last summer had done exceptionally well by hunting. He and another Kalmuck had quite the monopoly of the hunting ground. They were very sorry when we mounted our horses and commenced our second day's homeward journey up the hill towards the high Kalmuck pass bearing to the left from the Akkem valley. Several families had collected to give us a welcome, but they were only in time to bid us a hearty farewell. Half-way up the pass we met two Kalmucks, also on their way to visit us. They were fine specimens of horsemen, and were mounted on small sturdy ponies. They rode on one side of the exceedingly steep ice slope in order to let us pass. In the course of a short conversation they said they had run short of food because of the very severe and prolonged winter.

Judging by the experience Professor Sapozhnikoff had in the summer, and my own experience in the winter, the weather must be very changeable. Sudden blizzards and fierce north winds, with blinding snowstorms, occur in the winter, and excessive rains in the summer. The future explorer in the summer must expect very heavy rains about May and early June, and very fierce wind and heavy snowstorms in the winter.

After bidding our friends good-bye we were not very long in gaining the summit, where we gave the horses a rest. They were quite exhausted by slipping about on the frozen slopes. While we rested we could take in the view of the mountains.

We descended through forests, and most of the streams were free of ice. We found it was impossible to cross the

Q

stream at the place where we had come over, as it was flowing much too fast for the horses to swim across, so we crossed several small streams.

We passed a place where a Kalmuck rears marals in order to cut off their horns to sell them to the Chinese. We then came to a bend in the River Katun where the water was smooth. Hailing a Kalmuck on the other side, he paddled the canoe across. My interpreter and myself went in the canoe, while the hunters swam the horses across. After the Kalmuck had paddled us over, he offered us a duck he had just shot, for which we gave him 20 kopecks (5d.). When we joined the hunters and told them we had paid this small sum for the duck, they said we ought to get two ducks for the money, as 10 kopecks—2½d. each—was the usual price.

We noticed piles of bark on each side of the river, which had been cut off the trees in winter by the Kalmucks, who would take it up the river in a canoe as soon as the spring had returned. We waited for the hunters and horses and rode them up a steep bank and down through a wood, and soon entered the village of Katunda, where a crowd gathered in the post station.

The journey from Katunda, which had taken Professor Sapozhnikoff three days each way, only took us two. The hunters would have taken three days if I had not been very firm with them. So far as the hunters are concerned, it is not possible to get men who are either able or willing to climb, and, if serious mountain exploration is thought of, a good Swiss guide or porter is quite necessary. The traveller would also feel safer, and would not run the risk of being left in the mountains.

One thing that my hunters complained of very badly was that the camping arrangements were bad. Professor Sapozhnikoff, they said, had taken two large tents, one for the hunters and one for himself, and had not hurried or wanted to climb so often. Whatever may be said for the hunters, I should recommend any future explorer to be

KALMUCKS ON AKKEM PASS.

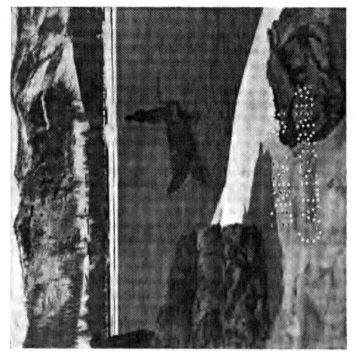

We cross the River Akkem in Canoe.

Akkem Streams were breaking up.

quite independent of their aid in the mountains, and only to take them to look after the horses; while an interpreter knowing English and Russian (probably some butter merchant who would like a holiday) could be found at Omsk, Novo-Nicolaëvsk, or Barnaul.

There is a lot of work to be done in these mountains, and, now that travelling on the Siberian railway is pleasant and a journey of 800 miles from civilisation brings you to the foot of the highest mountains, there is no reason why botanists, geologists, artists, hunters, explorers and climbers should not find these mountains quite as attractive as any in the world.

So far as photography is concerned, the air is much more actinic than the air in the Swiss Alps, and snap-shots or short exposure will be quite exposed enough in summer, while even in March a snap-shot was the most useful, and a very short exposure all that was necessary.

It is necessary for the climber to take crampons, which must be very sharp and of the very best steel; also a particularly sharp ice-axe. The axe I used is an old one and not sharp. This made it much more difficult to cut the ice; besides that, I had it cut down to pack into a cricket-bag, and was therefore unable to get much leverage on it.

The nails on the climber's boots are of vital importance, and the boots must be felt-lined. The cold is so intense, that even the temperature on Swiss peaks in winter is nothing compared with the cold on the summits of the Altai Mountains.

The climber must make preparations, both in summer and winter, for much colder mountain tops and much colder winds than on the Swiss Alps. It is of vital importance to have the thickest underclothing, a short seal-skin or bear-skin coat down to the knees, and a very thick "shuba" (all-fur coat) to go over all.

Great care should be taken to have all instruments packed carefully, because there are no springs on the sledges or droskies. The explorer will do well to protect himself, when camping, from the severe Arctic wind, and avoid a valley if possible, because the wind comes very suddenly and from all points of the compass.

The pass to the west of the Akkem valley is very long and narrow. This valley leads straight to the Katunskië-Belki, and gradually rises from 3800 feet high to the Akkem lake, at an elevation of 8000 feet, a rise of 4200 feet in 40 miles. The Akkem river has a very strong current. The road, for about 30 miles out of 40, is over forest-clad slopes. Before my visit, no one had ever been there in winter, and, considering the frozen state of the slopes, we were fortunate to get our horses there and back without any serious accident. Professor Sapozhnikoff, whom I have already mentioned, was the only man who had been up this valley before, and his expedition was in the summer. The Akkem valley, or any part of the Belukha mountain, is thought to be inaccessible in winter, and, after my experiences, I do not recommend exploration of the Altai Mountains during that season. The cold is so intense, that every living thing, from bears to birds, is either hibernating or has withdrawn to a more congenial climate, and we did not come across any animals except a few herds of wild sheep, ibex and stags, and a flock or so of ryabchiks. The best and most delightful time for a journey in these regions would be the month of July, as the aspect of the Altai flora alone would repay the visit.

There is a great deal to be learned in regard to the mountain districts of Siberia. My own theory of their formation is that the earth's pressure must have pushed them up, and at no distant date. The rocks are quite new and soft, yet the edges have not been worn smooth. Notwithstanding their softness, moreover, there is very little crumbling. The pieces of rock at the head of the mountains indicate that falls have taken place on a tremendous scale. Lightning could not have caused such havoc, and traces of ordinary denudation are quite absent. The only explanation which seems probable is, that the mountains, which resemble huge fins, have been pushed up by pressure of the earth's crust, and then, becoming top heavy, have split and crashed down on either side. Glacial action would have polished the base of the mountains very effectively, owing to the softness of the rocks, but there are no signs of glacier scratches higher than the course of the existing glaciers. I feel quite sure, from my study of the Katunskië-Belki, that it would not take a scientific geologist long to prove conclusively that mountains are formed by pressure.

Of the great mountains in the world, the Himalayas form the largest semi-circle. The ends of the ranges point north, and the range bends like a bow to the south. The Himalayas and the Caucasus form a semi-circle, which stretches across a large portion of our earth's surface. The ranges of the Altau and Altai are branches of the Thian Shau, which joins the Himalayas. The same semicircular structure is still more apparent in the Katunskië-Belki range. In the Akkem valley, and by the side of the Akkem glacier, there are four or five mountains of rock similar in shape to the seracs of the Glacier de Géant. The Siberian mountains grow smaller and smaller, until the great Siberian plains reach the Arctic circle. If the earth's mountains are formed by pressure this is as it should be. Mount Everest, which is the highest, has been pushed up highest, because the rock gave the greatest resistance, but the east and west end of the great main range project in a northerly direction.

I throw out these suggestions in the hope that they may encourage an expedition to the Altai Mountains for the purpose of studying mountain formation and to consider whether mountains are produced by pressure or cut out by glacial formation. If by glacial formation, how could the glaciers make these circles of mountains and climb over passes to get out? The theory that mountains are formed by the earth's pressure has been proved clearly to my mind by my visit to these previously unknown mountains.

The fauna and flora of the Altai are very varied and their examination would repay tenfold anyone who would take this trip to the mountain districts. From information I gathered I find that in summer the flora of the south Altai is magnificent and surpasses anything in the world. Specimens of plants known in Europe are also found there, but they are of enormous size and grandeur. There are also specimens not seen elsewhere. I am indebted to Professor Sapozhnikoff for permission to publish his information on the Altai flora, which has never been published in Europe or America before. It shows what a marvellous country the South Siberian Altai is, and there are, no doubt, a large number of species not yet discovered or known to science.

CHAPTER VIII

WE had promised to visit the village church, before leaving
Katunda, on the last day of our stay, therefore we called
for the priest and were conducted by him to the church,
which is the only one within a radius of 100 miles. The
churchyard is also the village cemetery. We were struck
by the absence of tombstones, the graves being marked by
plain wooden crosses, or square posts with V-shaped heads,
innocent of inscriptions. The wooden church is painted
to resemble brick, it being the great ambition everywhere
along the Siberian railway, and more particularly in so
remote a spot as Katunda, to possess buildings of that
material.

After taking a photograph of the priest and his two
children, we were shown the humble grave of his late wife.
He is a priest of the Orthodox Russo-Greek Church and is
permitted to marry once.

Inside the church were rough wooden seats, candles and
icons. The greatest care is taken of these, and the chapel-

251

keeper is apparently always on guard. One of the icons, which I attempted to photograph, had been brought all the way from Palestine by the Eastern route and over the Siberian railway to Bysk. It weighs 10 poods (3 cwts.) and was carried from Bysk to Katunda by relays of eight peasants.

As we were leaving the church the priest was accosted

KATUNDA PRIEST AND HIS CHILDREN.

by one of his parishioners. It appeared that the man was in trouble and wanted the *batushka's* assistance. Another peasant owed him 5 roubles (10s. 6d.) for a rather ancient horse—if I remember rightly the animal was seventeen years of age—which he refused to pay on the plea that the horse, while too old to work, was the possessor of a very vigorous appetite. It appears to be part of the priest's office to settle disputes of this character, and, in the case of this particular priest, the duty of arbitrator was one for

which, both from his ability and personal character, he
was very well suited.   For my own part, I developed quite

KATUNDA CHURCH, BUILDER AT WORK.

an affection for this homely priest and his two motherless
children, and was truly sorry to bid him good-bye.   He
pressed us very hard to stay, but we were afraid of the thaw,

which could be expected at any moment; therefore we arranged to start the same afternoon and spend the night at Ouemon, 10 miles distant, at the house of a merchant of that place. We promised to meet once more before we took our final departure.

Our next visit was to the mansion of one of our hunters. One would hardly have expected anyone to be able to live in so miniature a style, yet his wife and himself appeared to be quite comfortable, and gave us a hearty welcome and a good cup of China tea. Our friend was very anxious to present me with a pair of skis as a memento, he having taught me to use them to good effect in our hunting expeditions and when climbing the mountains. I was very reluctantly compelled to refuse them, as our trophies, in the shape of ibex and stag horns, were already more than we could conveniently take with us; in fact, we had to leave some of them to follow.

The woman in charge of the post station baked some white bread for us, and we called at the village creamery to buy some butter. The dairy-maid, bare-footed and rosy-cheeked, her head tied up in a handkerchief, stood at the dairy door laughing shyly, while I took a photograph of her. On a shelf above her, at the front of the dairy, was an assortment of all shapes of tin cans, in which the milk is allowed to stand until the cream forms. A small, cheap separator, costing about £3 or £4, the most wonderful machine these peasants had ever seen, produced some butter, the quality of which was scarcely inferior to the best Colonial. Yet, when this butter reaches London, or Germany, or Denmark, or even a Russian market, it is quite 10s. lower in quality. The reason is not far to seek. From Katunda, the most southerly village, it would have a journey of fourteen days by sledge in winter, or drosky in summer, to Bysk, with nothing to protect it but some well-dried hay. In order to do the journey in less time, it would have to be carried day and night—the speed being very slow—and would still be stale when it reached Bysk, the selling depôt for the Altai butter.

At Bysk the butter changes hands, together with the weekly output of other neighbouring dairies, which would be about three to six casks; the casks are branded, one mark, and the whole parcel is sent on to Barnaul for sale,

MY HUNTER, HIS WIFE AND MANSION.

when not sent direct to Europe. In winter the butter will keep fairly well, but, in the very hot weather of mid-summer, it is literally boiled before it reaches the refrigerator waggons on the Siberian line, having travelled over 700 miles, taking from three weeks to one month, and when the roads are broken by thaw as much as two months to make the journey.

As a result, the butter deteriorates 10s. per cask at least, a loss which is borne by the peasants. It will be obvious that the consequent waste and loss are enormous. The Government would be well advised if they adopted a system of refrigerator vehicles, in which the butter could be conveyed from the dairies to the depôts. It would represent a profit to the Altai peasantry, of at least £200,000 per annum. It is scarcely to be wondered at that the peasants are over head and ears in debt to the Government, for they have absolutely no means of disposing of the produce of their toil under favourable conditions. £50,000 of the £200,000 saved could be taken by the Government in payment of the cost of introducing the suggested refrigerator vehicles. It would also be well to take the most stringent measures to prevent delay in transit. Thus, the butter should not be exposed to the sun at the different collecting stations, particularly that of Obi. The law should, further, make it compulsory that all butter be carried in refrigerator waggons, whether in summer or winter, lest a sudden change of temperature, particularly in the spring, should destroy the quality of two or three train-loads of butter loaded in ordinary trucks. Having these considerations in mind I drew up a petition this year, which was signed by a number of interested merchants, and forwarded to the Russian Minister of Ways and Communications, in which I requested that thermometers in the refrigerator waggons should be read and recorded at mid-day every twenty-four hours, in order to ensure a uniform low temperature while the butter is in transit. This the Ministry promised to do.

Another drawback is in the appearance of the Siberian cask and the quality of the wood of which it is made. English buyers are prejudiced against the butter before it is tasted, and argue, that if the dairies are not sufficiently up-to-date to pack their butter in neat, handsome casks, similar to those used by the Danish dairies, they may also neglect to employ the best methods of making the butter, and that, on the other hand, the wood may interfere with the quality of the butter. The wood used in Siberia in the manufacture of butter casks is altogether different from that of which the Danish casks are made. It appears, that there are no trees in the Altai of which the wood could be obtained, and very little elsewhere, so that there is no possibility of the Siberians making casks of the same quality. On the other hand, the hoops on the casks are brown and coarse, which makes them look primitive and clumsy. The real difference is, that the Danish cask and hoops are cut by machinery in enormous numbers and are all of the same size and dimensions. The reason that the Siberian casks are made now is because they can be purchased cheaper, the Government having lately imposed a tax on foreign casks, which should be taken off without delay.*

The right kind of cask reaches the dairies cheaply enough, in view of the keen competition of the firms who sell them, but, owing to the tax already referred to, the clumsy Russian article can be sold as dear as the superior Danish cask was sold before the tax was imposed.

A number of important reforms will be necessary before the butter industry can be placed on a footing to give complete satisfaction alike to producer and consumer. At the same time, it must be admitted that the Government has shown marvellous insight and sympathy with the industry, and the peasants are quick to adopt new ideas.

It was while reflecting upon the conditions of life in that remote portion of the Czar's wide dominions that I was induced to name the three mountains of the Katunda district Faith, Hope and Charity, as a silent appeal to the native from a sympathetic stranger that they should endeavour to cultivate these sentiments towards the Czar and his active and energetic representatives who, it was plain to me, were doing their very utmost to conquer the natural obstacles in the way of rendering this enormous stretch of wild country a happy home to those who had settled in it.

* I understand that this tax has since been repealed.

R

I am firmly of opinion that His Majesty the Czar could not choose a more grateful task than that of opening up the Altai and other remote districts of Siberia, by introducing, with as little delay as possible, a system of quick transit in suitable conveyances. By this means the industry would be encouraged and the resources of the country developed. The dairies would be able to obtain at least 10s. per cask more for the butter, and the earnings of the peasants would be increased in proportion.

Before the Government decides upon refrigerator vehicles, I think it would be advisable to investigate thoroughly as to whether well-built, strong boats, of a suitable size and type, could not be sent up the rivers to relieve the traffic. A weekly collection of the butter from all the villages would be quite sufficient under such circumstances, as I believe that all the Altai rivers are navigable, or would take very little to make them so. I am well aware that, in the hot summer months, the level of the rivers falls very considerably; at the same time, the rivers I crossed in different parts of the country, and even at Koksa, Ouemon and Katunda, could easily be made navigable and used for the transport of dairy produce, or even cereals. This would encourage farming on a considerable scale where at present the rich soil of the district is almost entirely neglected.

I am equally convinced that the numerous small tributaries of the larger rivers could be utilised in this manner, and might, if properly managed, develop a not inconsiderable passenger traffic. There is, for instance, no reason whatever, that I can see, why pleasure-steamers should not extend their trips from Bysk, into the very heart of Mongolia and the Altai range, like the steamer that runs up the Irtish from Omsk.

We very much enjoyed our friendly call on the hunter and his house-wife. As we were coming away we met the Inspector of Forests, who, having heard of our being at Katunda, had come a distance of 20 miles to speak to us. It seemed a pity to me for the man to have come those 20 miles for nothing, so, in order that that should not be the case, and being determined to make as much as I could of a man who knew something about the great country I was so interested in, I began to ply him with questions.

Of the extent of the forests in Siberia he could tell me very little—they have never been properly measured or explored—all he knew was that it is enormous. The Inspector of Forests is an official who is responsible to the Ministry of Agriculture and the Imperial Domains, and he spends a large portion of his time in the saddle, riding from place to place, to enforce obedience and respect for the laws relating to the protection of forests. These men usually go through a special course of training at the St Petersburg Institute of Foresters. This may be described as the University of Forestry. There are, however, in the provinces, schools of forestry on lower educational scales. The course of training in these schools lasts two years. After a forester has gone through the prescribed course, he receives the title of conductor and is entitled to a post under the Crown as assistant forester. The Altai forests are the property of the Crown. The region contains 498,228,300 acres, of which the Crown owns 291,600,000.

The commonest tree is a fir (*Picea Excelsa*), which is particularly abundant in the north of Russia and Siberia. The European fir differs in certain marked respects from that of Siberia, as does that which grows in the extreme east, in the neighbourhood of the Pacific Ocean, from that in the Caucasus. In the northern forests of European Russia the fir tree very often attains a height of about 90 feet, stripped of branches, with a diameter at the top of 12 inches. Individual trees have been known to grow to the height of 120 feet, with a diameter at the top of 30 inches. Some of the trees are 350 years old.

Next in importance to the fir tree is the pine (*Pinus*

Silvestris). This tree extends much further south than the fir, and is particularly plentiful in the Altai, where one species, called the Siberian cedar, is of great value on account of the quantity of nuts it grows. Both the pine and the fir are distinguished in Siberia by the very high quality of their woods. Owing to the cold climate, they grow very slowly, and the grain is therefore exceedingly close. The pine tree attains a height of 100 feet, in some cases 130 feet, with a diameter of 12 to 45 inches at the top. In Southern Siberia the birch is also very plentiful, and in some localities produces "spanks," which are characterised by a very peculiar and pretty grain, and which are, therefore, extensively used in cabinetmaking, carving, etc., etc.

Next in importance to the birch is the aspen. This tree is gradually spreading more than the birch tree, as it grows better on land that has been cleared of forests. On good soil, and under good climatic conditions, the aspen in 60 years attains a height of about 90 feet, with a diameter of 17 inches at the top, and has a clean and healthy fibre.

The next place is taken by two coniferous trees, the larch (*Larix*) and a species of fir (*Abies Pextinata*). The latter grows mostly in Northern Siberia. The wood is of very high quality, and, if it is not exported to a very great extent, the circumstance can only be explained by the fact that it is not so well known as the other trees grown in Siberia. It frequently attains the height of 200 feet and the patriarchal age of 300 years.

The spectacle of hundreds of thousands of trees burnt down to their stumps convinced us of the necessity for good foresters to look after them. We gathered from the forester's conversation that the very serious burning of forests in these parts compels the authorities to be very strict. Peasants are allowed a certain quantity of wood, but they are also entitled to cut down dead trees. It is much to be regretted that the burning of forests cannot be

stopped in Siberia, as their wholesale destruction is
apparent from the enormous numbers of burnt trees
visible almost everywhere. The Forest Inspector was
there to stop the extermination and to distribute the right
proportion of wood from the forests among the peasants.
These parts are not so thickly wooded as the Barnaul
district, and it would be a serious matter if they were not
carefully watched.

We walked with him to the post station, where our
drosky and troika were ready to start on the first stage
homewards. A hearty good-bye from nearly half the
people of the village was a pleasant tribute from this unknown village where we expected to find a semi-
barbarous people, and it impressed me very forcibly that
Russian policy evidently has a civilising effect even so far
away from the seat of justice and the strong arm of the
law.

We had not gone far, before it became clear that we
were in for the very worst of the thaw, and that the 250
miles to Bysk would afford a very lively experience. We
took three hours to complete the first 10 miles, having
just managed to get into the thaw we had been trying to
avoid. We calculated, from all the information we could
gather, that the thaw would come while we were in the
mountains, but it was much later, showing that the
natives of Siberia are quite as uncertain about the proper
time to expect the season's changes as we are in England.
The fluctuations in temperature are also quite as rapid,
though the climate as a whole is much drier.

Our first stage cost double the usual price—10s. for
10 miles instead of 5s. charged in ordinary weather—and
the drosky stuck fast in the mud on several occasions.
When we reached the top of the Katunda Pass I took a
last farewell look at the mountains—the Saptam—and
the flat valley below, and, with an affectionate thought
for the priest and his flock, we drove down the Ouemon
side of the pass, through the forest. We put up at the

post station and left our luggage there, and then went out
to pay our merchant friend a visit. The village roads
were 4 inches deep in mud, and our high Wellington-
shaped goloshes were very useful.

A river flows through the· village, and this we
negotiated in a home-made canoe rowed by a youthful
native. The canoe had been hollowed out of the solid
trunk of a big tree, presumably with an axe. There had
been a bridge over the river, but the villagers had removed
it on account of the speed of the current, swollen by the
spring floods. So rapid was the stream, that we had to
pull some 100 yards up current before crossing, in order
to make a point opposite. We paddled as hard as possible
and managed to escape being carried away; but we were
nearly upset more than once. The water of the river was
beautifully clear, the stream at this part being about 40
feet deep, and swarming with fish.

Once across, we waded through the deep mud of the
village to the house of the merchant whom we had come
to see. The house itself is large and commodious for that
part of the world. The wooden gateway and boarded
railings enclose about an acre of land. We were heartily
welcomed and conducted to the best rooms, which were
very clean, handsomely furnished, and ornamented with
beautiful palms, which seem to flourish very well in
Siberia. We found our host very entertaining. He had a
German clock hung on the wall, the hands of which indicated two o'clock, although it was then about seven in
the evening. It was explained to us that the clock was
merely an ornamental feature, and that for the time of
day both he and the rest of the villagers went by the
sun.

We had a long and interesting conversation after
dinner and then retired. It was a pleasure to find ourselves confronted by two feather beds, made on the floor,
but scrupulously clean. After six weeks of very rough
quarters a night's rest such as we enjoyed on this occasion

was something to be grateful for. Among other advantages, this was the only house hitherto in which I did not see the "mites of our affliction" and had no occasion to use Keating's. After an early breakfast we took photographs of our friend and his family, and made a few inquiries about the life of the peasantry. By all accounts the average peasant in these parts will do just enough work to keep himself from absolute starvation, and this seems to be a rather common characteristic of the peasants in other parts of Southern Siberia, where Nature is so prodigal in her gifts.

Having bidden our host good-bye, we recrossed the stream and hurried back to our troika. The road beyond Ouemon is fairly level and runs through a valley, from which the mountains rise abruptly. On our arrival at Koksa — 25 versts from Ouemon — we learned that we would be obliged to continue our journey on horseback and take pack-horses for our luggage. The roads were in a very bad condition and the weather had become exceedingly warm, the thermometer registering 110 degrees in the sun at mid-day. This did not improve the roads, and there was deep soft snow in every direction. Our road took us down to the banks of the River Koksa. In the middle of the track was a stream of water quite 12 inches deep, caused by the melting snow on the mountain slopes on our right. Presently we crossed a shallow stream running into the River Koksa, and began to mount a hill on the other side, the river itself, now free of ice and flowing fast and furiously, being about 200 feet below us on our left. Our horses kept getting into deep snow, often up to their necks, and tumbling about in all directions. On such occasions it was very difficult to pull them out. My horse persisted in pitching forward on his knees and required a good jerk to bring him to his feet again without dismounting. Further on, we found that the small stream I have already spoken of had come to stay and ran persistently

right in the centre of the track, so the horses splashed
their way merrily through it. Four hours after dark the
moon came out, flooding mountain and valley in an ocean
of light. It was very beautiful and grand and inspiring,
yet we were very glad indeed when we reached the village
of Koksa. There is nothing very noteworthy about this
village except that the man in charge of the post-house
had been compelled to abandon it on account of the
tarakans. We found, however, that although abandoned
by its legitimate tenant we were expected to sleep there,
there being no other place available. Fortunately, it had
been newly white-washed throughout and thoroughly
cleaned, so we resolved to make the best of it, and, after a
grand supper, rolled on to the floor and slept the sleep of
the weary, oblivious alike of tarakans and everything else.

We were up betimes in the morning and at four o'clock
were on our way through the valley, this time in a sledge,
for the valley, to our surprise, was covered with deep, firm
snow. The sledge track had been badly worn in the
middle by the horses, so that the runners of our sledge ran
along two ledges of hard snow, except when one of them
lost its footing, so to speak, and then one side of the
sledge would go down into the hollow and we would be
dragged along with our heads nearly touching one of the
ridges. As anticipated, we found the road hard, owing to
the intense night-frost, and made very good progress. We
ascended the pass over the Korgomskië Mountains, and
about mid-day came to a lovely spot not far from Abbi,
where cattle were grazing on a slope from which the snow
had been blown, leaving the grass open for the cattle to
graze on. We had some difficulty from here owing to
patches of bare dry earth, over which we had to drive the
sledge.

We decided to rest the horses outside the village of
Abbi and walk through the deep snow to the village
cemetery, which lay away to the right near the slope of the
hills—a lonely spot. The cemetery is about 20 yards

CATTLE GRAZING ON THE KORGOMSKIE MOUNTAIN SLOPES.

SLEDGE NEAR ABBI VILLAGE BOUNDARY RAILINGS.

square, railed in on all sides, and has no gate. The monuments were of the same simple description as those in the churchyard at Katunda, and, like them, bore no inscriptions. Some graves were marked by a wooden cross of the orthodox Greek pattern.

I regained the sledge, which was dragged laboriously over the dry ground, from which the snow had melted away.

ABBI CEMETERY.

It struck me that it would not be at all a bad plan to construct a sledge with small wheels attached to it, so that they could be used on bare ground. They would also be of service when a sledge turns over sideways and would prevent many an awkward spill. Some patent of the kind would be a boon to the peasantry, particularly at the changing of the seasons in spring and autumn.

At Abbi the man from whom we ordered the drosky developed a most unpleasant obstinacy, refusing to take us any further. We argued and persuaded and cajoled, and when we had finally prevailed upon him to take us, his stubbornness took the form of refusing to take a troika, although we pointed out the state of the roads and the difficulties we had experienced with a pair on the last stage. Argument was of no avail, nor could he be prevailed upon to hurry himself, but sulkily took his time to get the drosky ready and grease the wheels. This operation took him fully half an hour, at the end of which time he announced that he was ready to start.

I had found a word which I could use with considerable effect whenever I wanted the moujiks to "hurry up." This was the word "skoro," which means "quickly," and had never been known to fail, for the peasants really did try to be quick in their clumsy way. Our friend at Abbi, however, was proof against its charm and could not be prevailed upon to bestir himself, so that we were more than half inclined to saddle the horses and ride away without him.

At last we started. The roads were very heavy, and, just beyond Abbi, the wheels of the drosky were nearly a foot deep in the water. We tried hard to induce the moujik to select the best parts of the road, but he took no notice of us, and, from his manner, may have been contemplating the advisability of upsetting us altogether.

About three miles along the road we came to a Kalmuck settlement, which we had not seen before, having, doubtless, passed it in the dark. A fine-looking Kalmuck on horseback was driving a large number of horses, and he saluted us as we passed.

It was here that we decided to get out of the sledge and walk for a spell, in order to breathe the horses and give them a chance on the muddy road. As we walked, my interpreter friend shared with me some of the information he had gathered in the last village relating to the Kalmucks.

The majority of the Kalmucks in the Koksa district — the last stage we had passed through — profess

Christianity, but they have not been accorded the full rights of Russian peasants, possibly on account of their Mongolian descent. Possibly, however, the Russian Government may have other reasons for refusing them these rights and for not allowing them to serve in the army. The Kalmucks are the descendants of the Mongols, or Moguls, who, under Chingis Khan and his nephew Batui, invaded Eastern Europe in the fifteenth century, advancing as far as Hungary and Bohemia, reducing Moscow to ashes and dominating the Grand Duchy for two centuries. The race came originally from Tibet, and is for the most part nomadic in its habits.

The Kalmucks have no religious marriage ceremony, but the customs connected with that event are very picturesque. They indulge in a feast, killing what they have previously captured for the occasion, which is usually a wild sheep, but if no sheep is available they kill and eat a horse. The father and mother of the bride build the couple a fairly commodious bark hut. This has two large doors, to enable the wedding guests to ride through on horseback. The bride and bridegroom stand inside and wait for them, and all they can pull off the back of the horse or the person of the rider becomes their property. The guests arrive with the wedding presents hung about them. These may be spoons, pails, or any other articles of domestic use. It is needless to say that the list of presents is not quite so elaborate or imposing as that which figures at some of our fashionable weddings, nor is it found necessary to enlist the services of detectives for their protection. The bride and bridegroom, however, probably value them none the less highly for that.

The Kalmuck is allowed three wives, but the baptised Kalmuck (the outward and visible sign of whose conversion is the negative one of an absent pigtail) only has one wife, like the other orthodox Siberians. In appearance the Kalmuck is short and wiry, with a dark, copper-coloured skin and dark hair. He usually wears a small skull-cap, which suits him very well. The Kalmucks are fairly intelligent and command respect.

The habits of the Kalmucks in the extreme south of Siberia resemble those of other Mongolian races. As a rule, their diet consists almost entirely of flesh-meat and dairy produce, as there is not a single square inch of land under cultivation in the whole of that part of the country through which I passed, that is, from Belukha to Chorni-Anni, and it is only the rich who can afford the luxury of millet, procured from the Russian peasants at Chorni-Anni. Although they use oxen instead of horses, we never saw them eat beef; but they consume enormous quantities of mutton, four or five Kalmucks being quite equal to finishing a whole sheep at a sitting. Our Kalmuck friend, in fact, accounted satisfactorily for half a sheep himself at one meal, while camping with us in the mountains. The animal was killed and hacked into pieces, the meat was put into an enormous caldron full of melted snow, without salt or seasoning of any kind. The Kalmuck seated himself at the fire, drew a knife from its sheath at his belt, and took each piece of meat out of the pot with his fingers as he wanted it. For beverage he took tea boiled with milk.

The Kalmuck rides from the cradle to the grave. One very rarely sees him on foot, and even to visit a tent only a few yards away the horse is requisitioned. When dismounted, their gait is clumsy and ridiculous, but their horsemanship is magnificent, and there are few things better worth looking at than a Kalmuck on horseback.

The drosky having overtaken us, we took our seats once more. The horses, tired as they were, struggled heroically, but it was quite evident to us that they would never be able to reach the next stage. We did not neglect to acquaint the driver with our views on the subject and to remind him of our request for a troika. The climax came when, with a thud, the wheels stuck fast near a wood, and, although the driver plied his whip lustily, further progress became out of the question. We held a

council of war and decided that the moujik was to rest the
horses and then return with them and bring fresh ones.

While waiting for him to take the horses out we heard
a woodpecker attending to business in the wood and
several other birds in full song. The scenery was wild
and rugged, but most picturesque, and, for a time at least,

OUR DROSKY STUCK IN THE MUD OUTSIDE ABBI.

we forgot our difficulties in our admiration of the landscape.

We had not been seated very long when we became
aware of the approach of two men on horseback. Thinking that they might be induced to lend us their horses, we
waited until they came nearer, when I recognised in one
of them the boy who had driven us from Koksa to
Ouemon. We explained our plight to him and persuaded
him to let the immediate author of our misfortunes, the
stupid driver from Abbi, return there with his horses,
while he harnessed his own to the drosky. The other

S

peasant, who was riding to Abbi, helped him with the horses. We decided to pay nothing until we should arrive at the next station.

Our young friend informed us, that his late master having most unjustifiably refused to pay him any wages, he had determined to run away and seek fresh woods and pastures new at the identical village for which we were bound. He told us that he would be able to get fresh horses when we arrived there, and that he would be our guide, philosopher and friend for the next stage. This was good news, for we had begun to feel afraid that our chance of making progress was likely to become somewhat precarious.

It was hard work climbing up the pass, and the downward journey on the opposite side was not much easier, on account of the snow not having melted away. The drosky insisted on sliding down sideways, and we were compelled to hang on to one side of it to prevent its turning a somersault.

When we reached the farm at Kirlick, where the youth was employed, there was trouble because the horses were very hot. We came to the boy's rescue by explaining how very bad the roads were, and presented the farmer with an extra rouble by way of peace-offering. This had more than the desired effect. In his anxiety to show his appreciation he gave us his best troika, and graciously acceded to the request of our young friend to be permitted to drive us to Ouskam.

We fortified ourselves with a cup of tea and then drove slowly out of the village. Presently we saw a horseman quite a mile away, riding at full gallop down the hill towards us. When he drew near to us we saw him to be a very rich Kalmuck. He was dressed in a well-fitting suit of velvet. He drew up to us and asked a number of questions in good Russian. He wanted to know where we had come from, where we were going, and was very pleased and interested when we told him

that we came from England and described to him what
kind of a village London was. When we told him about
the telephone and phonograph, however, he seemed to
have some polite doubts. He had himself never been
further than Bysk. He informed us that he made a living
by dealing in horses and cattle. After he left us we
stopped at a clear stream and had our first wash for weeks
in a stream of clear water. It was delightful, but we
would have been still better pleased if we had been able
to visit a barber. Our razors had got rusty and useless,
and our beards were becoming conspicuous.

The scenery in this district was still pretty, but the
mountains had dwindled down to hills. Our young
friend drove us at a very good pace through fertile valleys
such as we had not seen before on our journey, in which
the Kalmuck horses are allowed to graze at their own
sweet will and unattended. Yet they multiply freely
without attention, which explains how the Kalmucks are
able to sell their horses so cheaply. On one of the
mountain slopes we saw a herd of about 200 of them,
besides a number of sheep and cattle, while, in the
neighbourhood of one Kalmuck hut alone, the group of
horses numbered from fifty to sixty. I am sure that a
large trade could be done with Siberia when the projected
railway through the Altai district is completed, and that
one day the Siberian cattle - dealers may become as
wealthy as the famous rancheros of America.

The country is an ideal one for cattle-breeding. In
the numerous level valleys the snow only falls sparingly
in winter, the vegetation is luxuriant, and the mountains
are a magnificent barrier against the bitter winter winds,
while their slopes are not too precipitous to supply well-
drained, succulent grass for the cattle. As regards richness
of pasture land this country is vastly superior to Switzerland, and should, under suitable conditions, produce in
abundance the finest cattle and the richest milk in the
world.

As I have said elsewhere, a system of rapid transit is an essential condition. Given that, Siberian produce will work a revolution in the agricultural markets of the world, for no other country could hope to compete with a region where labour is at its cheapest and the pasturage at its best, both as regards quality and abundance.

We saw numbers of wild ducks and game birds of every description. At times the sky was literally blotted out by large flocks. Our driver kept a watch on the birds, while my fellow-traveller held his gun ready for a shot. We came across one large flock on the water, where the spring floods had invaded the low-lying portion of a valley, and my companion proceeded to stalk it. He got within 30 yards, and, as they began to rise, bagged one and wounded another, which made off, flapping its wings on the water as it flew. I took the reins from the driver and told him to run after it, and just then my friend fired another shot, at which all three horses took fright and bolted. I rather enjoyed the fun of it and gave the horses their heads, but when they had galloped about 100 yards they turned in the direction of the stream, and, as I had no taste for a ducking, I began to pull them in. This was not by any means an easy thing to do, and I was pretty well exhausted when I brought them to a standstill. They had jaws like iron. I made them gallop back to my companion and the driver, who, I was pleased to find, had managed to bag a good supper. With the exception of an occasional shot at geese and ducks on the wing we had very little sport.

We arrived at Ouskam in the evening. We had been provided with an introduction to a friend of his by the merchant at Ouemon, but, as it was dark when we arrived and the moon had not yet come out, we experienced some difficulty in finding him. We succeeded at last, however, and drove triumphantly into his yard, where we were accorded a noisy welcome by his numerous dogs, whose efforts were presently seconded by all the other dogs in the

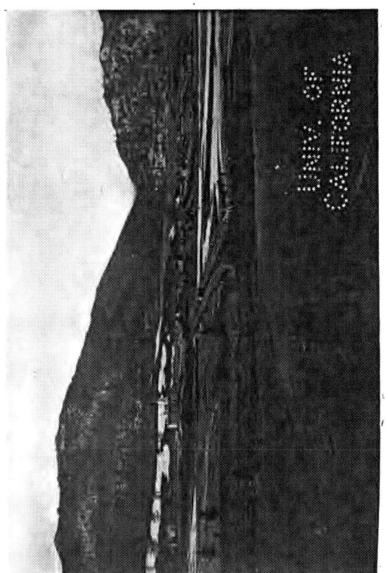

THE VILLAGE OF OUSKAM.

village. We knocked for about five minutes, at the end of which time a peasant came into the yard and informed us that the gentleman we wanted had gone on a wolf-hunt with a number of the villagers, and that they would be away all night. He invited us to stay with him, an invitation which, needless to say, we accepted with alacrity. He informed us that the wolves were very numerous in the district and that the villagers had been obliged, in the interests of their own safety, to organise a wolf-hunt, which was then in progress. Our only regret was that we had arrived too late to take part in it.

It is impressive to drive through a Siberian village in the darkness of a winter's night. The only sounds are the tinkling of the bells and the responsive barking of the numerous dogs which are kept to hold the wolves in check. Occasionally the darkness is intensified by the solitary glimmer of a candle kept burning in a window to guide the wayfarer.

We sent instructions to the post station that we should want horses by five o'clock the following morning and retired to rest on a feather bed made on the floor. It was very clean and comfortable, although the room, as frequently happens in Siberia, was much too warm.

The next morning we were outside waiting for our drosky at seven o'clock and took a snapshot of it as the troika galloped over the wooden bridge at the bottom of the road. I shall never forget the view from where we stood. It was as pretty a village scene as I have ever seen. However, we were in a hurry and were not sorry to bid our host farewell and commence our next stage of 16 miles to Chorni-Anni.

The scenery along the route was exceedingly pretty, and we saw enormous quantities of game, but could not spare the time for shooting. We had made inquiries about the state of the road from Chorni-Anni to Bysk, and had been informed that it was impassable. This, though trying to our patience, did not surprise us.

For six miles beyond Ouskam the road is on the level, after which it ascends a long hill and crosses a pass, with a sudden dip on the opposite side. The road was very slippery and the horses fell more than once. The weight of the drosky, which had no brake, forced the horses into a run every time we were on a down gradient, with the result that, on one occasion, one of the horses fell and was dragged a considerable distance. Shortly before reaching Chorni-Anni we descended into a valley which was under cultivation and saw a Russian peasant actually sowing seeds. I had seen no land that had ever been touched by a plough from Katunda to Chorni-Anni. This was civilisation once more, and the sight was truly pleasurable after so much wild country. We also noticed a huge forest, fired fully four to six square miles, on the slope of a mountain to our left. Finally we reached Chorni-Anni, which is the central market-town of the Kalmucks, and, in comparison with the villages through which we had just passed, is quite civilised. It contains a spacious market-place, in which the annual Easter fair was being held when we arrived. All transactions are conducted on a system of barter, and one respectable London corn-dealer's shop would stock all that this huge market has to offer. The principal article of trade at the fair is flour; but boots, bread, butter and other articles are also bought and sold. All business was stopped as we drove through the village to the post station, the peasants, in long, shirt-like overalls and enormous fur caps, dragging themselves out of the way in the most leisurely fashion to make a passage for our drosky. Every one of them, as far as I could see, raised his cap to salute us as we passed, to which we naturally replied by raising our own.

Arrived at the post station we learnt that the road we had come by from Bysk had been impassable for six days, and that no one had ventured to attempt it. We decided, therefore, to be guided by the man at the post station, who was willing to direct us as to the best road to take. As for the road we had come by, neither he nor anyone else would attempt it, and there had been no communication with Bysk for fully seven days. We discussed the matter

CHORNI-ANNI VILLAGE.

at considerable length, and finally decided upon a road which started away west from Chorni-Anni, whereas the one we had decided to abandon runs east by Tavourack. For some distance we had a rapid river on our right. The mud on the roads was very thick, and our progress was very slow in consequence. Presently we descended into a valley, and the horses had to swim a stream which had only recently been spanned by a bridge, but the swollen waters had carried it away bodily. We perched on the sides of the drosky in order to escape a wetting, but the water was among our luggage and our feet were wet very soon. At about four in the afternoon we reached Tapoleoni. In the immediate vicinity of this village there is a dome-shaped mountain, snow-capped, which was much higher than any we had seen in the districts through which we had come, since we left the neighbourhood of Katunda. The peasants informed us, on inquiry, that it was the highest mountain in the district and that no one had ever thought of climbing it.

At five o'clock we started on a 20-verst journey to Solonishini. Some three or four miles out of the village our horses and drosky stuck helplessly in a snow-drift near the top of a mountain pass. The horses had been going very well so far, and it seemed a pity they should have so rough a time of it at this point. The three of us did our utmost to help the poor beasts out, but without avail. There was nothing for it but to give them a rest, after which they made a fresh effort, and with a pull that threatened to break the drosky into pieces we got out of the hole. The value of the small wheels of the drosky is apparent when the vehicle gets stuck in a snow-heap. Big wheels are difficult to extricate. The plan adopted of attaching a rope to the front axle of the smaller front wheels is a good one. By this means the drosky is pulled out of the holes, which are so frequent in this practically trackless country, with comparative ease.

On attaining the top of the ridge we entered what was, in effect, a second circle of mountains like the one we had just left, and were several hours descending through snow-drifts along a rough and devious road. In some places the hardy and vigorous steppe grass had withstood the winter colds and we came across great patches of it growing from two to three feet high. The sun set gradually while we were in the middle of our difficulties, and, when we entered upon the road which led to the village, pitch darkness had already come upon us. The snow had been shaken off the wheels of the drosky and mud had taken its place. We were just congratulating ourselves upon having surmounted our difficulties when we were warned by a scraping noise that something was amiss. One of the wheels of the drosky had come off, so we were obliged to tumble out of the vehicle and strike matches until we found it. It was a small wheel and required a great deal of fixing, but we succeeded in getting it in its place at last and drove for another quarter of a mile. Then it came off again, and the process of searching for it and fixing it in its place in the darkness was repeated. This happened every three or four hundred yards, but we reached the village at last in pitch darkness, having done the 20 versts (12½ miles) in about six hours.

It was a memorable journey. The drosky crawled through the darkness and the moujik groped about for the post station. When we did find it at last we had to knock up the people in charge, as they had already retired to rest. We ordered tea and food, and, before turning in, I went outside for a few moments to breathe the fresh air and look at the night. Everything was still, and the darkness indescribably intense. I could hear a dog barking in the distance and the steady munching of a horse, in a stable in the corner of the yard, enjoying its well-earned meal. The intense silence is only matched by the blackness of the night.

The villagers go to bed at sunset and rise in the morning with the sun. We turned in on the floor and awoke next morning at about half-past four. It was a Saturday. Daylight showed us that we were inside another fairly large circle of mountains, the average height of which appeared to be about 3000 feet. It had rained during the night, and the thermometer registered 42 degrees Fahr.

The sky was clouded, but there was no rain, and there were indications that the weather would clear up later in the day. Daylight came at about five o'clock a.m. and lasted till seven in the evening. We urged the moujik to hurry with the horses, as we were in doubt as to whether he would take us any further or not. The driver we had had over the last stage had told us that this man had refused to take two moujiks the week before, on account of the hopeless condition of the road. But he insisted on telling the man that we had a pass, the result of which was that we found the village secretary waiting for us in order to inspect that document.

I produced my letter of introduction from Prince Khilkoff, Minister of Ways and Communications, requiring the officials to help me on my journey, and, while the secretary was trying to make out what it meant, I practised my Russian upon him, which prevented his understanding my letter too well. I also held out my pocket-book, from which I had taken the letter, and waited in an impatient attitude, and with hand outstretched, to receive it back again. This worked like a charm; the puzzled village wise man handed me the letter without a word, and the owner of the horses, evidently impressed, arranged for us to proceed. In this manner we escaped being stranded in an out-of-the-way place, and continued our journey at the usual post rate, meeting with every civility and attention on the way.

We passed through the village at the very moment when the usual Easter procession round the church was in progress. The priest, followed by the congregation, marched in solemn procession, bearing the icon and lighted candles. Before the early service on Easter Eve the Russian Church has a service similar to the watch-night service in some places of worship in England.

One great defect of Easter in a remote Siberian village is the restriction of diet to eggs. For ten days we had little else to eat. The eggs are small but good, yet eating five eggs to a meal, two and three times a day, becomes monotonous, and I felt that I did not wish to see another egg as long as I lived.

The moujik had informed us that there was no road fit to travel over, and it was soon abundantly evident that he was right. There was no track. We drove straight through the deep snow and presently descended into a valley. Twice we crossed a swollen, formidable-looking stream, and, when at last we arrived at our next station, we found the main street of the village at least 2 feet deep in mud. After inquiring our way, we crossed the stream once more—it was about 3 feet deep at this spot—and soon arrived at the post station of Chiranchanka.

While the horses were being got ready, we paid a visit to the creamery. This is a very small affair, having been erected, so the owner told us, at a cost of £40, including the separator and all working utensils. The proprietor was not in a position to produce the best butter, and, if he had been, the village is so remote and so small, and the supply of milk so inadequate, that by the time a sufficient quantity was ready for the market the best half of it would have turned stale. For this reason they were making the butter and afterwards melting it down, and packing in large barrels holding about 2½ cwt. each. This used to be the method of preparing Russian butter before the Siberian railway was constructed. The butter was melted down into barrels and conveyed to the fairs for sale. The reason for melting the butter was that after it cooled again it could be kept for months; but the deterioration, both in the quantity and the quality, was very considerable. The owner of the Chiranchanka creamery informed me that he experienced considerable difficulty in inducing the peasantry to send their milk to him to be-made into butter, as they did not understand, and were suspicious of, the separator, and were afraid that they would never see their money after the butter was disposed of. As he was short of capital and could not pay cash for the milk, he was unable to obtain a sufficient quantity to keep the creamery going. The place itself was in an exceedingly dirty condition and resembled a coal-house more than a creamery. A few years of education will effect a

CHIRANCHANKA CREAMERY.

great alteration. Whatever instruction in dairy farming the peasants receive is imparted by Government officials. The priests in Siberia do not, so far as I can see, do anything to aid the development of the industry. If the priests in Siberia were only one-half as zealous and intelligent as those in Ireland, to whose efforts the development of the Irish creameries is largely due, Siberia would make rapid strides, but everything appears to be left to the Government. The priests should be encouraged to study dairy farming, in order to be able to teach the peasantry. By this means the Siberian moujiks would very soon become prosperous and self-dependent, and able to hold their own with the agriculturists of other nations.

The Government instructor is unable to visit the individual creameries very frequently, so that a given establishment may work for months producing bad butter, where a little intelligence brought to bear upon the matter would have remedied the defects on the spot and prevented serious loss.* Russian theorists of the Tolstoy type would do well to consider these matters and turn their talents to better effect by helping to train the people to utilise the wealth at their doors, instead of dreaming their lives away in a fairy-land of impossible Utopias. The Government has done much and will do more, but it needs the practical assistance of the people themselves, and particularly of those who have had the privilege of attending the magnificent universities and colleges, and who repay that privilege by defying the Government that grants it.

Our horses being now ready we mounted, and were soon on the way to Lejanova, a distance of 13 miles. We were obliged to ride, as the road was hilly and difficult, and our progress, even thus, was slow. We had to wait for horses at the post station and, when at last they were supplied, they were young and frisky, and from Lejanova to Solonofka, a stretch of 17 miles, we had a lively and exciting time. The road was swampy, owing to the thaw, and the horse I was riding regularly refused to pass a pool of water, and would rear and dance sideways until I dismounted and led him round it.

We met a number of peasants leaving Solonofka on horseback and, as it was quite an unusual thing to pass

* This refers to creameries 400 to 500 miles from the Siberian line.

anyone on the way, we inquired the meaning of the
cavalcade. We were informed, that as there is no church
at Solonofka, the peasants were going to a neighbouring
village to church for the Easter service, and were taking
provisions with them to be blessed by the priest and
sprinkled with holy water.

As we approached the village we found that the snow
and ice on the slopes had not quite thawed, and were very
slippery for the horses. It was about five o'clock when
we reached Solonofka. We at once made inquiries about
the road and were told that the postmaster had taken a
peasant on to the next station, Starebrolikave, seven miles
further and on the other side of the River Katun, and that
he would be back before long. When we asked how long
that meant we were told "seychas," which means
"presently." We had some tea, dyed Easter eggs and
Easter fruit cake. This cake was the only one that had
not been blessed at the Church, so it was given to us as we
were not supposed to be particular.

After tea we decided to allow the two sons of the postmaster to guide us on the next stage, as they were quite sure
they knew all about the road. A description of our
experience in travelling the next seven miles may serve as an
illustration of the pleasures of travelling in Siberia in early
spring. As a preliminary step we inquired our way to the
station. We were informed that we would have to cross
the river, which had shortly before been spanned by a
bridge, but the spring floods, which had come very suddenly
that year, had carried it away bodily. What was worse,
however, was, that we seemed to have arrived in the
village when the floods were at their highest. We were
assured by our guides that they were quite certain of the
road and would take us along the same route that their
father had taken that morning. This sounding quite
satisfactory we caught our horses, which were loose in the
yard, and proceeded to saddle and load them. Two horses
were loaded with our baggage, while the other four bore

my companion and myself, and the two guides with our
saddle-bags. I selected for myself what I thought was a
good strong horse. We started at seven p.m. and rode
through the village, and up a steep hill, on ascending which
we found ourselves in the steppes once more. At about
eight o'clock the leader of our little procession inquired
the way across of a peasant whom we met, and was
instructed, as it was then dark, to follow a line of
railings, till they came to an end some three miles further,
and then turn to the right. When we reached the end of
the railings I attempted to persuade the peasant who had
directed us, and who had accompanied us thus far, to go
further with us, as he seemed to know all about the road,
but he politely refused my invitation. We descended the
banks of a small stream, which we crossed. The soil
beneath our horses' feet now seemed as black as soot, and
we seemed to be riding into the darkness. I could scarcely
see the leader, although he was only some few yards ahead
of me. Suddenly we pulled up abruptly by the side of a
lake, into which he had very nearly walked. We called a
halt and rested. A flock of ducks rose quite close to us
beating the water with their wings, but we could not see
them. They seemed so near that one of our company fired
a shot at them, causing considerable commotion among
their numbers. Then we made a circuit of the lake,
wading through three streams as we did so. Presently we
came to a fourth stream, which ended in a cataract some
fifty feet high quite close to us. We could hear the water
tumbling over the ledge about three yards to our right,
which made it necessary for us to ride very carefully, as a
slip would have meant a good ducking—if not worse.
We next encountered an accumulation of melting snow,
which had lodged in a hollow, and through which we had
to guide our horses with great care. Just as I reached the
other side of the drift I heard a splash. My companion's
horse had stumbled, depositing him in the slush. We
helped him up as well as we could, but he was thoroughly

T

wetted. If it had been daylight the ride might have been fairly enjoyable, but in the pitch darkness the uncertainty of what was going to happen next was rather trying to the nerves. A little further on we came to what, by the sound made by the water, appeared to be a very heavy stream. The leader decided to attempt it but, from the splashing, I concluded that the water was both deep and swift, the horse appearing to have been carried off its feet. A little more splashing and the horse reappeared, but without its rider, and immediately bolted into the darkness. The moujik hailed us from the other side, telling us that he was wet through but safe and would try to get back again, as we could not proceed without the horse. Very shortly the moujik reappeared, and, after a brief council of war, we decided to retrace our steps, more especially as the runaway horse had taken with it some of the luggage belonging to my companion. The young peasant mounted beside me and we turned our horses very cautiously towards the village again. We had not ridden for more than ten minutes when a cry of "Volk! volk!" (Wolf! wolf!) from one of the guides caused us to pull up rather suddenly. I got my revolver in readiness and prepared to shoot what, in the darkness, certainly looked very much like a wolf, but on approaching nearer it was discovered to be the missing horse. It was clear, from the horse not having made its way home, that we were surrounded by water. The horse having been found, I wanted to wait until the moon came out, but the others were against me, so I was obliged to yield with as good a grace as possible and return with them to the village. We had been out four hours and a half when, at last, we emerged into the village street, and groped our way to the post station. The postmaster had returned. The peasant whom he had conducted that morning had been thrown, through his horse stumbling, and was the richer for a broken leg.

The following morning we had our first meal of flesh meat for the past fourteen days, and we did it ample justice. It appeared that this was the customary Easter calf. It was cooked entire—head, tail and collaterals— but the cooking had been well done, and the flesh tasted delicious, the more so, no doubt, as we had been without food of the kind for so long.

Breakfast over, we began anxiously to make arrangements for continuing our journey. We were assured by the postmaster that we would experience very little difficulty on the way, but we were not easy to convince, and wished to put his assurances to the test. As we drove through the village, the name of which is Solonofka, we awakened quite a flattering interest in the breasts of the native population, who turned out in their strength to see us take our departure. After a ride of about half an hour we came to the river, at the spot where the vanished bridge had stood, to find a very convenient canoe waiting for us. We paddled across, the horses swimming after the boat. The river was swollen and the current very swift. A second drosky was waiting for us on the other side, into which we climbed, rejoicing exceedingly as we rattled over the flat steppes and soon forgetting our adventures of the night before. We had a journey of seven miles to Seechofka. As we drove into the village we passed groups of peasants standing idly at the street corners—celebrating Easter. The people at the post station had not expected visitors on a Sunday, but they willingly gave us horses and harnessed them to a drosky. The moujik who drove us was, no doubt on account of the holiday, dressed in a handsome suit of velvet. He was smart and clean shaved. Nearly every peasant in Russia and Siberia wears his hair and beard long—probably to protect him from the severe cold in winter.

The road to the next post station was very bad, owing to the accumulations of deep snow, which the sun had not yet melted and, although the distance to Starahelokura is only six miles, the journey took us more than six hours. The peasants had congregated on a hill not far from the post station, where they appeared to be enjoying themselves. The women were dressed in very striking, brightly-hued costumes, the prevailing colour being red. We arrived at Starahelokura at two o'clock and dined at the station. We had made a detour of about six miles to avoid two rivers, and had consequently left the post route, which we rejoined at this station.

The next station was Tochilna. We started as soon as we had finished our meal. The road led us over the hills and, as we approached the village, we had a splendid view of the flat-roofed huts lit up by the sun. Large flocks of ducks and game of all kinds flew past us, but we were anxious to reach Bysk as quickly as possible, as we did not know what might be in store for us. We were driven to the post station and here the driver left us. He should have taken us on to the next station, but, in spite of our eloquence, he categorically refused to go any further. We discovered his reason for this when we got on the way again. This took some arranging, however, as we had the greatest difficulty in persuading anyone to take us, and, when at last we did induce one of the moujiks to give us a drosky, we had to pay him three times the ordinary fare. Even then he did not appear to be altogether happy, but walked off sulkily to make his preparations and to fetch the drosky from the other end of the village. Our meal on that occasion consisted of tea without sugar, and black bread without butter, on which we feasted sumptuously and with relish. I then realised how it is that the Russian and Siberian peasant is so easily satisfied with the dry black bread which forms the staple article of his diet. The keen, bracing air is a glorious whet to the appetite.

The walls of the post station were ornamented with a number of cheap and badly-executed chromos, illustrating martial scenes such as the Russian peasant loves. I found little difficulty in making out their meanings. One of them was entitled "Our Hero" and

SOLONOFKA—CROSSING KATUN.

represented General Skobeleff, composedly washing his
hands during the bombardment of a Russian fort in the
Russo-Turkish war of 1877, to a lively accompaniment of
shot and shell. A fierce battle was being waged in the
centre of the picture. Another bore the legend : " On the
6th of January Grabbe led the storming party, and as the
columns were about to take the fortress the Duke was
wounded in the side and fell dead. At that moment the
battle was won." A third picture included representations
of the fighting forces of all the white nations, the " handy
man " being depicted on top of the Chinaman. The fourth
showed a Chinaman, with the representatives of four
nations on his back instructing him in the methods of
Western civilisation.

We learned that the Government pays the postmaster
from 1000 to 4000 roubles, or something over £100 to £400
per annum, according to the number of horses kept, while
the post station at Altaiskoë, which is a rather important
junction, receives 5000 roubles, or upwards of £500.

At 5.30 the moujik drove up to the door of the post
station and declared himself ready to proceed. We packed
our luggage in the bottom of the drosky and took our
seats. Half-way through the village he pulled up, and
called to a young moujik, who tightened his waistband,
drew up his valenky and vaulted on to the drosky with
much of the air of a man who is not particular whether he
tumbles off again or not. His cap was crammed tightly
over his head. It turned out that he was to be our driver
for the next stage. We started away at a splendid pace,
and, as the stage to Smolensk, our next stopping place, was
only ten miles, we calculated we would get there by 7.30.
All went well for the first hour. Large flocks of wild
ducks kept rising to right and left of us, some of which we
shot at, but shortly afterwards we emerged into a portion
of the steppes which, as a result of the thaw, was almost
entirely under water. My companion and interpreter
usually turned to me to ask whether the drosky was to go

straight through the pools or to make a detour in order to
avoid them. I had hitherto been very fortunate in my
judgment, fording streams and rivers and crossing marshes,
calculating that the ice under the water was strong enough
to bear. I had also contrived to select the proper places
at which to drive through the water in the steppes, and
had never found it much deeper than about three-quarters
of the height of the wheels. Here, however, the road was
.lost. We dismounted and tried to find it. Our driver was
obviously puzzled, and admitted that he had never been
that way before. Not being able to find the road, we
decided to drive through a small lake. I directed the man
to drive to the right, where the water appeared to be
reasonably shallow, but to our general regret he turned to
the left, and, before we quite knew where we were, our
horses were up to their necks in the water and it was
barely possible, by jumping from the back of the drosky,
to reach dry ground again. We suggested that the driver
should wade into the water, detach the horses from the
drosky, and then, with the aid of the horses, try to pull it
out of the water backwards; but he failed to see the
matter in the same light. Indeed, he attempted to drive
the horses through the water, nearly drowning one of the
team and jeopardising the safety of our luggage. He then
tried to undo the traces by standing on the shafts, but,
failing again, essayed to turn the horses round, nearly
capsizing the vehicle in the attempt. After that we called
a halt and pointed out to him that the only possible course
was the one we had suggested, and that he himself, as the
author of all our woe, was the right and proper person to
go into the water and free the horses. Very reluctantly
he fell in with our views and waded waist deep, detaching
the horses and leading them out one by one. He then
hitched the rope to the back of the sledge and pulled, while
I took hold of the horses' heads. The drosky gave a
lurch, there was a splash, and it was out again. The
driver removed his tall boots and poured out the water.

He wore no stockings, his legs and feet being swathed in strips of calico. These he wrung out and squeezed, and was on the point of replacing, when we discovered that we had a pair of spare valenki which were only wet on the outside. These we gave him to put on. We decided to leave that particular pool severely alone and drive round it, but we had not proceeded very far when we arrived at another and considerably more formidable one. We tried to find a way round it but without success. There being nothing for it we made up our minds to drive through it, my companion leading the procession on horseback to ascertain the depth of the water, and the drosky following respectfully in the rear. The night had fallen and the darkness was intense. Flocks of ducks rose on either side as we splashed through the water. A light showed somewhere in the distance, which our driver informed us came from a lonely flour-mill. We could only guess our way. There was, however, some slight indication of a track in the ridges of frozen snow made by the sinking of a cart wheel and which the slight frost had rendered solid. This ridge could be recognised by the bumping of the drosky, and very welcome the bumps were. The Siberian drosky is not provided with springs, but rests on two horizontal poles and two other poles at right angles to them and a little higher, which serve the same purpose. A more elaborate system of springs would be broken many times over on those rough roads. The poles, however, are made of a specially selected wood of extraordinary toughness. The harness is of very poor quality and comes loose every two or three miles, when the driver has to dismount and tie up the traces anew. However, we surmounted all our difficulties at last, and at eleven p.m. drove triumphantly into the village street of Smolensk. The tinkling of the bells had awakened a watchman, who opened the door of a house as we passed and immediately used his rattle, although he was more than three parts asleep. From his remarks he took us to be officials, for he appeared very anxious to

convince us that he had only just entered the house. He
directed us to the post station, but we had some difficulty
in finding it. We drove up and down the narrow streets
in the mud and the darkness, looking for a lighted window
where we could knock and make inquiries. The villagers
were in bed and their houses in darkness. We found the
station at last, however, and having had our supper were
glad to stretch our tired limbs and snatch a few hours of
sleep.

On rising next morning we were rather surprised to find
that it was snowing. We showed our letter of introduction from the Minister of Ways and Communications
to the postmaster. It had been of great assistance to us
so far, but this particular moujik was too near Bysk, and
therefore too enlightened, to be persuaded that it was quite
as good as a postmaster's letter, so he required us to pay
full fare, stating that he would refund the balance to the
postal authorities. Our principal object being to avoid
being delayed, we had no objection to paying more; our
reason for showing the letter was that we were afraid of
being stranded, the more so as several peasants who were
travelling the same way had been refused horses at any
price.

We started in a driving snowstorm for Katunsky, the
last station before reaching Bysk, which is situated on the
River Katun, at a distance of about eight miles from Bysk.
While crossing a stream, the ice of which had thawed, our
drosky broke through the ice-sheet about half-way across
and turned over sideways, depositing my companion in
the water and myself on top of him. As we were both
enveloped in large fur overcoats, which were wrapped
tightly round our legs, the situation was not without a
certain measure of inconvenience, especially as the water
was extremely cold and quite two feet deep. My
friend struggled to his feet and walked out, while I,
having reassumed the perpendicular, helped to turn the
drosky over again and rescued one of the boxes from a

watery grave. We afterwards discovered that one of the
gun cases had got wet, spoiling the gun. The horses
struggled ashore, and my companion insisted that it
would be folly to go on; but I was determined not to turn
back, so, seeing that my mind was made up, he consented
to continue the journey. We removed our stockings and
poured the water out of our valenki. We then tied our

THE PLEASURES OF A THAW.

luggage more firmly and resumed our journey, singing
"Soldiers of the Queen" in order to keep up the circulation. We were beginning to congratulate ourselves on
having got over the worst of our difficulties when our
drosky plunged into a drift. The horses were in up to
their necks, and the cart was buried over the wheels.
Once more we had to alight and wade into the snow up to
our hips in order to extricate the drosky, while the stupid
driver managed to free the horses. This was, however,
our last misadventure. Thence to Katunsk, a drive of
about an hour and a half, the road was smooth and easy.

We dried ourselves at the post station, an operation which practically wasted the morning. When we were about to start we heard singing in the street and became aware of a procession, consisting of the priest bearing a crucifix, followed by a crowd of peasants making a hideous noise. This was the usual Easter procession, a rather lucrative institution for the priest, who blesses the people and, in exchange, receives presents of money or goods, according to the means or inclination of the giver.

A mile beyond the village we came to the River Katun, which we had to cross. We were surprised to find the ice only partially started, the nearer half of the river being open for boat traffic, while the remainder had to be negotiated on foot, half-a-dozen carriers assisting to convey the luggage. Just before crossing we met a friend with whom, when starting on our journey, we had arranged to do some bear-shooting at Pestchan, a day's journey in a south-easterly direction from Altaiskoë. We had contrived to get lost in the steppes, however, the night on which we should have arrived at Altaiskoë, and the idea was given up. It was a coincidence that he should be crossing the River Katun at the same time as ourselves. He was armed with a long coil of rope with which to face the dangers of the crossing, while one of his friends carried a long pole. These precautions were, probably, by no means superfluous, as the current of the river is very swift, and the depth in that particular spot pretty considerable. A person missing his footing, while jumping from one piece of ice to another, would run considerable risk of being drowned, unless supplied with something of the kind. Notwithstanding these considerations, however, I considered it my duty to chaff our Russian friend about it.

Once across the river we had a drive of about six miles to the banks of the Bye, where the steamers were being cleaned and burnished for the coming summer season.

The weather was beautiful, the air balmy and spring-like. We hired six carriers and proceeded to negotiate the

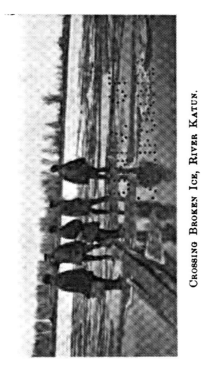

CROSSING BROKEN ICE, RIVER KATUN.

EASTER PROCESSION, KATUNSKY.

broken ice of the river—by no means a simple task. We were advised to be particularly careful, as several people had fallen in the day before. At this point the Bye is about one third of a mile across. For the last 30 yards we secured the aid of a boat, from which we piled the luggage on to the bank while my fellow-traveller went off to find a drosky. He returned in about three-quarters of an hour, having made a mistake in the house. The inmates of the house into which he had strayed were celebrating

BYSK STEAMERS ON THE RIVER BYE.

Easter and insisted on his staying to partake of some of the Easter cake and the "vodka." Our drosky man demanded an exorbitant price, but we paid it gladly, as we were anxious to return to Bysk and comparative civilisation. The journey to Katunda only occupied three days and two nights, but the return journey had taken us five days and four nights of very difficult travelling. Our average daily journey commenced at about five a.m. and finished at ten p.m., with very little rest in between.

The news of our return spread throughout Bysk in a very short time and we had quite a royal reception. Our friends had made up their minds never to see us alive again, which was strikingly illustrated by the words of Mr N. A. Sitcheff, who had lent me his heavy "shuba" (fur overcoat). He said, when I handed it back to him very much the worse for wear, that he had not expected to see either me or his "shuba" in this world again. It was Easter Monday when we arrived, so, as we had several invitations for dinner, and one or two business friends to interview besides, we decided to stay over Tuesday. We made the very best of our time, and, judging by the splendid reception accorded to us, and by the profound interest that was taken in the expedition, I think it very probable that the people of Bysk will be visiting the mountains, either by themselves or in company with some other travellers, if the expedition is undertaken in the summer months and not, as mine was, at the worst possible time of the year for the purpose. Mr Sitcheff and his friend, Judge Vinnitsky, both said they would be pleased to accompany an Englishman.

Several of the richest men in Siberia reside at Bysk, and the architecture of the place, considering its remoteness, is exceedingly fine. Mr N. A. Sitcheff has presented a pretty church to the town, the great bell of which stood in front of the building ready to be raised to the belfry when we arrived. It was a very fine bell, about 16 feet in height and about 2 feet thick. Bysk possesses several other pretty churches, and is, in many respects, a very nice little town. It is, besides, a most important market centre. The drainage, however, is very unsatisfactory, and the supply of drinking water is obtained directly from the river, being either filtered or boiled before use. In the spring, when the ice melts and the rubbish which has accumulated on its surface sinks into the water, it is very far from pure, and a source of great danger to the health of the populace. The water is taken from the river by public or private watermen.

After the long and tedious journey of five days, during which time we had met no one to speak to, the change to this elegant town, with access to good food and every other comfort, was truly delightful, and the discomforts and difficulties through which we had lived were soon forgotten. If we remembered our journey at all, it was to recall the magnificent sunsets and glorious after-glow reflected on the still, smooth waters of the flooded steppes, spread out for miles and miles on either side of the route ; or to imagine travellers skating long stretches of many scores of miles over the frozen surface of those pools, pursued by packs of ferocious wolves. As a matter of fact, the skating on these unbroken stretches of smooth ice after a stiff frost should be something magnificent. I am at a loss to describe the impression produced upon us by those endless steppes. The dominant sensation is one of utter loneliness, such as one would expect a traveller to experience who knew himself utterly alone in the heart of a dark and unexplored region.

On the morning following our arrival we were up betimes and sallied forth to make calls. We hired an isvostchik. The ordinary fare per hour is 30 kopecks (7½d.), but, as it was Easter, which is the principal holiday of the year in Russia, the tariff for Easter Sunday, Monday and Tuesday, the chief holidays, had been raised to three times the usual amount.

There are altogether too many holidays in Siberia, and their variety is wonderful. Not including the feasts of patron saints (name days), of which there is a host, the holidays amount to a total of one month in the year. The following is a list:—

RELIGIOUS HOLIDAYS:—*January*—New Year's day and Epiphany; *February*—Feast of the Purification; *March*—Annunciation, Easter; *April*—three days; *May*—one day; *June*—two days; *July*—one day; *August*—one day; *September*—three days; *October*—two days; *November*—two days; *December*—two or three days at Christmas.

OFFICIAL HOLIDAYS:—The birthdays and name days of

U

the Csar and Csaritsa, the Dowager Empress, the Cesarevich, and the Anniversary of the Coronation of their Majesties.

Until June 1904 there existed legal penalties for openly engaging in working on festival days, but these penalties are now abolished, owing to the harmful effect which the enforced idleness had upon the agricultural interests of the country. It happened very frequently, for instance, that crops were completely spoiled through the absence of hands to attend to them. The abolition of compulsory holidays is bound, therefore, to make a difference in the agricultural development of the country, by assisting the peasant to acquire habits of industry. So many holidays would make most people lazy.

The snow fell unceasingly during the whole of that night, nevertheless, next morning, we proceeded to pay a visit to our friend the trader. On the way I took a photograph of a Chinese cow, which appears to be a cross between an ordinary cow and a small buffalo.

The house occupied by our friend was small and built of wood, but it was scrupulously clean. We were welcomed, and partook of lunch with him and his wife. He talked long and interestingly about trade with Mongolia, and as he spoke, I took down the substance of what he said in my notebook. I have since had the opportunity of verifying most of the statistical information I received from him, and I believe the rest of the particulars communicated by him are equally reliable. The Russian merchants of Bysk are decidedly more enterprising than those of most other nations. Some of them will ride for eight or ten days with little more to eat than a few rusks, and dry manure to burn at their camp fires. They travel through Mongolia, to Kobdor and other places, visiting, among others, such towns as Uliassutai. They take pieces of silver with them, which they cut and weigh as required, to serve instead of money. I could not discover the

A Chinese Cow, Main Street, Bysk.

prices they pay for skins, but was able to ascertain the
selling prices to Moscow and Leipzig, and to some other
German towns. Mongolian wool that year was sold at
£2, 7s. per cwt., ready washed, and packed in bales of 3 to
4 cwt. each. The one firm of which our friend was the
representative had made considerable sums out of the
business, having exported 7000 tons of wool during 1902.
They expected to ship between 10,000 and 15,000 tons in
1903. It is surprising that this trade has not yet been
directed to Great Britain. John Bull is, obviously, behind
the times in this particular.

The following articles are exported:—Mongolian sheep's
wool, as already referred to, at £2, 7s. per cwt.; wool,
£2 to £2, 3s. per cwt.; camel hair at £2, 2s. per cwt.;
goat's hair (Angora, sorted) at £2, 2s. per cwt., and un-
sorted at £1, 10s. per cwt. A big trade is also done in
skins. A buffalo skin fetches 2s. 1½d.; maral, 2s. 1½d.;
goat skins, 7½d.; sheep skins, in four qualities, from 6d.
to 1s. 6d. each. Small curly kids (Astrakhan or Caracoul),
10d. to 2s. 1½d.; bear skins, 17s. to £1, or if very large,
£1, 15s. The market for these commodities varies with
the supply and demand. The smartness and energy of
the merchants of Bysk is exhibited in every branch of
business they undertake. The merchants and peasants
who own dairies are forming an Association similar to
those at Kourgan, for the control of the produce and its
better disposal.

The Association was anxious to learn the best method
of packing eggs for the London market. I gave them
full particulars, and my directions were promptly understood and applied. In view of the fact that eggs can
be bought at most of the villages at 50 to 60 for the
1s., the trade promises to be a very lucrative one. Eggs
have been exported during the last three years from
other parts of Siberia, with the result that the prices
on the London market have declined considerably. Importers of eggs in this country will do well to remem-

ber that still larger supplies will find their way from Siberia to London in the near future, and that advances against consignments should be made with an eye to the ever-increasing quantities of eggs imported. What may look, when the credit is opened, like a fairly modest advance with a good margin for possible fluctuations, may be above the market prices by the time the goods arrive on the spot, and considerable losses may easily result to the trade. The import of eggs from Siberia figures in the returns as from "Russia," in the same way as Siberian butter is shown as Russian butter; but, whereas the Russian eggs and butter industries are well developed, those of Siberia are still in their infancy. In a year or two prices will reach the lowest point, and Russia and Siberia alone, by reason of their immense resources and the cheapness of labour, will be able to hold their own, to the gradual destruction of the dairy industries in other countries, many of which already import large quantities of the cheap Siberian butter and eggs, in order to release their own produce for export. In course of time, as the London market cheapens, this policy will cease to be remunerative, and the Siberian article, having killed all competition, will command slightly better prices. The merchant and peasant of Siberia will then be able to place their business on a firmer basis, the peasant labour will be better paid, both in European Russia and in Siberia, and the remuneration for agricultural labour throughout the world will be reduced to a common level. The increased supply of foreign agricultural products, however, cannot seriously affect the home industry, provided British farmers are willing to adopt up-to-date and scientific methods. The British farmer has always a ready market for his milk, for which he can usually realise a good price, while, if we except the artificial product, he has no foreign competition to fear. Again, in the case of butter, if he is able to produce the best quality in sufficient quantities, the difference in the retail price is so great that

it will always be able to compete with the imported article,
while the British public is at all times prepared to pay
more for the home-made article than for a foreign substitute. In the present state of the market, as much as 2d.,
3d. and even 4d. per lb. more is paid for best English
butter than for the foreign-made article, whereas 25 per cent.
to 30 per cent. more is readily paid for English eggs than
for those brought from abroad. In the case of articles of
so exceedingly perishable a nature as eggs and butter,
therefore, the English farmer, and in a slightly less degree
his Irish colleague, from their proximity to the market, are
practically beyond the reach of serious competition, provided the quality of their produce is satisfactory. Then, if
the English and Irish farmer were able to make their produce as good as that of Denmark, or to organise its sale on
as practical a basis, the extra advantage of being so near
to the consumer, which enables them to place the produce
before them before its freshness has gone off, as in the
case of the foreign article after a long overland and oversea
journey in refrigerators, would make it quite unnecessary
to protect the English farmer by legislative acts, a policy
which can only result in converting the common necessaries
of life into luxuries. The best protective policy that the
English or Irish farmer can adopt is that of educating
himself in the most approved scientific methods of dairy
farming, and devoting the same industry and energy to the
work as are displayed by his Danish rival. These remarks
only apply to the farmer who is able to produce the best
quality of butter, as a second-rate article, whether of English
or Irish production, has to face the competition of quite
two-thirds of the produce that is dumped on to the English
market from abroad. As a matter of fact, the English
farmer who cannot produce the best quality of butter
should sell his milk, as it is only for the very best quality
that he can hope to obtain the advantages I have
mentioned.

I have already pointed out that it would be a mistake to

impose a tax on dairy produce imported into this country. The notion that it would bring about a rise in the wages of the working classes is also erroneous. It will be obvious to anyone who gives the matter a few moments' serious reflection, that even if foreign countries were compelled to send all their products to us and to keep on producing the same quantities, which they are not, a protective tax would only mean that the amount of that tax would be added to the price of the butter. There is, however, a greater danger even than that. If a tax, say, of 5 per cent. were imposed upon imported goods, that fact would have to be taken into consideration both by the importer in England and the exporter in Siberia, or wherever the imported article may come from. The English market would thereby be rendered less remunerative by 5 per cent. to the nation producing the commodity in Siberia. This would be borne in mind when considering the relative advantages of selling to us or to our competitors in Germany, Denmark, Norway and Sweden, etc., who are also extensive purchasers of Siberian produce. If these latter countries were to impose no extra tax on such imports, the Siberian exporter would obviously find that it paid him better to sell to them. The quantity imported into this country would, therefore, decrease and the market price would rise in proportion. On the other hand, the producers would be obliged to reduce their production, the standard of wages would be lowered, and the cheap labour diverted into other channels—possibly the manufacture of goods which would compete on our own markets with the products of our own manufactories—in which case the home producer would not have the advantage of freshness, as in the case of dairy produce.

There was, however, one broad idea which appealed to me very forcibly as I travelled through this vast country, and that is, that the more food-stuffs are produced in the world, the more remote will be the danger of famines and deficient food supplies, and that, therefore, the interests of the human race at large are directly concerned in the development of those industries which have for their object the supply of the food-markets of the world.

Although, at present, racial and national animosities stand in the way of so desirable a consummation, a day is bound to come when the farmers and cattle-breeders throughout the world will be able to produce largely and find a market for their produce. When that day arrives the country which enjoys the most suitable natural conditions will take the lead, while those that are less favourably situated in this one respect will turn their energies into other channels. Each country will supply the specialities for the production of which, from its natural conditions, it is best adapted.

CHAPTER IX

LEAVING BYSK

In order to take advantage of the heavy fall of snow, we
decided to leave Bysk the next day, April 23rd. My interpreter was successful in obtaining a pass from the postmaster, which read as follows:—

"From the Chief of the Bysk Post and Telegraph
Station. April 1903, No. 739. To postmasters and
secretaries of all post stations between Bysk and Novo-
Nicolaëvsk. In accordance with the command of
superior officialism I order to let pass without any delay
(not less than three horses on each stage), and to show
every assistance to the under-mentioned British subject,
Mr Samuel Turner.—(Signed) Chief of the Post-Office,
M. A. BASCHENKA."

Armed with this, our reaching Nicolaëvsk was assured,
although there was every possibility of the roads breaking
up and imprisoning us in some out-of-the-way village. I
recommend all travellers in winter to make a point of

procuring such a postmaster's pass, the importance of
which can hardly be over-estimated. In summer it can be
dispensed with for the portion of the route between Bysk
and Novo-Nicolaëvsk, as the river steamers ply there, but
beyond Bysk it is useful both in summer and winter. The
post road is specially kept for the mail and for the use of
Government officials, all other traffic being prohibited, and
this renders possible a more rapid rate of progress. Our
sledge was brought into the yard and loaded with our
belongings, much to the regret of our host and hostess,
who were very sorry we were leaving them and expressed
their longing to be back in dear old England. We
noticed that the bells on our drosky were tied up, and
were informed by our moujik that it was not permissible
for the bells to sound when passing through a town. The
change was so agreeable, after the incessant clanging to
which we had been treated for so long, that when we got
out of the town we preferred to continue without freeing
the bells. The first stage to Skubensky is down dale and
over hill. The cold north-east wind had dried up the
roads, and we managed to cover ten miles in the excellent
time of 1½ hours. Just after reaching the village we
went through a stream 18 inches deep, then over a bridge.
Although the boundary railings and gate are reached
after a drive of eight miles, the village itself extends
for another two miles further. Like most Siberian villages
it lies in a hollow, surrounded by a circle of picturesque
hills, which protect it from the north and north-east
winds. Skubensky is some six miles in circumference.
As we drove into the village we noticed the peasants
standing about in small groups, apparently, in their way,
enjoying the Easter holidays. We made a short stay at
the post-office, but, as the priest happened to be in
possession of the best room, we were forced to content
ourselves with the kitchen.

In twenty minutes' time we resumed our journey, over
the same kind of country as on the previous day, until we

reached Bulanka, twelve miles distant. The snow was lying thickly, whilst our progress was much impeded by marshy ground. The sky was clear and bright, but the wind was excessively cold, the thermometer showing 10 degrees below freezing point. The snow, however, was in splendid condition, and we completed the twelve miles in 1½ hours,

ALTAI POST STATION, SKUBENSKY.

the light sledge taking the road very smoothly. We arrived feeling exceedingly cold, and, after ordering a "samovar" of hot water to make tea with, much enjoyed a light lunch. The "samovar" in nearly every house in which we stayed appeared to represent the most costly piece of furniture. As a rule the fittings were of a very primitive and homely description, bearing distinct marks of home manufacture.

Taking a sledge we drove through the village, which is about 1½ miles across and three miles in circumference. Few of the houses were of brick, in fact, there are none to be seen in any of the villages and only a few in the larger towns. The weather was still very fine, in which respect we had been consistently fortunate. We were undecided whether to wait for the river steamers, which were almost ready to start, when snow came on to a depth of about five inches, which decided us to proceed. When fairly on our way again, however, the weather became once more settled.

Those of our friends who had predicted terrible roads for us would have been surprised to learn of the way we had been favoured. The condition of the Bysk streets, of course, could afford no clue to the condition of the roads in the country, as the heat from the houses had melted the snow and made the streets muddy and difficult for traffic. Owing to the severe cold wind one could get over the ground about three miles an hour more rapidly than ordinarily, but this was only a mixed blessing, as the wind was so cold as to make it extremely uncomfortable for the face and ears.

The journey from Bulanka to Haruzofsky was about twelve miles, the snow lying firm and not too deep for the horses. The sun went down, leaving an after-glow which reminded one of a perfect sunset at sea.

We arrived at Haruzofsky at nine in the evening, having traversed thirty-four miles since three o'clock in the afternoon.

We read the official particulars of the road to the next station—Petrofsky—which is fourteen miles distant, and learned that we should have to cross the River Belle at six miles, and a larger river at eight miles, and, as we were informed that these rivers were rapidly breaking up and were not bridged, we decided to retire to rest that night and make as early a start as possible in the morning. The peasant who was to take us was well pleased with the arrangement.

At four o'clock the next morning we were up, and at five had resumed our journey. Out of the wind the temperature had now fallen to 22 degrees, whilst in the wind it was 35 degrees below freezing point.

We were inclined to take some credit to ourselves for our early start, but, on looking round, we observed white smoke issuing from nearly every hut in the village, showing that early rising was not confined to ourselves. On the steppes there was plenty of hard snow, and the road was very good, although rough in places. A sunrise is always a beautiful spectacle, but that at the commencement of this stage was enhanced by the beauty of the trees on the banks of the River Belle, which were covered with hoar frost. The most beautiful of sights, however, could not have helped us to forget the intense cold, which troubled my interpreter to such an extent that I had to improvise some protection for him out of one of my old Alpine caps, by cutting holes in it for the eyes and mouth and pulling it down to the neck.

Telegraph poles skirted the roadside for some distance, and, where they left the road, small impoverished trees had been planted to serve as guides to the traveller across this pathless part of the steppes, which is much subject to snow drifts. The black-and-white striped verst posts, eight feet in height, also acted as guides, and every one of them was welcomed as a sign of so much progress made. We counted every verst in our anxiety to get to the next station. On passing the twentieth verst post we came in sight of a very handsome church, a certain indication of a village being near, and sure enough, a little beyond it, in a shallow valley, lay the village, which we went through, noticing, as we did so, the partiality the pigeons and other birds very properly displayed for the warm roofs of the houses.

Just beyond the village was another forest covered with hoar frost, a hoar frost which had by this time covered ourselves and the horses. In 2¼ hours we completed the journey, the temperature having fallen still further to 45 degrees below freezing point, so that we were fully able to appreciate the warm post station at Petrovsk. While the roads remained in good condition,

HORSES OUTSIDE PETROVSK POST STATION.

however, we were obliged to make the best use of our time, so our stay here was very brief.

The road to the next station, Ovchinikovskaya, fourteen miles distant, was over a very narrow track. So narrow was it indeed that one of our horses got off the track into very deep snow, and some valuable time was lost in extricating it. After this episode the moujik tied one of the horses behind the sledge and drove the other two tandem. Not a cloud was in the sky, and the country we passed through was uniformly attractive, being richly wooded with birch trees. We reached the village, which also lies in a valley, but only stayed long enough to pack another sledge and procure fresh horses, and were soon on the way to Jelensky, 16½ miles further. The road was good, lying, in fact, over the typical steppe country, without a tree to be seen and only a few wild bushes showing themselves here and there. During this stage we had some good shooting, bringing down a large crane, in Russian, "jouravl." Being shot in the wing, it lay on its back with its legs in the air, ready to attack us with its formidable beak. We could hear the cries of its companion as it soared out of reach of the gun. We pretended to go away, in the hope that it would return and enable us to have another shot at it, but the creature was too sagacious. Large numbers of these birds are to be seen in this part of the country. The specimen we obtained was three feet across the wings and stood about three feet high ; when walking together in pairs they present a very striking appearance.

In 2¾ hours we arrived at Jelensky, the roads still being in good condition, and, after a light lunch, started on the next stage to Chelofsky, a distance of 18½ miles. From Jelensky to Barnaoul by the post road is forty miles, but there is also a more direct road which is only twenty-five miles. We took the latter road, covering the distance in three hours, through a fairly well-wooded district. Nine versts beyond this station it was necessary to cross the River Obi. When we arrived at Jelensky, and went into the room to see the master, we found him seated with about twenty other peasants round a table, all of them about three-parts drunk. They were unanimous in the opinion that the Obi was too dangerous to cross that night, but we told them we had heard nonsense of that kind before and were determined to proceed. The master then

announced to us, that if we were willing to pay for two
carriers, and to give him 5s. for the six miles to Barnaoul,
he would take us, to which terms we agreed, only stipu-
lating that the start was to be made without delay.   Ten

WE SHOT A LARGE CRANE.

minutes later we were seated in a drosky and driving
through the village.   Two of the drunken men, who had
gone on before us to get their horses, for the purpose of
accompanying us, hailed our driver and jumped on the
drosky, the one behind and the other at the front.   From
the reckless manner in which these men jumped on the

X

drosky, and the way they tumbled off again to go into the
yard for their horses, we were very doubtful as to their
ability to retain their seats upon the animals. We drove
along slowly, and in about twenty minutes turned round at
some shouting. This was from the two moujiks, who,
seated on one horse, were galloping furiously, one of them
waving his arms frantically to frighten the horse into full
speed. The spectacle they presented was irresistibly
comical. They trotted behind us all the way, chatting to
our driver, until, as we were going through some deep snow
quite near the riverside, they rode up alongside us. Just
as the first moujik was turning round to shout something,
the horse stumbled in a snow heap and rolled him off like
a log. As he crawled out of the snow we expected to hear
him swearing in those terribly long and ugly Russian
words, but he only remarked that he had "nearly" fallen
off, a euphemism which made us all laugh so much that
our driver was forced to stop the drosky for two or three
minutes. The other moujik only managed to struggle
back into a sitting posture after he had been nearly pulled
off by his companion in his fall.

The journey to the river took us 1½ hours. It
was not so broken up as we had expected it to be,
though we found that the horses were of no use and that
it would be necessary to carry everything across the broken
ice. The three drunken men were the only help we had,
so we were forced to assist ourselves, and the five of us
commenced the journey across the Obi, which was at this
point about 150 yards in width. Just below the Irtish, however, it increases to 3512 yards. We fully expected some
trouble before we reached the other side and were not disappointed. We weighted the three moujiks according to
our estimate of the quantities of vodka they had respectively
imbibed, giving the most incapable the lightest weight, and
so on. They staggered across with great distances between
them. In the middle the strong current had broken the
ice, so that we had to cross this portion in a boat, pushing

our way between large blocks of ice. We resumed the
crossing on the ice and were nearing the other side, when
we missed one of the moujiks and turned back to look for
him. We found him lying on the ice. On being expostu-
lated with he said he had had no sleep during the last week,
as he had been celebrating Easter. We lifted him up and
reloaded him. Eventually we crossed in a boat, which connected the last piece of ice with the banks, and at nine p.m.
carried the luggage up the banks of the river. That day
we had been on the move sixteen hours, and had covered
seventy miles.

We sent one of the moujiks in search of a drosky,
whilst our sleepy friend huddled himself on the ground
just as naturally and contentedly as I would have taken to
a feather bed. The weather had changed again that afternoon, so we decided to start at midday on the morrow
and go back that way, which was supposed to save crossing
the River Obi many times, to Novo-Nicolaëvsk.

Arrived at Barnaoul, I paid a visit to a few business
friends, and also to the Barnaoul Bank. The manager of
this establishment was astounded to hear that we had come
from Bysk, because he had intended to go there to open a
bank but had given it up as impossible, and was waiting
for the thaw. This is only typical of the general ignorance
which prevailed as to the state of the neighbouring roads.

I noticed in one or two of the business offices cedar
nuts are placed on the table for business men to partake of.
I called upon Mr Gransky, who is the chief Government
Dairy Instructor in the Barnaoul district, and is doing good
work, the farmers being very well organised. Altogether,
Barnaoul left a very favourable impression upon me. At
four o'clock in the afternoon we again crossed the river, a
difficult matter, as it was now thawing hard and the
various blocks of ice which required to be negotiated were
very unsafe. When we reached the other side, we observed
about a score of peasants who were turning a gigantic
windlass, walking round and round and singing a popular

song, whilst the thick block, like the hub of a cart wheel, was winding a stout rope on to it and dragging the ferry boats—long narrow vessels of a shape similar to the turbine boats—out of the ice. They were exceedingly joyous

MAIN STREET, BARNAOUL.

because the spring had arrived. The motion of the boats was breaking the ice up very much, and it was doubtful whether we would have succeeded in getting across the river on the following day.

To reach the first station we had to cross a frozen

PEASANTS DRAWING FERRY-BOATS OUT OF ICE.

marsh about fifteen to eighteen miles in circumference and
ten miles in diameter, which would have made an admirable
skating rink in winter. In summer the people row across
it from the village to the ferry.

We reached this station — Beleraska — which lies
10½ miles from Barnaoul, in 3½ hours, which included
the time taken in crossing the river. Without much delay,
we started for Povolicha on a very narrow and badly worn
sledge road seven miles long and through a dense forest.
In some places, for three feet below the level of the snow,
where there were no forest trees to ward off the rays of the
hot sun, the track was half full of water.

We found the postmaster at Povolicha reluctant to
take us on at so late an hour, but we were determined to
cover the next stage before retiring to bed. It was a cold
journey of 10½ miles. For half of the way we had good
roads, but after that they were very bad, and it took us
two hours and forty-five minutes to cover the distance.

When we reached Ozjorka we proposed to travel all
night, but the owner of the horses, who should have taken
us further, declared that the river had broken up, a sledge
having broken through the ice that day, which made it very
dangerous to cross at night-time. He induced us to stay
by saying he would get up very early to take us on the
next morning, and we gave instructions to be wakened
promptly at four. As a general rule we found the people
fast asleep when we awoke in the morning, and on this
occasion the rule was not broken, as it took us quite half
an hour, by rattling a chair on the floor, to elicit the sleepy
answer "seychas." About an hour afterwards we were on
the road to Talmanskalyar, 16 miles away.

The road was in good condition, passing through some
very fine forests. At 5.30 the temperature was 5
degrees below freezing point. Our driver informed us
that the post sledges were coming in the opposite
direction. These were the only sledges we had met on
the road for 400 miles, as the general traffic had been

stopped. When they got near us I stood up to photograph them, shouting, in Russian, "Stop." Whether it was owing to my bad Russian I do not know, but the officer clutched at his revolver, and it was not until he was shown the camera that he would relax his hold.

The dreaded river near Talmanskalyar, which was supposed to be impassable, proved to be quite safe, and looked as though it would hold out for another two weeks.

THE ONLY SLEDGES WE MET FOR 400 MILES.

During this stage we enjoyed some very fine shooting, there being very large flocks of woodcock and ryabchiks. These and many other species of game birds are very numerous from May to the end of August, the ryabchiks, woodcock and quail being found in the Altai district from Bysk to Novo-Nicolaëvsk. During the threshing season close upon 5000 birds are netted, the majority of which are quails. The brown fox also is common in this part of Russia, while squirrels are scarce. Other birds are the magpie, the blackbird, the pigeon, and a little bird similar to our robin, but much prettier. Pigeons are found in large quantities in the villages and are quite tame. Owing to their being considered sacred by the peasants they are never killed or meet with any ill usage.

We reached Talmanskalyar at about eight o'clock, and left again in half an hour for sixteen miles over a beautiful sledge road, through forests and down hill for a long dis-

DURING THE JOURNEY WE HAD SOME GOOD SHOOTING IN THE FORESTS.

tance, and afterwards up a steep valley, the weather all the while being perfect. We arrived at Anisimofsky at eleven o'clock, the thermometer registering 5 degrees above freezing point. There were still 130 versts to cover before we would reach Novo-Nicolaëvsk, and this we had an idea of doing before midnight, so we promised each driver something extra in the way of remuneration to go at an increased speed. For three miles after we left the road was very good, and we travelled the first sixteen miles in two hours, According to the post-house table for this station the journey should take 2¼ hours, with half an hour's rest, and the return journey five hours, the horses to stand for three hours after their return. We therefore did the journey in one hour less than the official time. On the way one of the horses had a nasty tumble. If it had turned out to be a serious accident we should have had to pay a fine of £4 for instructing the driver to go beyond his speed limit. On this particular journey we had made record time up to then, just when we had expected to be hopelessly imprisoned in some village or other owing to the thaw. By a little strategy we managed to escape the risk of being fined, which we certainly should have been for telling the moujiks to hurry. This was accomplished by telling them what the previous moujiks had done and asking them if their horses were as good. In addition, and this was the most important point, we took good care to pay the extra kopecks for good speed to the last moujik in the presence of the new one. At this station, Garogekira, the dodge worked splendidly, the moujik driving his horses at a terrific pace, frightening them into increased efforts by the most hideous shouts and yells. We arrived at the next station, Medvedviseom, thirteen miles away, in an hour, once more the best time on record by a long way.

The horses were harnessed in a curious manner, two being in front and one behind. We did not stay long and were soon rumbling along to Koivoviva—twenty-two miles—over a fairly good road, occasionally up and down hills, with soft snow. We covered this distance in 2½ hours. The general description of the country was flat with plenty of forests. All kinds of game were plentiful, but we had now no time to waste in sport, and twenty minutes after arrival at Koivoviva we were on our way again to Bersk, the last station before Novo-Nicolaëvsk, which was reached by us, after a journey of 2¼ hours, at 8.30 in the evening. We covered the last stage much more quickly than we expected, considering the bad condition of the roads, there being hardly any snow on the way and the sledge being heavy and the district generally very hilly. · As we entered the village we heard the watchman's rattle, and being very tired, decided not to go on that night to Novo-Nicolaëvsk. Besides, at that hour, my interpreter's people would have retired for the night. I think we created a record that day for travelling at the end of the winter, having covered in all 154½ versts, or equal to 103 miles. We were travelling from 5.15 a.m. to 8. 30 p.m., and during the 15 hours and 15 minutes we changed horses and sledges, besides transferring and repacking luggage, six times. It surprised us very much that we had been able to utilise sledges all the way, with the solitary exception of the first station, as at this time of the year it is usual to find the country thawed.

From Bersk, the next morning, we again made a very early start, as it was necessary to cross the Obi twice before reaching Novo-Nicolaëvsk, and in the early morning the ice would no doubt be in better condition than later on. This district was well wooded and we were not long before we reached the track leading across the river. It stood some two or three feet higher than the level of the ice, as the accumulated dirt and refuse had protected the ice under it from the rays of the sun. Half-way across we were nearly in a hole, but the horses overcame the obstacle splendidly. We were evidently just in time, as in a few hours more the river would have been quite impossible to travel over. Overhead the clouds were fleecy and very high. These were the first clouds we had seen for three days. The sky was beautifully clear at 4.30 a.m. that morning, and the temperature was 10 degrees above freezing point, but it had risen by the time we reached the river. Our horses got into difficulties several times, but at length we got within thirty yards of the banks. The moujik then wanted to go back and try another route, but I would not listen to this but pointed him out a way which he must risk. When however we

had gone a little way we could see that if we did not leave
the sledge we should go under, so we jumped out onto the
ice, which luckily held us until we reached the bank.
Only fourteen miles remained now of the journey to Novo-
Nicolaëvsk, and as the roads were now good, we arrived
at the River Obi, near the Obi Bridge, at 9.45. Just before
we commenced the crossing the rain began to fall heavily.
This made us realise what splendid weather we had been
favoured with, as the rain-storms break up the ice very
rapidly, and, if they had started any sooner, our difficulties
would have been increased a hundredfold. We had to
abandon the sledge six yards from the bank and, placing
our luggage on a high four-wheeled cart, we rode on to
the banks of the Obi. My interpreter said "Home at
last" as if it were too good to be true.

I cannot help feeling intensely grateful to my interpreter, Mr P. Cattley, who showed exceptional pluck in
taking this journey, which had never previously been undertaken by anyone in the winter. All his friends were bitterly
opposed to his going, prophesying all kinds of dreadful
calamities, such as being frozen to death or devoured by
wolves or bears. They were quite sure they would never
see him back again. In addition there was the danger to
be anticipated from the mountains which he intended to
climb with me. It is not surprising, therefore, that when
we arrived at Bysk, it took all my powers of persuasion
to get him to continue the journey with me. His friends
were still busily engaged in trying to convince him that
the journey if continued would mean certain death, and in
addition the journey up to Bysk had really been a very trying
one, what with the intense cold and the wolves. He had
no mountaineering ambition to propel him onwards as I
had. I can only account for his exceptional courage by
the fact that he is a true-born Englishman and that his
father is an honorary member of the British Geographical
Society, which compliment was conferred upon him for
his plucky expedition with Captain Wigans. In this

expedition, Mr Cattley's father was on board the ship
which was instrumental in re-opening the passage of the
Kara Sea in 1874. That the re-opening of this passage
was a very important event, will be seen when it is remembered, that although opened in the first instance in
the seventeenth century, it remained closed for 200 years
after that time until the Wigans expedition accomplished
its mission and proved that it was possible for a steamer
to go from London to the heart of Siberia. Owing to the
short winter, however, the passage was closed again in
1890, so far at least as steamboat communication is concerned. This came about through one of the steamships
getting jammed in the ice, compelling the others to return.
From a commercial standpoint this passage is of the
utmost importance to Siberia, as the saving of carriage
on goods, which would otherwise have to be sent by rail,
amounts to £3 per ton. Under these circumstances it
would pay to continue to run the risk, more especially if
the Russian Government would lend assistance by making
a railway line from Tomsk more to the centre, which
would reduce the distance the boat would have to come
down the river. As far as the wheat trade is concerned,
the expense of the land carriage destroys any prospect
of Siberia supplying the western nations of Europe at
present, and the proposed short route would probably
encourage the central trade, which otherwise must remain
undeveloped for want of cheap carriage. The return to
Novo-Nicolaëvsk and the welcome from an English
explorer of such high repute as Mr Cattley made me feel
that Siberia was not so inhospitable a country as most
people think. We hired a drosky, and as we pulled up at
the front door we found we were not mistaken in
supposing that we should receive a hearty English
welcome. That evening all the merchants and friends of
the family gathered round a well-spread dinner-table
expecting to hear a little about the unknown Altai
regions. I hope they were not altogether disappointed.

I shall never forget the great amount of comfort I felt on being able once again to enjoy a good night's rest on a real English bed.

The road by which we went to Bysk was longer than the road we returned by. The latter was the post road reserved for the post sledges, whilst the one we went by was the trade route, which I trust no travellers will attempt to travel in winter, as it is not fit for anything more sensitive than a load of unbreakable luggage. I give the best route to and from Bysk for the benefit of any travellers who may find themselves in that locality, as even the inhabitants do not seem to know that there is any choice of routes.

That day the thaw began in real earnest, streams running down the middle of every street, whilst everywhere there were about six inches of mud. In another week or so a large number of boats would be sailing up and down the river and the large quantities of goods that had accumulated during the stoppage of traffic would be loaded into the steamers and floated down the flooded rivers in company with the drifting ice-floes. Merchants wishing to open offices and all varieties of business people would crowd the first available passenger steamer, and the summer would be here again in all its glory.

Siberia has altogether 27,843 miles of navigable rivers —20,000 miles of which are navigable by steamers—and the change of spring brings life everywhere on these rivers, and cheap transit for goods and cheap fares for passengers. So the importance of spring to Siberia can hardly be over-estimated.

Spring even made the gloomy, long-faced peasants appear happier, and a walk in the market-place that evening was sufficient to impress one with the increased cheerfulness of manner of the small merchants, who were now anticipating renewed business activity after the slackness of trade they had experienced owing to the severe and prolonged winter. Birds had already settled

in the town and were chirruping songs of gladness, and
all the inhabitants seemed to be raised from a depressing
dulness to vigour and freshness.

The marked contrast in character the change in
weather had caused made one reflect upon the large effect
climate has upon national life and character. Place the
average Englishman in the conditions of the Siberians,
give him a winter as severe, and he would undoubtedly be
quite as morose and lifeless as they are. And the sudden
change of spring would just as surely change his tempera-
ment in the opposite direction.

The peasant labourer has cause for rejoicing when
one considers that he earns from 1s. 3d. to 2s. 6d. per day
of twelve hours in summer against 10d. to 1s. 8d. per day of
eight hours in winter. The mines are closed in the winter
and open in spring, and work is carried on eighteen out of
twenty-four hours in the summer, the summer night in
Siberia only lasting for about five hours. In the depth of
winter this is the length of the day, and the labourers work
from sunrise to sunset. These and many other advantages,
which I shall not enumerate, easily account for the bright-
ness which pervaded the atmosphere of Novo-Nicolaëvsk
that day.

The warmer weather was such a relief to me after the
excessive cold I had experienced that I was quite prepared
to fall in love with the Siberian climate. It is altogether
a mistake to suppose that because an explorer or traveller
is accustomed to all kinds of climate and temperature any
kind of weather is enjoyed by him. On the contrary, it
is he who can best appreciate fine weather when it comes
his way. The lucky mortal who has always lived in a
fairly even temperature does not assess his privileges at
their true worth.

There was no necessity for early rising next morning, so
we indulged in a larger share of sleep than we had been
allowing ourselves for some time. When we did rise we
determined to have a day of rest, with no more arduous

work than making a few purchases or taking stock of the customs of the inhabitants. At one of the Novo-Nicolaëvsk confectioner's shops we bought some well-made sweets and cakes. We were reliably informed that the proprietor was a banished murderer. When I commented on this I was further informed that there is one man who is practically known to have committed two murders in the suburbs of Novo-Nicolaëvsk, but as no witness saw him commit them he is at large, in company with several other banished murderers, in the same town. We also bought some Moscow-made biscuits from a banished convict in a grocery store. All the pickles, jams, sauces, and nearly all manufactured articles, come from Moscow. The Cattley family imported a small consignment of biscuits from Carlisle, but the duty and carriage were too dear to make the continuance of such a trade useful. I afterwards had a stroll round to a new red-brick church, where a religious service was in progress, as I much wanted to see how a Siberian service was conducted. As I approached the doors I was reminded of one of those scenes depicted in the Bible, where the maim, the halt and the blind gathered together to hear the Gospel. Here, however, the crowd was composed of beggars, whose chief object was the solicitation of alms from peasants who, if appearances went for aught, were quite as poor as they were. However, the occupation seemed to be remunerative enough, as the beggars were receiving Easter eggs, bread, and all kinds of eatables, and occasionally money. I pushed my way through the doorway, up four steps, and into the porch, from whence I could see right through to the altar, at which the priest was officiating. Peasants were buying candles at prices ranging from five to fifty kopecks, and these they were lighting and passing up to be placed on the altar. I was informed that the priest was particularly desirous that his congregation should buy those which were sold at fifty kopecks instead of those at five kopecks, as his profit on all transactions amounted to 90 per cent.

From information I collected from several sources, I gathered that the priests of the Altai, generally speaking, are not very much respected. I heard that in the Bysk district, for instance, the squeezing of money out of the peasants is conducted on such a scale, that the peasants sometimes protest, the protest taking the form of beating their priests.

Whilst in Novo-Nicolaëvsk, I obtained what I should suppose is very accurate information on this subject. The priests in Novo-Nicolaëvsk have so obviously an eye to the main chance, that it borders on the scandalous. There is competition with the midwife when the young Siberian makes his first appearance into the world, competition when the child is to be christened, competition to perform the marriage ceremony, and, worse than all, competition when a burial has to take place. If the child is of Christian parentage, nine days after birth the midwife takes it to be christened. When this ceremony is over the godmother presents the child with some useful article, and the godfather gives a cross of silver or gold, which is worn by the child all its life. This cross is blessed by the priest at the christening, but, to make it doubly sacred, before the priest puts it on to the child, a form of baptism has to be gone through and the child is immersed in water. After this the godmother provides a dress for the mother, also a sheet for the child to be wrapped in. Then the priest cuts off a little of the child's hair, fastens it together by applying a little wax taken from a burning candle, and then places it on the top of the water. If it sinks the child will die within a year, if it floats the child will live. This superstition is very deeply rooted. Afterwards the midwife receives the guests. She hands round a tray, on which are vodka and other drinks, and, when the guests take their glasses, they put down money according to their means. This money is given to the midwife. The godfather and the godmother are supposed to be related to one another. The only duty of a godfather and godmother

Y

is to see that a child receives its first communion ; after the age of seven it no longer receives communion without confession and absolution. This information was given to me by an English lady, and, although there may be some people to whom these habits and customs appeal, they did not at all satisfy her. Like two other Englishwomen I met there with their families, she had an intense longing for London and London life. To even hear of anyone going to London seemed to cause her torment.

The evening before I left Obi station I went for a stroll along the main promenade. This is the great Siberian railway, the longest promenade in the world, but the train service is not so considerable as on English lines, so the chance of being run over is very remote.

I noticed that a large barracks was in course of erection, as well as a large factory for the making of rusks and war biscuits for the soldiers. On my returning to my friend's house I noticed that the torrents in the middle of the streets had been considerably augmented, which made their negotiation a matter of no small difficulty ; in fact, it took us all our time to successfully manage one of the large rivulets near the railway embankment.

We had a farewell supper and concert, at which the élite of Novo-Nicolaëvsk, including an exiled count, were present. Then I was driven to the station by the Cattley family in a drosky, as by this time the roads were almost clear of snow.

I joined the Wednesday morning post train at 1.25 a.m. with the intention of catching the Siberian express at Kourgan, which would leave two days afterwards. I thought that possibly a rouble judiciously applied would secure us a first-class berth with a second-class ticket, but this experiment in the palm-oil business, which so many writers about Siberia have commented upon, failed to succeed, and I was shown into a second-class compartment. This experience lessened my faith considerably in all those who enlarge upon the proneness of the Siberian officials to

339 BRIBERY AND CORRUPTION 339

accept bribes. I do know, however, of one well-authenticated case of this. A certain veterinary surgeon was required to inspect some cattle and to grant a certificate testifying to their perfect health, which was necessary before they could be sent by rail. It so happened, that he had spent the night previous in card-playing and had lost heavily, so that he was too tired or too lazy to get out of bed to do it. It was only when a payment of so many kopecks per cow had been agreed upon that he signed the certificate. This he did without making the slightest inquiry. Of course, if the Government knew of such cases they would very quickly be stopped and an act would be passed such as it has been found necessary to pass in England, but there has been no agitation to this end. The person who informed me of this incident knew both the peasant who owned the cows and the veterinary surgeon who had selected this means to recoup his losses at cards. Card-playing and vodka drinking appear to account for the downfall of a very large number of officials, who land eventually into the clutches of the money-lenders. They are then in a hopelessly bankrupt condition, so that it is not surprising that they stop at nothing when it comes to taking bribes. The amount expended in card-playing exceeds the budget for national education, it is estimated, by £600,000, so that it is not at all unnatural if it leads to bribery and corruption in Russia and Siberia. Of course, before a man is capable of accepting bribes he must be morally, and probably financially, bankrupt, and the few men who answer to this description may be looked upon as akin to the common thief who commences pilfering to regain his lost position. There is very little doubt that the Russian Government were robbed in a wholesale fashion in this manner in the construction of the Siberian railway. Being on the Siberian steppes they had a splendid chance, and they took full advantage of it, but robbery of this description is not confined to Siberia.

I have read articles by men who pretend to know the reason for the Siberian railway being built, who freely express their opinion that it would not act for military work, it being liable to all kinds of break-downs. As my business has, in the main, been dependent upon the Great Siberian railway carrying butter during the war, a few remarks from me on this head may to some extent be valuable. Having examined the line with some care, I came to the conclusion that the Great Siberian railway is well entitled to rank with the seven wonders of the world, being, in fact, a stupendous undertaking, and that its chief object was not to menace Japan but simply to develop the country. We must remember that in sparsely-populated countries railways are built primarily to increase the population of that country, whilst in thickly-populated countries the railway is built to benefit the people. One very strong proof that the Trans-Siberian railway was not built for war purposes is the fact that when General Kourapatkin went over it to Manchuria in 1903 he did not alter or relay any of the numerous curves, while, in addition, there are places on the line where the work of the jobber and plundering railway contractors can very easily be seen. In times of war, these unnecessary curves are a very serious matter, and General Kourapatkin had afterwards to set to work to relay the railway line, making the curved places straight, when the war had actually started. This would all have been done in the first place if war with Japan had been thought of. Although the line is a single one there are, at each station, two and sometimes four lines, the distances between stations averaging about twenty miles. This makes it, for all practical purposes, just as convenient as a double line, as trains do not pass one another many times during the week, and when they do, the returning train can easily be timed to reach a siding so as to let the full train pass without delay. This system has worked very well, in fact so well, that since the war commenced consignments of Siberian butter have regularly arrived at

Riga from Kourgan, a distance of 2500 miles, in the space of ten days. If Russia had engineered the railway for the purposes of war it is difficult to see why two lines were not constructed throughout. The fact that Lake Baikal was not girdled by a railway also tends to show that Russia did not anticipate warfare.

CHAPTER X

ON THE WAY HOME FROM NOVO-NICOLAËVSK

My train companions—Tea and conversation—A steppe thunderstorm—
Kainsk—Dining facilities—A *menu*—Siberian cats—Kourgan—Boarding
the Siberian International Waggon-lits Express—We meet General
Kourapatkin—His personality—My fellow-passengers—"A good old
English gentleman"—Missionaries—Naval officers—Mountaineering—Big
game in the Far East—Russian officers—A pleasing incident—Unfair
criticism—Zlatoust—The Birmingham of Siberia—Emigrant trains—Bashkirs—Ufa—Other aboriginal tribes—Samara—The Volga Bridge—Tula—
Moscow.

THE slow post train on which I was leaving this interesting
country was composed of five carriages. I secured a berth,
having as companions a post-office clerk and a merchant
bound for Moscow. They could not speak a word of
English, so I thought it an excellent opportunity to
increase my knowledge of Russian, and after making them
understand my mission to Siberia, and thoroughly scrutinis-
ing them to see what kind of characters they were, I fell
off to sleep feeling quite comfortable and satisfied that I
was in the company of honest men, which is a consideration
when travelling alone in this country.

I dreamt of good Old England and home, and that the
sledge which was taking me there had fallen through the
ice of the River Obi. Just as I was gliding comfortably
under the ice I awoke. It was about seven o'clock. The
morning was lovely, with a clear, pale blue sky. My
Russian postman friend had just drawn the sliding door to
with his left hand, while in his right he carried a tin
kettle full of hot water. When he saw that I was awake
he bid me good-morning very politely, and asked me if I
would have a glass of tea with him, to which I gladly

assented, sitting up on my flat mattress to enjoy breakfast with my fellow-travellers.

We had great fun owing to my being deficient in a number of Russian words, which I supplied by all manner of gestures. I found it was by no means a disadvantage to be ignorant of the language, as, when I made any particularly strange remark, it brought out roars of laughter, and all nations understand a good laugh.

The day was very warm and the steppes were flooded in every direction. It became very apparent that the region of the River Obi was more backward than the district we were now passing through, which was about 250 miles nearer west, as all the snow had melted. The railings, which had kept the snow from covering the railway line, had been taken down and piled up at intervals.

We opened the windows to let the delicious air into the carriage, and they were no longer heated and unbearable to an Englishman, as in the winter, but comfortable and cool. Towards mid-day I sat down and wrote two letters, which I posted on the train by dropping them into a small tin box attached to the last carriage and distinguished by a small red cross painted on it.

That morning I was treated to a Siberian thunderstorm. From behind the train I could see the effects of each flash, without the interference of buildings. The lightning was very vivid, and the rumbling of the thunder rolled right around us. The rain came down in sheets. The darkness was intense. The storm lasted all day, the train travelling about 25 miles an hour, the storm area must therefore have been very extensive.

We stopped for dinner at Kainsk at 1.30 p.m. local time (10.30 a.m. St Petersburg time). I enjoyed a good lunch for 2s., served by two young waiters in conventional dress. This was about the dearest lunch I could buy, and it would cost 3s. at an ordinary London hotel. I could have had one for half the price. The tariff at Kainsk station, which was posted under a shed outside the refresh-

ment rooms, was about the same as at other stations. The
prices were 2¼d. for butter; 1¼d. to 2½d. for a bottle of
exceptionally rich milk; 5d. for a large fresh cooked fish;
6d. for a very nice well-cooked ryabchik, more delicious
than our English partridge; 9d. for a well-cooked goose
sufficient for four people, and 1½d. for a small loaf. All
kinds of wine and lemonade could be obtained at reasonable prices. This station was being enlarged to double its
size, and will be a very fine one when it is completed. I
found out that my post-office friend and his companions
were going from Tomsk to Moscow. Although the
journey is one of nearly 3000 miles, they did not think it
much. They estimated their expenses to Moscow with the
train, including second-class railway fare, at £3, 6s. 4½d. (31
roubles), and the same for the return journey, and they
spent 3s. per day for food and 1s. 6d. per day for best
Russian cigarettes, which appeared to be the one indispensable necessary for the journey. They had a friend
travelling third-class, whom they introduced to me, and I
accepted tea at his invitation in the crowded third-class
carriage with its wooden seats. It was 5.30 and quite dark,
but that was St Petersburg time, the local time being three
hours behind. The tea, which I tried hard to enjoy, was
accompanied by fish, sour cream, cheese (Swiss Gruyère),
lemon for the tea, sugar, biscuits, sweets, black bread,
which they ate with sour cream and buttermilk, and a
good supply of caviare, which has a great reputation, and
last, but not by any means least so far as they were concerned, "vodka." The third-class carriages were badly
lighted, with only one candle to each compartment. My
host and hostess had another candle stuck in the neck of a
vodka bottle to help the light. They remarked that it
was necessary to take your own candle if you want to read
or write. In this carriage there were four compartments
with six berths to each of them, including the sides of the
corridor. In the next compartment were a man and his
wife and two children, who were going back to Moscow

because Siberia had not been kind to them; and in the one next to them were two young ladies, very poorly dressed, who were going to seek their fortunes in Moscow, having grown tired of Siberia. Most of the third-class passengers had their food with them and only got hot water from the large samovar or the hot-water house at the stations. On the train were two Siberian cats which were being taken to Moscow. They were finer than any Persian cat I have ever seen. I learnt that the climate of Russia does not agree with them, and they nearly all die, while several have been brought to England with the same result. They are beautiful animals, with very long hair and of good size. They fought all the time and made a terrific noise, which disturbed all the passengers. It was annoying when the passengers wanted to sleep, although sleeping on bare boards on a long journey by post train is not so comfortable as some people would like. There were in all thirty-six passengers, whereas in the same space in the second class there were only 20.

Including stoppages at eight stations we were 40 hours on the way from Novo-Nicolaëvsk (Obi Station) to Kourgan, and I arrived just after midnight. Instead of risking driving through the town at such an unearthly hour I bought 40 picture post-cards, upon which I scribbled the information that I had not yet been devoured by wolves and dispatched them to my friends. From Cheliabinsk to Irkutsk is practically the mid-Siberian section of the railway, which runs through the lonely steppes, and there are 103 stations along this section, which is 2015 miles in length. According to the official time-table the post train takes 118 hours to make the journey, allowing for all stoppages. These vary from 15 to 50 minutes at 27 chief stations and several minor ones. The chief engineer of the Siberian railway, Mr Pavlovsky, had his special carriage switched on to the back of our train, and the priests at nearly all the stations met and had a conversation with him. He was going to Cheliabinsk to meet General Kourapatkin, Minister of War, who was bound for Manchuria.

I left the train to spend a day at Kourgan. I discovered that I had left my sealskin overcoat in the carriage, but the train had gone so I telegraphed to Cheliabinsk. I spent the day at Kourgan transacting business. The weather was beautiful, the thermometer registering 71 degrees Fahr.; all the ice had cleared off the river and the mud had cleared away, the streets being very dirty. When I informed a few people that the River Obi was frozen over two days before, they were very much surprised. The thaw had come upon them ten days earlier.

I rejoined the Siberian International Waggon-lits Express train. The day I left Kourgan was the commencement of a 25 per cent. quicker service, and four trains a week had been adopted for the summer instead of three. Two stations farther we stopped, as General Kourapatkin's special train stopped here too. All the passengers were interested and went out to look at the General, so, being interested myself, I left the train and saluted him on the platform as the others did.

The Minister is dark-complexioned, with keen eyes and a serious and rather stern face. He is of medium height and wears a black beard. He had a tall Caucasian soldier in attendance, who was dressed in the Caucasian dress, and with his copper-coloured skin looked the handsome mountaineer he no doubt was. The train was a special one and consisted of eight strong carriages. One contained a drawing-room, another a dark room— probably stores—then the travelling kitchen and five carriages for the General and his attendants. The train was very well made to protect the passengers from the shots of the robbers in Manchuria. For two feet from the bottom the lower part of the carriages was of steel. The General seemed to realise his responsibility and his manner was grave and solemn. Like most powerful men he has risen from a relatively humble position.

The thirty passengers on the train I was travelling with were on their way from the East, and as far as I could gather I was the only passenger who joined the train in Siberia. Nearly all the passengers use that railway to get from the Eastern to the Western world.

There were three English missionary ladies on the train. One, from Pekin, had been a doctor in Pekin during the siege. Another of the missionary ladies was from Amoy and another from Foochow, China. They were returning to England after several years' absence. There was also a good old English gentleman coming for the first time by that route to England. He had been in business in Hong-Kong for forty years, and he informed me that he sent an anonymous wreath to the Nelson Monument, Trafalgar Square, every year. Before he left Hong-Kong his Chinese friends had been afraid that something would happen to him and that he would never get back to England by the Siberian route.

This gentleman has a house in Piccadilly. He said his wife could not stand the sea and would not go to China, but he was so very favourably impressed with the Siberian railway, had received such politeness and attention from the officials in charge of the train, and had been able to procure such excellent food, that instead of dreading the journey as when he started he had come to look upon it as one of the pleasantest holidays he had ever spent and felt in the best of health. Another of the passengers was a German who was on the way from Pekin. He said he thought it very silly to attempt to prevent Russia from occupying Manchuria, as that country would keep Russia occupied for the next 100 years on account of its being overrun by robbers, which require quite a little army to keep them under control. This is no doubt one of the reasons why there were so many soldiers in Manchuria. When Japan began the war the Russian nation was not prepared, and apparently had no idea of war, which goes far to prove that the Czar's desire for universal peace is sincere.

There were two naval officers on the train, and a General with his daughter. There was a merchant from Odessa, and a stout lady who smoked more Russian cigarettes than many men. The passengers were a very sociable party. The German language will carry you almost anywhere near the Siberian railway. All three naval officers spoke English and German fluently. They were very polite and friendly, and I got on very well with them. Baron von Raden, one of the naval officers, was returning from Pekin after the siege. He told me that one of the missionary ladies, Dr Lillie E. D. Saville, of the London Mission, then on the train, had proved herself to be a very brave lady. He had come in contact with her during the siege of Pekin. She had attended to the wounded and dying soldiers amidst all the turmoil of battle, and had been highly admired and esteemed by both the officers and the men of the Russian and English armies. The soldiers particularly thought her an exceptionally fine character.

We afterwards drifted to the topic of the Altai Mountains, which he was eager to hear about, and he told me that there was good climbing in the Kamchatka Peninsula. The highest mountains were Klutchevis (Sopkyar), a volcano 22,000 feet high, and Korertskyar, 16,000 feet high, which had never been climbed. A German doctor had climbed 12,000 feet of it. The best way to get there was by rail to Vladivostock, and thence to Petropavlovsk for Klutchevis, forty miles away, or for Korertskyar from Petropavlovsk to Negi Kulchka by steamer, the mountains being twenty miles further. There is plenty of hunting; sables, red, white, blue and silver fox, bears, squirrels, sea otter, seals, ermine, wolves and white hares abounding. The average yield of skins per annum is about 7000, but when there is little snow in the winter it is difficult for the natives to travel and the quantities

decrease to about one half. The best time for shooting
is August or September, at other times fogs abound and
it is very cold at night. The hunter waits by the rivers,
which are full of fish, chiefly a variety of salmon. The bear
comes down to the river to feed on the fish, and is easily
shot, if he does not get scent of the hunters.

The Baron informed me that he had shot nine bears in
fifteen days, which averaged 9½ feet standing up. They
have a light brown-grey fur, similar to the grizzly of
America. It is necessary to take a good gun, because if
the bear is only wounded he becomes very dangerous, and
will come straight for the hunter, anxious to enclose him
in an affectionate embrace. My informant told me that
when the British men-of-war were stationed very near
Vladivostock the officers organised a bear hunt and were
successful ; they expressed themselves highly delighted.
He told me of several big game hunts that made me
admire his pluck, and he also informed me that the
organised big game hunts were general with all the
officers, proving they were not lacking in courage. He
also said that it was possible to go from Petropavlovsk
to Kamchatka any day and shoot a bear or two, returning
in the evening. All kinds of birds abound, including big
eagles, and the wolves are particularly troublesome,
especially in the winter, when they are short of food.
The polar fox can be shot 300 miles from Petropavlovsk ;
in other places the fox is red or black. From the conversation I had with the Baron and the other naval
officers, I formed a very high opinion of them. I cannot
speak as to their fighting qualities, but as highly-educated
men I have never met their superiors. There is one
incident I should like to relate which is an index to the
character of at least one of these officers. We were walking up and down a station when some little peasant girls
offered us cages full of birds, something like our English
canary, at 5 kopecks (1¼d.) each, or 1 rouble (2s. 1½d.) for
twenty birds. This officer, who by the way had been

imprisoned in Pekin, bought the whole cageful and
opened the door, letting the birds fly away. The action
showed thought and feeling, and is typical of the highly-
educated Russian, who is kind, sensitive and intelligent,
but not excitable. I also formed a very good opinion
of the soldiers I came in touch with, who are also well
educated. They are to be seen at the stations, and are
fine handsome men, nearly six feet high, clothed in long
grey overcoats, which are most picturesque. From my
experience of the Russian and Siberian soldiers, and the
Russian naval officers, whom I have seen often enough, I
think that they compare very favourably with the
British, and the book entitled *Russia As It Really Is*
contains a very unfair criticism of them. I was delighted
to meet with a strong criticism of this book in the columns
of the *Daily Telegraph* of the 3rd July 1903, which I
reproduce verbatim: "It would be hard to find a book
written in more violent language than this, the natural
result being that the author defeats his own aim." This
criticism is not by any means too strong, and to my mind
could be applied with almost equal truth to the writings
of many pretended authorities on Russia and Siberia who,
through an excess of anxiety to belittle and traduce
Russia, only succeed in discrediting their own sincerity.

Other writers, having visited Siberia, have found that
the subjects of the Czar are disinclined to talk about or
criticise the actions of the Government, and have been
obliged to rely upon the stories of the exiles, who are the
Government's bitter enemies, and are secure against being
banished further into Siberia. I myself have listened to
stories from exiles here and there, but owing to my
business training, which causes me to sift and prove a
statement before I accept it, I have found that many of
them will not bear investigation, and I have not thought
fit to repeat them. If our own murderers and convicts
had been banished to a country like Siberia for the last
seventy-five years, instead of being imprisoned or executed,

it is open to us to imagine the grievances they would conjure up and pour into the ears of irresponsible critics sent over to rake up sensational stories. I had a unique opportunity of learning something of the truth from un-prejudiced merchants who were not afraid to talk to me in confidence, and have felt it my duty to give my opinion of this much-talked-of Empire, in order that I may correct false ideas that have been created by prejudiced or mis-guided writers.*

As the train slowly forged its way to Europe the weather became more spring-like. At almost every station peasants were selling flowers. As soon as the train stopped at Zlatoust the Russian naval officers made for the stall on the station to buy some of the manu-factured articles which this district is noted for. They brought some handsome presents into the carriage, pro-bably for those whom they had been thinking of while locked up during the siege of Pekin. I bought several articles, including a dozen knives and forks, which are a speciality of the town's manufacture. They were of beautiful white metal, like silver, and were engraved with the name of the town in artistic Russian letters.

Owing to its being situated in a hollow, Zlatoust was seriously affected by the spring floods, and, in one part of the town, the water had risen as far as the second storey windows of the house, and the inhabitants were using boats. From Zlatoust to Ufa we passed over the Ural Mountains. The line ran through extensive cuttings of chalk, and, as it passed along the banks of the River Ai, we could see that this stream had done very serious damage by overflowing its banks. All day long we passed emigrant trains loaded with rough-and-ready Russian peasants. The carriages indicated that they were ordinarily used for carrying horses, but the peasants appeared to consider them good enough. There is a stove in

---

* There is a club being formed to help to promote a better feeling be-tween Great Britain and Russia, showing that others share my opinions.

the centre of the carriage, and seats all round the sides.

It was spring and everything had blossomed into life. The trees were beautiful. The people seemed brighter and more cheerful at every station, and life appeared altogether different from what it had been when I made the outward journey in the winter. We were passing through the Birmingham of Russia. Not far from here the famous Bakal iron mine is situated, which turns out 6,000,000 tons of ore per annum. The scenery about here is very fine in the spring, particularly after the long stretch of level plain of Siberia.

It is interesting to notice the difference in the people of the different countries along the line. In this part we pass through Bashkiria, and, as we approached the capital, Ufa, the Bashkirs were easily to be distinguished from the European Russian. The Bashkirs have been known to Russia since the Mongol conquest, but their nearer acquaintance dates from the time when the Muscovite Government was struggling for the possession of the horde of Kazar. Wearied by intense family dissensions, persecuted by Kirgiz-Kasaks, and seeing the growing power of Moscow, the Bashkirs voluntarily submitted to the Russian dominion and paid, in 1557, the first tribute in furs.

Ufa was the first Russian town established in Bashkiria for collecting furs. As far back as 1760, twenty-eight factories, including fifteen copper and thirteen iron works, were in full operation. In 1798 the people were employed as irregular troops, and were noted for being good and very effective shots with the bow and arrow.

The origin of the Bashkirs is not yet scientifically ascertained. Some suppose that they descend from the Ugor-Finnish race, and only in course of time acquired the Mongolian type; others believe that they are Voguls, who represent one of the Ugor tribes and form part of the great Altai family. The present Bashkirs are of two marked types. Of these, one is the more common Bashkir of the steppes and resembles the Kalmuck or Mongolian. He has a large, flat face, a broad nose, sometimes bent inwards at the root. He has a protruding chin, a large head, and is usually of middle size. The other type, which is more like the Caucasian, and is common to many central Asiatic nations, is characterised by a hooked nose, a marked profile and high stature. To this type belong the forest Bashkirs, who inhabit such mountainous and wooded regions as are situated at the source of the Belaya.

The Bashkirs are Mohammedans, and the majority of them write and read Tartar. They are provided with a certain quantity of land, and engage in agriculture and cattle-breeding. They settle in groups, forming small villages. Most of them had left their huts, which is their usual custom in the summer, to live in felt "kibitkas," which they pitch in fields and pastures, returning to the smoky huts in the winter. The Ufa Government contains about one million Bashkirs. The majority of the native population of Ufa is represented by Teptairs and Mesh-cheriaks, who mostly live in the north of the Government. Their mode of living differs but little from that of the Bashkirs, but they are at a much lower stage of civilisation, and are heathens. The whole of the population, comprising 2,277,158 people, is distributed amongst the six following districts—Belebei, Birsk, Zlatoust, Menzeisk and Sterlitomsk. Amongst them are 100,000 peasants. One-tenth of the population live in the towns.

After leaving the foot of the Urals the difference in the people is very marked. We crossed the very fine bridge over the River Belaya. This river had overflowed its banks in both directions, making the country look like one large swamp. About forty miles before Samara we came across what appeared to be a huge lake, but which turned out, on a nearer acquaintance, to be caused by the enormous spring floods of the Volga. The town is elevated

z

and out of reach of the water. We did not stop long at the station. From Samara the line takes a more southerly direction and runs several miles from the Volga, but the water of the floods came a little way up the railway embankment. When we arrived at the Volga Bridge all cameras were got ready and quite a number of snapshots of this famous bridge were taken from the rear of the train.

SUMMIT OF URALS IN SPRING.

The next station we stopped at was Tula, noted for the manufacture of "samovars." Several of the passengers bought samovars, which are here very good and cheap. I purchased one myself at the stall, which had a large assortment. A little further on we were buying lilies of the valley and other beautiful flowers.

At 1.45 that afternoon we beheld Moscow's golden domes and spires from the distance, a welcome sight not only to myself but to all the home-sick passengers. At two o'clock we had reached that ancient city.

CHAPTER XI

CONCLUSION

Exploration and commercial success—The expedition to Russia of 1553 and its results—How British trade was made—Advantages of life in Siberia—Russia and our alliance with Japan—Cotton and the Lancashire mills—Japan and China.

As the greatest maritime and commercial power since the world began, Great Britain owes much to her explorers and travellers, from the earliest pioneer to the latest scientifically-equipped expedition. The discovery of new countries and the exploration of those which, although not new in the sense of not having been known before, are yet a *terra incognita* in other respects, is essential to our national prosperity, and the day on which the Briton ceases to be an explorer and an opener out of new worlds will mark the beginning of the decline of our national supremacy.

The expedition which resulted in the establishment of trade relations with Russia in 1553 was organised at a time of unusual depression in English trade. New markets were an imperative necessity, and merchants of London were prompted to combine in a practical business spirit with a view to discovering new outlets for the products of British industry, while the support of royalty conferred on the expedition the character of a national undertaking. The energy and determination which had been applied to the project were not without their reward. The expedition was a success; business relations were established between the two powers, and have continued without interruption ever since. There is, however, very little eagerness to trade with Russia to-day, notwithstanding that our markets are being taken away from us by foreign competition, and that by importing Russian raw products we would be enabled to fight our commercial battles with much greater effect. It is very clear that this lack of enterprise is due in the first place to a peculiarly-distorted form of national independence and, secondly, to insular prejudice. There is hardly a person in the British Isles, whatever his degree of intelligence or historical equipment may be, who does not consider himself qualified to pronounce judgment upon Russian affairs. I have endeavoured to show in the foregoing chapters that neither the people nor the Government of the country deserve a hundredth part of the journalistic venom which is daily distilled for them in Great Britain. On the other hand, it is not good policy to permit our pharisaical notions of what is and what is not the proper method of running the Government coach to interfere with our commercial operations, or to allow prejudice to interfere with business. One hundred years ago a display of these ethical idiosyncrasies on the part of the British mercantile world would have seriously interfered with the commercial development of the country, and it is doubtful whether Great Britain would have reached the exalted commercial position which she holds to-day. If we inquire into the sources of our commercial prosperity we will find that blind unreasoning prejudice has had no place among them. Justice and equity, and an attitude of absolute straightforwardness towards his customers and clients, are a business man's best commercial assets. Ruskin objected to a statement by Adam Smith that the honesty of tradesmen is guaranteed by the competition of their rivals. Ruskin was evidently thinking of the fair policy which British trade has always adhered to, of fostering the development of business by means of low prices, even on markets where there was no competition to be feared. Competition never kept a nation honest; it may easily have the opposite effect of encouraging devious methods on the part of those who are less able to hold their own.

Helped by honesty and fairness, British trade has been pushed in the face of the most deadly odds. British pioneers, sailors and merchants have braved the dangers of unknown climates and countries, have established relations with savage, barbarous races, often at great personal peril; trade has been forced upon nations against almost insurmountable difficulties, and not seldom at considerable loss to ourselves. We seem to have penetrated everywhere in pursuit of trade. The obstacle of language does not exist any longer. English is spoken throughout the world, and no absurd prejudices against a nation or its methods of internal government have been permitted to interfere with legitimate trade. Yet we have made very little headway in Siberia. The country, as I have tried to show, offers ideal conditions for trade, and is a paradise to live in compared with some of the countries in which our commercial men are ready enough to settle, yet we have permitted the Danes, Germans, and even the French and Americans, to get ahead of us in nearly every branch of trade with the country. Surely there is room for national self-reproach.

I believe that the maintenance of our commercial supremacy depends more upon a friendly understanding with Russia than upon our military alliance with Japan, and will endeavour to give good grounds for that opinion. In the first place, it should be remembered that Japanese commercial success depends upon open markets in Asia, as she does more trade with Asia than with all the rest of the world put together. Japan resembles England in many of the characteristics of her people and in her commercial requirements and prospects. She is as dependent on the development of her foreign trade as we are on the development of ours, but is considerably freer from commercial prejudices than we are. Japan possesses a further advantage over us in that she has not ceased to be an agricultural nation and that she has an abundance of cheap labour to draw upon in the development of her manufacturing industries, which will enable her to compete with her rivals on exceedingly advantageous terms, and very much to our detriment, as we shall learn by bitter experience very soon. Our reason for allying ourselves with Japan was that we were afraid of interference by other nations with the 43½ million pounds' worth of trade per annum between the United Kingdom, her colonies and dependencies and China. Japan, in her turn, was desirous of securing our support in order to preserve her own trade with Asia, which amounts to about 30¼ million pounds annually. Although the trade which Japan does with Asia is thus seen to be some 13¼ million pounds sterling less than that which is done by Great Britain, it should be recollected that the former can show an increase of no less than 50 per cent. in five years, while the amount of trade done by Japan with China alone increased in one year (1902-1903) by 21 per cent. The figures for these two years show that the exports from Japan to China alone increased from £4,595,000 to £6,627,850, or by £2,032,850. The worst feature about this increase, however, is that one million sterling of it represented an increase in the export to China of cotton yarns, at the cost of the staple industry of Lancashire. The reasons for this increase in Chinese trade are not far to seek. The Japanese are able to speak with the Chinese in their own language, they are intimately acquainted with the conditions of native trade, and they are well endowed with the energy and enterprise that are necessary. In 1896 Japan imported cotton yarn to the extent of £1,243,812, and exported £436,522 worth; but in 1903 she only imported to the extent of £78,225 and exported £3,205,233. These figures are significant, and clearly show that Japan will shortly dominate the cotton trade of Asia. Her power over Asiatic trade, if recent developments are any evidence, will become very harassing to us, and will enable her to benefit by the open-door policy in China very much more than we shall be able to do. In any case it is obvious that she has secured a very powerful hold on the commerce of China, while Japanese teachers and publicists are labouring hard to remodel the Chinese language, and Chinese military officers are being trained in Japan. It is our duty, in our own interests, to watch Japan very carefully, although we are on friendly terms with the country. For instance, a Chinese law encourages Japanese merchants to enter into business partnerships with Chinese. The result of a piece of favouritism of this nature can only be that Chinese business will be conducted according to Japanese methods and invariably in favour of Japan. Ever since the last war the Chinese and Japanese have been growing increasingly friendly, and, although China may wish to be left alone, it is quite certain that if her isolation is broken at all she will prefer to have it broken by the Japanese rather than by any nation of Western Europe. At present Japan is certainly the most favoured nation in China; she is also the best represented, numerically speaking, and from her natural energy and enterprise, is the one nation in the world calculated to awaken China out of her old-world torpor. The few concessions to which I have referred are not likely to be wasted by the Japanese; railways are being built, and other reforms are in contemplation. Moreover, Japan has shown China that it is possible to beat one of the chief industries of this country—the 120-year-old cotton industry of Lancashire—and has actually brought about the closing of two large cotton-mills in Canada. The next lesson will be to export as well as manufacture her own cotton. They are well aware that labour is cheaper in China even than it is in Japan, and will know how to avail themselves of the knowledge when the time comes. The lessons to be learned from the increased competition and growing independence of the East are many; suffice it that, so far as the Lancashire cotton trade is concerned, it is only in one or two articles of cotton goods used for special purposes that business in British yarns will be done in future with Japan. At present Japan is no longer dependent upon American supplies for her raw cotton, as may be seen from the fact that imports from America to Japan have, in 1903, decreased in one year by £1,600,000.

The independence which Japan enjoys of the evils of cotton gambling shows her supply to be on a sounder footing than ours, and taking the advantages which Japan further possesses in her geographical position into consideration, we shall require to be very fortunate and very wary if we are to hold the trade we now possess. The power of the Trades Unions to coerce and fetter capital will have to be curtailed. This might be effected by some system of compulsory arbitration which would prevent strikes. On the other hand, labour-saving machinery should be produced to reduce the cost of production. Advantage should be taken by British capitalists of the cheap land suitable for cotton-growing in the Russian Empire, which, with cheap Russian labour, will produce cheaper cotton than we can buy at present. It might be possible, also, to break the German monopoly which exists at present for the purchase of cotton in Russian Turkestan, in which case we would be in a better position to compete with Germany and Japan in the Eastern markets. There is a further advantage in this arrangement in the fact that, owing to the want of capital, Russian merchants would not be able to gamble in cotton, even if the Government would permit them to do so. With these advantages and better-organised trade to enable British manufacturers to deal directly with the Eastern markets, we may succeed in getting back a portion of the trade that is done in the East, more especially in the Chinese market. This would be a very much better way than for British capital to be taken to China to be invested in cotton-mills in that country.

The problem of whether China will become more powerful than Japan in the future, and succeed in shaking off the influence of the latter country, is one that I do not propose to enter into here; but one thing at least is certain, and that is that China's military and commercial resources, if properly organised by Japan, would be a more formidable combination than any other that could be suggested, and could only be met by a counter-alliance of the Western powers—a most improbable thing to look forward to. And if a military invasion is, at least at present, not to be feared, and the spectre of Chinese cheap labour is laid, that of a commercial "yellow peril" of cheap products, as the result of a Chino-Japanese commercial combination, is still to be confronted.

It is not my wish to speak derogatively of our alliance with Japan, as I do not see that as matters now stand we could very well have improved upon it, but I would wish to draw careful attention to the other side of the picture as I have attempted to show it in the preceding pages, in order that we may be led to take our own affairs in our own hands, remembering that Japan, with all her virtues, has her own fish to fry and is the last nation in the world to neglect her duty to herself. We must look forward either to surrendering the greater part of our commerce with Asia to the Japanese, or we must fight them by finding a field of cheap products, and this we can only hope to find in Russia and Siberia.

I would not advocate investing money in Russian and Siberian companies—the French have lost money that way —but we should try to work Russian resources with British capital and under the guidance of British managers, while utilising Russia's cheap labour and cheap land.

In conclusion I would strongly urge the policy of seeking at all times to preserve to ourselves the goodwill of a generous and friendly nation, and of refraining from that gratuitous animosity which is becoming so predominant in certain sections of the British Press towards the Russian Empire.

APPENDICES

APPENDIX I

Expenses for a Ten Weeks' Expedition to the Altai

N.B.—*There are about 95 roubles in £10 ; 100 kopecks (equal to farthings) in 1 rouble.*

	Roubles.
Riga to St Petersburg by rail	25
St Petersburg to Moscow by rail	35
Moscow to Novo-Nicolaëvsk and return by rail	168
Place card to secure seat in train	15
Two fares, one sledge or drosky, return, to Barnaoul and Bysk	65
Novo-Nicolaëvsk to Tomsk, return, for two	60
Moscow to Riga by rail, 1st class	25
14 days' expenses for interpreter	84
40 days' hotels, including train, food, expenses and gratuities, about 8 roubles a day	380
Saloon (on boat) expenses from Riga and back	40
Fur coat, gloves, cap, goloshes, etc.,	230
Sundry sledge drives	22
Return from London to St Petersburg by boat	80
Two sheets Russian 40 verst map at Standford's, Long Acre, W.C.	3

I had no Customs duty to pay, but it might cost £10 to £12 according to the bulk of luggage and eatables.

Roubles.

Conveyance for two persons and luggage on two
sledges or two pack horses, and two riding-
horses, 600 versts 300
Hunters and six horses for ten days—hunters, 1
rouble per day ; horses, 50 kopecks per day . 50
Interpreter's pay—5 roubles per day.

Particulars of boat journey from London to St Petersburg
or Riga can be obtained from Messrs Tegner, Price & Co.,
107 Fenchurch Street, London, E.C., and W. E. Bott &
Co., 1 East India Avenue, London, E.C. The shippers will
procure the passport.

The whole journey would cost, at the outside, between
1600 to 1700 roubles, or about £168 or £178. The
expenses for the climbing and exploring outfit are not
dealt with.

OUTFIT, ETC.

If bear, wild sheep or ibex shooting is contemplated,
the following additional equipment is necessary :—

One ·450 bore Cordite Express rifle, weighing 10 or
11 lbs., for large animals. A gun is required for small
game. It is necessary to have a sling affixed to the gun,
as you have to ride with it on the shoulders. I took a
pistol, but did not find any use for it.

A Zeiss binocular will be found useful.

Camera—I took a Goetz lens fitted on a No. 3
folding pocket Kodak, and 24 rolls of films, packed in
watertight tins. The air is clearer than Switzerland, and
a snapshot or short-time exposure is sufficient.

Clothing should be similar to the climbing outfit
described in the *Hints to Travellers* published by the
Royal Geographical Society, London. A pair of dark
spectacles are necessary to prevent snow-blindness. You
require valenkis (felt top-boots) and goloshes (high
topped), which can be bought in Moscow.

A compass is not very necessary on the road, as

there are good land-marks, but you require one for the mountains.

I should recommend a small green canvas mummery tent for the mountains, and a larger canvas explorer's tent for the camp at the base of the mountains. The largest should weigh about 30 lbs., and accommodate two men; the small one 12 lbs., and also be suitable for two men to crawl in to.

All luggage should be taken separately and not in boxes, or you will almost certainly be taxed for the weight of the boxes as well as the tents. Benjamin Edgington, Duke Street, London Bridge, makes a suitable tent.

An interpreter is necessary unless the traveller knows Russian, and even then he will want a companion. In selecting a hunter I recommend one Siberian hunter, who can speak Kalmuck, and one Kalmuck, who is generally a good hunter and knows the district better than the Siberian.

The hunters' pay includes food, which they find themselves, also fodder for their horses. You will be able to shoot what fowl or meat you require. See that your hunter and Kalmucks take plenty of food, or they will eat yours and you may run short.

A pony will carry about one and a half cwt., but this must be reduced to one cwt. on the mountain slopes. To get along quickly you commence hustling the peasants immediately you get out of your sledge or conveyance, and do not sit down to tea until you see him on his way for horses and sledge. One word, "skorey," is very handy, as it means hurry. You stop on the road at wooden huts, which in winter are heated by a stove and are very warm. The peasant is very sociable, and willingly brings out the best he has, leaving the price to you. Plenty of Keating's powder is a necessity. The tarakan is the insect that will trouble you most, but this insect is not caused by dirt, as the post stations are kept clean.

The pleasure of Siberian sledging or travelling by drosky depends upon the condition of the roads. The country interests you, and you are able to look about with freedom. You can stop the bells if you object to the noise they make. You have to take pack horses and saddled ponies at times, and this is very slow travelling, probably not more than 30 miles a day, while on a drosky you may cover 75 miles a day. Beyond Bysk you must arrange for your own food, etc. Take methylated spirits in liquid and a good methylated spirit lamp and stove, also blocks of spiritine, which are very handy, as they go in your pockets. June or July are the two best months for the mountains. If you start on the 1st of May the following programme could be carried out :—

Leave London 1st May.
Arrive St Petersburg 6th May.
Leave St Petersburg (evening) 7th May.
Arrive Moscow (morning) 8th May.
Arrive Novo-Nicolaëvsk 14th May.
Leave Novo-Nicolaëvsk (by steamer) 16th May.
Arrive Bysk 20th May.
Leave Bysk (by tarantass) 23rd May.
Arrive Katunda 26th May.
Leave Katunda 28th May.
Arrive Akkem Valley 29th May.
Base of Peaks 30th May.
Fourteen days' hunting and climbing 13th June.
Arrive back to Katunda 15th June.
Arrive back to Bysk 18th June.
Leave Bysk 20th June
Arrive Novo-Nicolaëvsk 24th June.
Leave Novo-Nicolaëvsk 25th June.
Arrive Moscow 31st June.
London 7th July.

A day would have to be spent at Bysk in making

purchases. The return journey down the river with the fast current only takes two and a half days. To go by boat from London to Riga and back is about £14 cheaper, and there is no worry with the frontier Custom-house officers. I was helped by the Russian Ambassador, London ; the British Ambassador, St Petersburg; the Minister of Ways and Communications; Prince Scherbatoff, the President of the Russian Imperial Geographical Society ; Professor Sapozhnikoff of Tomsk University and the Governor of Tomsk. It is wise to make the acquaintance of the police at Barnaoul and Bysk and let them know where you are going. Introductions are unnecessary.

The best hotels are the Hotel d'Europe, St Petersburg; Slavfansky Bazar, Moscow. There is only one at Novo-Nicolaëvsk.

You can procure guides at the hotels at St Petersburg and Moscow to show you the towns.

If you go in winter, you require particularly thin underclothing and very thick overcoat and furs, as the temperature inside the trains and houses is very warm, whereas outside it is very cold. Warm underclothing is very uncomfortable in the warm trains. In camp you require very warm underclothing; it cannot be too warm, as you have not the slightest idea of what a winter in Siberia is until you have been through one.* Take plenty of note-books and pencils. Do not attempt to develop photographs except at Tomsk, where you can go to the university. No explorer should visit the Altai without obtaining information from the Tomsk University. If possible he should also give them a lecture on the result of his tour. They are all keenly interested in the Altai.

The climber should take exceptionally good steel crampons, specially sharpened for the very hard ice, and sharp long steel nails in Alpine boots, also a particularly sharp ice-axe, somewhat larger and heavier than the

* Even during the months of May and June there is sometimes frost at night.

largest Swiss Alpine axe of the very best steel, and
with a very sharp head. The ordinary Alpine axe would
have no effect upon the intensely hard ice. Take an ice-
axe as a present to the University professors; it would
be a nice present, and would repay them for their information.

APPENDIX II

SKETCH OF SIBERIAN HISTORY

THE history of the Siberian peasant is very different
from that of the Russian peasant, which I have alluded
to elsewhere.

After the free Cossacks had conquered Siberia in the
sixteenth century, seekers of adventure poured into Siberia
in large numbers. The first raids upon a tribe inhabiting
the present Government of Tobolsk were made as far back
as the twelfth century by traders from Novgorod, but these
had always ended in the levying of a ransom from the
natives in the shape of rich furs. It was after Russia
had destroyed the Tartar kingdoms of Kazan and Astrakhan, and had taken possession of the basin of the River
Volga, whose branches brought pioneers to the rich Ural
Mountains, that proper relations between the Russian and
Siberian inhabitants commenced.

In the year 1555 several Siberian princelings, oppressed
by their more powerful co-tribesmen, sent their ambassadors to the Tsar, praying to be accepted as his subjects
and agreeing to the imposition of a tribute, on condition
that he should afford them military protection against
their oppressors.

A very prominent part in the settlement of Siberia at
that time was played by the well-known family of the
Stroganoffs. They possessed vast tracts of unsettled
lands, and very liberally assigned them temporarily to
enterprising tradesmen, on the condition that they should

settle there and cultivate the land. The settlers were afforded many privileges, such as freedom from taxation, trade duties, etc. In the reign of Ivan IV. these pioneers penetrated into the region of the River Kama, and in 1558 the Stroganoff family petitioned the Tsar to grant them that land for the purpose of building a town, to enable them to develop industry, and to raise troops for defence against attacks by the wild hordes who constantly troubled them. The petition was granted for a period of twenty years, during which the settlers bound themselves to build stockades and maintain troops. Several small towns soon appeared in the district, industries increased, and the population spread into regions until then unknown and undeveloped.

In the second half of the sixteenth century, during the reign of Ivan the Terrible, many people fled to the newly-populated country. There the fugitives found liberty, ease, and plenty of scope for activity. Bands were soon formed, which completely severed themselves from the State and led the life of free Cossacks, engaging in robbery, and threatening the territory under the authority of the Tsar. For this, however, they were prosecuted by the Government.

Amongst the most important of these fugitives was a party of Don Cossacks under the leadership of Yermack Timofeiev, who had been a constant trouble to the Tsar's Government through his freebooting expeditions on the River Volga. This party, being pursued by troops, managed to escape up the Kama and reach the Stroganoff possessions. The Stroganoffs availed themselves of the opportunity to invite the Cossacks to enter their service. The latter, equipped and under the leadership of Yermack, started across the Ural Mountains, and, in 1580, on the banks of Tura, defeated the Tartar princelet—Yepancha— and took by storm the town now known as Tumen. In the spring of the following year Yermack moved to the capital of the Kuchum kingdom, the town of Isker, or

Siberia. Having navigated the Tura, Tobol and Irtish in barges, the Cossacks reached the Khan's residence, and after a fierce fight took possession of it on the 26th October 1581. Yermack immediately sent his trusty associate—Koltso—with the news of this conquest to Moscow, supplied him with costly furs, and commanded him "to humbly acquaint the Lord Ivan Vasilievitch the Terrible of the acquisition of the new Siberian kingdom." The Tsar forgave Yermack his former crimes, presented him with a cloak and medal, and sent the leader —Glukhov—to his assistance. Yermack, however, was not long fated to rule Siberia. In 1584 he perished, together with his band, in a fight with the Tartars on the banks of the river Irtish. In Moscow, meanwhile, nothing was known of Yermack's death, and in 1586 a fresh reinforcement of 300 men arrived on the Tura. They founded there the town Tumen, and began to spread Russian authority over the Siberian natives. In 1587 another 500 men were sent from Moscow, and orders were given to build a Russian town—Tobolsk—in place of the ruined capital of the Kuchum kingdom.

As soon as the Siberian kingdom was united with the Russian possessions, the Government concerned itself with its colonisation, and established strongholds against attacks. The strongholds founded beyond the Ural Mountains in the sixteenth century were, besides the already-mentioned Tumen and Tobolsk, Verhoturee, Polim, Beriozovo, Surgoot and others. In the seventeenth century the Russian dominions rapidly extended further and further east. From 1604 many strongholds subsequently grew into towns, amongst others, Tomsk, Yeniseisk, Kainsk, Krasnoyarsk, Yakutzk, Irkutzk and Nerchinsk, and Russian power was extended over the basins of the great rivers of Siberia, the Obi, Yenisei and Lena, and along the coast of the Arctic Ocean, the Sea of Okhotsk, Kamchatka and the Amur river.

The name which is most commonly associated with the

2 A

exploits on the River Amur is that of a Cossack—Yerofei Khabaroff. This man, who occupied himself with corn-growing and salt-boiling, resolved at his own cost to subjugate the Amur country. Having obtained authority from the Chief of Yakutsk, he, in 1649 and 1650, reached Amur and destroyed a few native towns. After convincing himself of the riches the country contained, he returned to personally excite interest in and draw attention to that hitherto unknown and remarkable place. He gathered about 150 volunteers and three guns. In 1651, Khabaroff again appeared on the banks of the Amur and wintered at the station Albazin, which he had founded. Notwithstanding the armed opposition which he met with during two years from the Manchurs, who surrounded him on every side, he succeeded in his operations and reported his success to Yakutsk.

The rumour of the wealth of the new country conquered by Khabaroff soon spread all over Siberia and reached the capital of the mother-country. In 1654 Khabaroff was called to Moscow to make a personal report on it.

From 1654 till 1685 there were many fights with the Manchurs, and in that year a horde of 15,000 men overcame the Cossacks, numbering 500, at Albazin. As soon as reinforcements arrived the Cossacks returned and built earthen entrenchments in place of the former wooden fortifications. Seeing this, the Manchurs undertook a second siege in 1688, but becoming, in 1687, perfectly exhausted, were compelled to raise the siege. In 1688 a congress of plenipotentiaries was appointed, at which the Chinese gained a diplomatic victory; on August 27th 1689 the Nerchinsk treaty confirmed the Amur to the Chinese, and for over 180 years deprived the Russians of the possession of that outlying Siberian province.

The actual colonisation of Siberia commenced only towards the end of the seventeenth century, when its boundaries, in the large sense of the term, were indicated more or less by the points of defence. Cities and post stations were-built and the Government strove to create a class of peasant artisans and to spread corn-growing. With this object, by command of the Tsar, volunteer ploughmen were sent out, who received every privilege, besides agricultural implements and financial assistance. Grain was imported from Perm, Viatka and other places to provision the people whom the Government had thus settled there.

The spread of agriculture and the establishment of fixed settlements within the limits of the new country were ensured by repeatedly sending out fresh ploughmen, and girls to be married to the Cossacks.

In 1723 parties equipped by a well-known trader, A. Demidoff, penetrated to the Altai Mountains, where they found several ore mines. Works were quickly built there, and the first one taken over by the State was called Kolyvansk.

Owing to the development of mining in the Ural, Altai and Nertchinsk, the need for workers considerably increased, and hundreds of families from the interior of Russia were sent there annually to augment the population of Siberia. In addition to this colonisation encouraged by the Government, many discontented people at home fled to the new countries in search of better conditions and greater freedom. In later years political and other exiles have considerably added to the growth of the population.

The settlement of Siberia necessitated its exploration, and in the course of the eighteenth century the Emperor Peter the Great initiated this matter.

An attempt to establish regular sea communication with Kamchatka having failed for want of ships, Peter the Great sent Swedish prisoners acquainted with shipbuilding to Okhotsk, and by this means a regular communication between Okhotsk and Kamchatka was established.

Peter the Great then interested himself to discover

whether or not a sea passage leads into the Arctic Ocean between the Asiatic and American continents. An expedition for this purpose left St Petersburg in 1725, the year of Peter the Great's death, and, after a period of three years, reached Kamchatka through Siberia. The existence of a strait between Asia and America was thus proved.

A land expedition to explore the whole of Siberia, under the leadership of the best men of science of that time, was carried out from 1733 to 1743. A further expedition from Okhotsk to Japan and the Kurile Islands was also attended with great success.

In the second half of the eighteenth century, during the reign of the enlightened Empress Catherine II., a new and brilliant era in the history of the geographical and scientific exploration of Siberia began.

Particular attention was directed to the exploration of the southern districts, and also of the extreme east, the Behring Sea, and the north-western corner of America.

From 1789 to 1799 many islands in the Behring Sea were discovered, and Russian settlements arose upon them, as well as on the peninsula of Alaska, which had been discovered in 1770.

In 1799 a great company was formed in St Petersburg, under the name of the Russian American Company, for the purpose of working Russian possessions on the American continent and on the shores and islands of Behring Sea and the Sea of Okhotsk. This Company was granted many privileges, to secure which a convention was made with the United States in 1820 and with Great Britain in 1825. The Company existed until 1867, when the Emperor, wishing to cement the good relations which existed between his Government and the United States, surrendered the whole territory, with its adjacent islands, to America. On the 25th April 1875 Russia entered into an agreement with Japan, by which the latter surrendered to Russia the island of Sakhalin, receiving for it the group of Kurile Islands.

The name of Muravieff is closely connected with the annexation to Russia of the whole of the Amur. Muravieff was Governor-General of Eastern Siberia, and was afterwards known as Count Muravieff Amourski. Immediately on his arrival in the region entrusted to his care, Muravieff clearly saw that without the command of the great River Amur, which flows through the length of Siberia from the west to the east, and leads to a sea free from ice, the prospects of further development in Eastern Siberia were very small. He set himself the task of acquiring the whole of the territory through which this river flows, and successfully accomplished his purpose after many difficulties and much opposition.

A treaty was subsequently signed in 1857, by which the left bank only of the Amur, from Argun to the mouth, was ceded to Russia, and the right bank, as far as Ussuri, to China. Only Russian and Chinese vessels were allowed to navigate the Amur, Sungari and Ussuri, the Manchurians inhabiting the left banks to remain under the Manchurian Government.

In 1860 there were already as many as 12,000 Russian colonists and 61 Cossack stations on the Amur. In the same year another treaty was signed at Pekin, by which the Chinese Government recognised the Russian rule over the River Amur and the entire region of Ussuri, and thus restored to Russian possession the whole of the territory previously acquired by Khabaroff and Muravieff.

The descendants of the ancient Siberians are a bold, free race. The Russian serf, when liberated, mixed with them in Siberia, and the descendants of this mixture are a self-reliant, strong-willed people, with a striking in-dividuality, and afford a great contrast to the humble, man-fearing peasant of European Russia. The Siberians will, some day, become a great nation like America. At one time the Americans were made up of what might have been called adventurers, but that bold, fearless character was a good foundation for the future history of America, and it will be for Siberia. The people are very much more free in Siberia, and if politics are left alone the Siberian's life is the life of the brave and free.

———

APPENDIX III

ALTAI FLORA

Flowers of the Siberian Alps

As the Altai is the natural home of some of the most beautiful of our cultivated plants, it will be of interest to know the names of the flowers discovered up to the present in the Altai. The list is not by any means exhausted, as the number of classes, species and varieties appears to be endless, while very little has, as yet, been done in the matter of their discovery and classification.

The flora of the mountains is very varied.

In the Kuzneski Altau, a branch of the Altai Mountains, the flora is even more magnificent. In the provinces of Bysk, Barnaoulsk and Smernagorsk, where there is a sufficiency of water, heaths are very plentiful, but farther away from the mountains, where the rainfall is less abundant, the heaths are scanty.

The fact that 50,000 tons of honey and 150 tons of beeswax are exported from this wonderful district annually, gives some idea of the abundant flora. The following list of the flora of the Altai is a translation from Professor Sapozhnikoff's book on the flora made with his consent. It has never before been published in the English language.

I am greatly indebted, too, to the Royal Horticultural Society for translating the names of all known plants. Those that are not translated are not known in Great Britain.

RANUNCULACEAE

A natural order of herbs dispersed all over the globe. Upwards of 1200 species have been described ; many of these species are highly ornamental plants.

1.	Clematis glauca .	. Glaucous-leaved Clematis
2.	Atragene Clematis alpina	Alpine Clematis
3.	Thalictrum alpinum .	Alpine Meadow-Rue
4.	Thalictrum petaloideum	Petaloid-sepaled Meadow-Rue
5.	Thalictrum foetidum .	Fetid Meadow-Rue
6.	Thalictrum minus .	Lesser Meadow-Rue
7.	Thalictrum simplex	
8.	Anemone coerulea .	Blue Anemone
9.	Anemone altaica	
10.	Anemone sylvestris .	Snowdrop Anemone
11.	Anemone narcissiflora .	Narcissus-flowered Anemone
12.	Anemone (Pulsatilla) patens . . .	Spreading Anemone
13.	Anemone(Pulsatilla)albana	
14.	Adonis vernalis . .	Ox-eye
15.	Adonis villosa	
16.	Adonis appenina	
17.	Ranunculus pulchellus	
18.	Ranunculus plantaginifolius	
19.	Ranunculus Cymballaria	Sea-side Ivy-leaved Crow-foot
20.	Ranunculus natans	
21.	Ranunculus radicans	
22.	Ranunculus frigidus	
23.	Ranunculus lasiocarpus	
24.	Ranunculus affinis	

25. Ranunculus auricomus . Goldilocks, Wood Crow-foot
26. Ranunculus polyrhizos
27. Ranunculus acris .   . Blister-plant,   Buttercup,
                            Butter Daisy,   Crow-
                            flower, Meadow Ranun-
                            culus, Upright Crow-foot,
                            Yellow Gowan
28. Ranunculuspolyanthemos Many-flowered
29. Ranunculus repens   . Buttercup, Butter Daisy,
                            Creeping   Crow-foot
                            Crow-flower,   Yellow
                            Gowan
30. Ranunculus glacialis . Glacier Crow-foot
31. Callianthemum rutae-
     folium   .   .   . Rue-leaved
32. Caltha palustris .   . "Boots," Common Marsh-
                            Marigold, Golds, Goldins,
                            May-blobs,   Meadow
                            Bright or Meadow-Bout,
                            Meadow Gowan, Water
                            Buttercup,   Water   or
                            Open Gowan, Yellow
                            Gowan
33. Trollius asiaticus .   . Asiatic Globe-flower
34. Trollius altaicus .   . Altaian Globe-flower
35. Hegemone lilacina
36. Isopyrum grandiflorum
37. Isopyrum fumarioides
38. Aquilegia glandulosa . Altaian Columbine
39. Aquilegia sibirica   . Siberian Columbine
40. Delphinium laxiflorum . Loose-flowered Larkspur
41. Delphinium dictyocarpum
42. Delphinium elatum   . Common Bee Larkspur
43. Aconitum Anthora   . Jacquin's   Yellow-flowered
                            Monk's-hood, Wholesome
                            Wolf's-bane,   Yellow
                            Helmet (flower)

44 Aconitum septentrionale   Northern Monk's-hood
45 Aconitum Lycoctonum .   Wolf's-bane
46 Aconitum baratum
47 Aconitum volubile
48 Aconitum Napellus   .   Bear's-foot,   Common
                               Aconite, Friar's, Soldier's
                               or Turk's Cap, Helmet-
                               flower, Luckie's Mutch,
                               Common Monk's-cowl or
                               Monk's-hood
49. Paeonia hybrida
50. Paeonia anomala .   .   Anomalous Peony

BERBERIDEÆ

51. Berberis siberica .   .   Siberian Barberry

PAPAVERACEAE

Old Latin name—Papaver

52. Papaver alpinum .   .   Alpine Poppy
53. Chelidonium majus   .   Cock-foot, Great Celandine,
                               Fetter-wort

FUMRIACAEAE

An order of herbs included as a tribe of Papaveraceae. The flowers are irregular. There are about 100 species altogether.

54. Corydalis pauciflora
55. Corydalis bracteata   .   Bracteata
56. Corydalis nobilis .   .   Great flowered Fume-wort
57. Corydalis stricta
58. Corydalis capnoides
59. Fumaria Vaillantii

CRUCIFERAE

Sometimes called Brassicaceae. Comprises about 170 genera, and about 1200 species, spread all over temperate and cold regions, but chiefly belong to the old world. All are nitrogenous (and contain sulphur), pungent, stimulant. Many of them are highly-esteemed plants, such as the Broccoli, Cabbage, Cress, Turnip, etc.

60. Barbarea vulgaris	Common Winter Cress, St Barbara's Herb, Winter or Yellow Rocket
61. Turritis glabra	
62. Arabis hirsuta	Hairy Rock-cress
Arabis pendula	
63. Arabis incarnata	
64. Cardamine lenensis	
65. Cardamine pratensis	Bread and Milk, Common Cuckoo-flower, Cuckoo's Bread, Cuckoo - Spit, Lady's Smock, May-flower, Meadow-Bitter-cress, Meadow-cress
66. Cardamine macrophylla	Large-leaved Cuckoo-flower
67. Dentaria tenuifolia	Tooth-wort
68. Macropodium nivale	
69. Alyssum alpestre	Alpine mad-wort
70. Alyssum minimum	
71. Ptilotrichum canescens	
72. Draba alpina	Alpine Whitlow-grass
73. Draba repens	Creeping Whitlow-grass
74. Draba Wahlenbergii	
75. Draba hirta	
76. Draba incana	
77. Draba nemorosa	
78. Draba	
79. Draba	

80. Thlaspi arvense . . Boor's Mustard, Dish Mustard, Pennycress, Wild-
   cress
81. Chorispora exscapa
82. Chorispora sibirica
83. Hesperis matronalis . Dame's Garden, or White
   Rocket, Dame's Violet,
   Queen's   Gilliflower,
   Rogue's Gilliflower, Winter Gilliflower
84. Hesperis aprica
85. Dontostemon perennis
86. Sisymbrium junceum
87. Sisymbrium heteromallum
88. Sisymbrium Sophia . Flixweed
89. Sisymbrium humile
90. Sisymbrium salsugineum
91. Erysimum altaicum
92. Erysimum strictum
93. Camelina microcarpa
94. Hutchinsia calycina . Having a prominent calyx
95. Lepedium ruderale . Narrow-leaved Cress
96. Lepedium micranthum
97. Isatis lasiocarpa

VIOLARIEAE

A natural order of broadly-dispersed herbs. There are
21 genera and about 240 species. Many of these are well
known in gardens and require careful attention in England,
although they grow wild in Siberia.

98. Viola pinnata . . Pinnate-leaved Violet
99. Viola hirta   . . Hairy Violet
100. Viola canina . . Dog Violet
101. Viola arenaria . . Sand-loving Violet
102. Viola biflora . . Twin-flowered Violet

103. Viola uniflora	.	. Siberian Violet
104. Viola altaica		. Altaian Violet
105. Viola tricolor	.	. Call - me - to - you, Fancy, Flamy, Garden - gate, Heart's-ease, Herb Trinity, Jump - up - and - kiss-me, Kiss-me, Kiss-me-at-the-garden-gate, Live-in-idleness, Love-in-idleness, Pansy, Pink-of-my-John, Three - faces - under - a - hood, Tickle-my-fancy

DROSERACEAE

Sometimes called Drosera, from Droseros = dewy. The plant appears as if covered with dew, in consequence of being beset with glandular hairs. They are small everywhere except in Siberia. Here they are fairly large. They are treated in Great Britain as greenhouse plants.

106. Parnassia palustris . Common - Grass - of - Parnassus

POLYGALEAE

These species contain tonic and astringent properties, in fact several of the European Polygaleae are used as remedies for lingering diseases. There are 15 genera and about 400 species. The Polygala vulgaris varies in colour —blue, lilac, purple, pink or white—about one inch long. The Polygala Sibirica is a native of the Siberian Altai.

107. Polygala sibirica
108. Polygala vulgaris . Common Milk-wort, Crossflower, Gang Flower, Procession Flower, Rogation Flower

Sileneae

English name, "Catchfly." A very large genus—400 species are known. They are found in South Europe, North Africa, extra tropical Asia, about a dozen in South Africa, and eight are included in British flora.

109. Dianthus Seguieri . Seguier's Pink
110. Dianthus superbus . Fringed Pink
111. Gypsophila petraea
112. Gypsophila Gmelini
113. Gypsophila altissima
114. Silene inflata . . Bladder-Campion
115. Silene turgida
116. Silene graminifolia
117. Silene repens
118. Silene viscosa
119. Silene chlorantha
120. Lychnis Melandrium apetala
121. Lychnis Melandrium tristis
122. Lychnis Melandrium brachypetalam
123. Lychnis Melandrium pratensis
124. Lychnis Githago seg-
    etum . . . . Cockle or Cornflower

Alsineae

We get our Arenaria plant from this tribe, and the Arenaria has 150 species.

125. Arenaria (Alsine) verna . Vernal Sand-wort
126. Arenaria (Alsine) arctica
127. Alsine biflora
128. Arenaria formosa
129. Moehringia lateriflora
130. Stellaria Bungeana
131. Stellaria dichotoma

132. Stellaria davurica
133. Stellaria petraea
134. Cerastium trigynum
135. Cerastium pilosum
136. Cerastium lithospermifolium
137. Cerastium davuricum
138. Cerastium vulgatum
139. Cerastium arvense

LINEAE

A small order of herbs, rarely trees. Petal often blue, yellow or white, rarely pink. One of these species yields the flax and linseed of commerce. There are 14 genera and 135 species.

140. Linum perenne . . Perennial Flax

MALVACEAE

An order of herb, shrub, or tree with flowers, violet, purplish, pink or yellow, often showy. There are 39 genera known and 700 species.

141. Lavatera thuringiaca

HYPERICINEAE

An order of herbs, shrubs, or rarely trees, comprising 8 genera and 200 species. Many of them yield a yellow juice or an essential oil.

142. Hypericum perforatum
143. Hypericum hirsutum . Hairy St John's-wort

GERANIACEAE

A native order of herbs, shrubs or sub-shrubs, rarely

arborescent. Flowers often showy. There are about 20 genera and 750 species dispersed through the temperate and sub-tropical regions of the whole world, particularly in South Africa.

144. Geranium albiflorum
145. Geranium pratense   . Crow-foot, Crane's-bill, Meadow Geranium, Wild Geranium
146. Geranium pseudo-sibiricum
147. Geranium
148. Geranium
149. Erodium Stephanianum

ZYGOPHYLLACEAE

150. Biebersteinia odora   . Sweet Biebersteinia

PAPILIONACEAE

A sub-order of Leguminosae spread over the whole world, of which there are 295 genera and 4700 species.

151. Thermopsis alpina
152. Thermopsis lanceolata . Thermopsis with lance-shaped leaflets
153. Medicago platycarpos
154. Medicago falcata .   . Sickle-podded Medick
155. Melilotus alba   .   . Bokhara Clover, Cabul Clover, White Melilot
156. Trifolium pratense   . Common Clover, Purple Clover or Trefoil
157. Trifolium eximium
158. Trifolium Lupinaster . Bastard Lupine
159. Trifolium repens .   . Dutch or White Clover
160. Glycyrrhiza glabra   . Liquorice-plant
161. Caragana arborescens . Common Siberian Pea-tree

162. Caragana frutescens . Shrubby Siberian Pea-tree
163. Caragana pygmaea . Pigmy Siberian Pea-tree
164. Oxytropis alpina
165. Oxytropis argentata
166. Oxytropis recognita
167. Oxytropis nivea
168. Oxytropis glabra
169. Oxytropis altaica
170. Oxytropis caudata
171. Oxytropis pilosa . . Long-haired Oxytrope
172. Oxytropis
173. Oxytropis pumila
174. Oxytropis deflexa
175. Oxytropis setosa
176. Oxytropis rhynchophysa
177. Oxytropis ampullata
178. Oxytropis aciphylla
179. Oxytropis tragacanthoides
180. Oxytropis
181. Oxytropis
182. Oxytropis
183. Oxytropis
184. Oxytropis
185. Astragalus alpinus . Alpine Milk-Vetch
186. Astragalus penduliflorus
187. Astragalus vaginatus . Sheathed Milk-Vetch
188. Astragalus hypoglottis . Purple-flowered Milk-Vetch
189. Astragalus multicaulis
190 Astragalus semibilocularis
191. Astragalus Onobrychis . Saintfoin Milk-Vetch
192. Astragalus puberulus
193. Astragalus testiculatus
194. Astragalus kurtschumensis
195. Astragalus brevifolius
196. Astragalus follicularis
197. Astragalus Schanginianus
198. Astragalus Alopecurus

199. Astragalus frigidus
200. Astragalus laguroides
201. Astragalus rytidocarpus
202. Astragalus
203. Astragalus
204. Astragalus
205. Astragalus
206. Astragalus
207. Cicer Songaricum
208. Vicia sepium. . . Bush-Vetch
209. Vicia Cracca. . . Common Tufted-Vetch
210. Vicia tenuifolia . . Slender-leaved Vetch
211. Vicia magalotropis
212. Vicia costata
213. Vicia sylvatica . . Wood-Vetch
214. Vicia amoena
215. Lathyrus pratensis . Angle-berries, Meadow Pea
216. Lathyrus Pisformis . Pea Vetchling, Siberian Everlasting Pea
217. Lathyrus palustris . Marsh Pea
218. Lathyrus altaicus
219. Lathyrus tuberosus . Dutch Mice, Earth-nut Pea, Fine Tare, Tuberous-rooted Everlasting Pea
220. Orobus alpestris
221. Orobus luteus . . Yellow Butter Vetch
222. Hedysarum neglectum
223. Hedysarum obscurum
224. Hedysarum polymorphum
225. Onobrychis sativa . Common Saintfoin

AMYGDALEAE

226. Prunus Padus . . Bird Cherry
227. Amygdalus nana . . Dwarf Almond

ROSACEAE

A large natural order erect or prostrate, very rarely
2 B

climbing. Is one of the most important orders from a gardener's standpoint. The principal fruit yielded by members of the order are almond, apple, apricot, blackberry, cherry, medlar, nectarine, peach, pear, plum, quince, raspberry, service berry, and strawberry. In addition to these, many beautiful flowering plants are included in the Rosaceae, the rose of course taking front rank. Rose-water is obtained by distillation from Rosa-centifolia. The order comprises 71 genera and 1000 species known to Great Britain, but some authors place the number as high as 1500.

228.	Spiraea trilobata .	Trilobed-leaved Spiraea
229.	Spiraea hypericifolia	Italian " May "
230.	Spiraea crenifolia .	Crenate-leaved Spiraea
231.	Spiraea alpina	Alpine Spiraea
232.	Spiraea media	Intermediate Spiraea
233.	Spiraea chamaedryfolia	Germander-leaved Spiraea
234.	Spiraea Filipendula	Drop-wort
235.	Spiraea Ulmaria .	Common Meadow-sweet
236.	Dryas octopetala .	Mountain Avens, White-flowered Dryad
237.	Coluria geoides	
238.	Geum strictum	Upright Avens
239.	Geum rivale.	Water Avens
240.	Sanguisorba officinalis .	Great Burnet
241.	Sanguisorba alpina	
242.	Alchemilla vulgaris	Lady's Mantle
243.	Agrimonia pilosa	
244.	Sibbaldia procumbens	
245.	Chamaerodos erecta	
246.	Potentilla pensylvanica	
247.	Potentilla tanacetifolia	
249.	Potentilla sericea	
250.	Potentilla multifida	Much-cleft Cinquefoil
251.	Potentilla bifurca	
252.	Potentilla Anserina	Silver Weed

253. Potentilla chrysantha
254. Potentilla opaca
255. Potentilla flagellaris . Whip-like Cinquefoil
256. Potentilla cinerea
257. Potentilla nivea . . Snowy-leaved Cinquefoil
258. Potentilla fragiformis
259. Potentilla fruticosa . Shrubbery Cinquefoil
260. Comarum palustre . Marsh Cinquefoil
261. Comarum Salessowi
262. Fragaria vesca . . Common Strawberry
263. Fragaria collina . . Alpine, or Green Pine Strawberry
264. Rubus Idaeus . . Common Raspberry
265. Rubus saxatilis . . Bunch - berry, . Roebusk-berry, Stone Bramble
266. Rosa pimpinellifolia . Pimpernel-leaved Rose
267. Rosa acicularis . . Needle-pricked Rose

POMACEAE

Very little known in England.

268. Crataegus sanguinea
269. Cotoneaster uniflora
270. Cotoneaster vulgaris . Common Cotoneaster
271. Sorbus Aucuparia. . Mountain-Ash

ONAGRARIEAE

An order of inodorous annual or perennial herbs, rarely shrubs, or trees, a few being aquatic. They are found in all temperate regions, but are rare in the Tropics. The species contain mucous and occasionally somewhat astringent principles. The berries are sweet and edible, while the roots of several of the species are also eaten. The order comprises 22 genera and about 300 species.

272. Epilobium latifolium
273. Epilobium angusti-folium . . . Rose-bay, or French Willow

274. Epilobium montanum . Broad-leaved Willow-herb
275. Epilobium roseum . Pale-flowered Willow-herb
276. Epilobium alpinum . Mountain Willow-herb

HALORAGEAE

An order of herbs or under-shrubs, rarely annual, aquatic or terrestrial. These species are sparingly dispersed throughout the world, and are found in damp places. There are 9 genera and 90 species.

277. Myriophyllum spicatum
278. Hippuris vulgaris . . Bottle Brush, Common Mare's-Tail

LYTHRARIEAE

A natural order of herbs, shrubs, or trees with variable habits, natives chiefly of topical America.

279. Lythrum virgatum . Slender-branched Purple Loose-strife

TAMARISCINEAE

Flowers often white or pink ; very showy and striking colours.

280. Myricaria davurica
281. Myricaria davurica

PORTULACEAE

A natural order of usually smooth and more or less succulent, and sometimes long, pilose herbs, rarely small shrubs or under-shrubs, mostly American, some South African or Australian. A few Asiatic, North African or European ; 15 genera and 125 species.

282. Claytonia Joanneana

CRASSULACEAE

An order of usually succulent herbs or shrubs. Flowers in terminal or axillary cymes. There are 14 genera and 400 species.

283. Umbilicus spinosus . Spiny Penny-wort
284. Sedum quadrifidum
285. Sedum algidum
286. Sedum elongatum. . Elongated Stone-crop
287. Sedum purpureum . Purple Stone-crop
288. Sedum Ewersii . . Ewer's Stone-crop
289. Sedum hybridum .

GROSSULARIEAE

Little known.

290. Ribes aciculare . . Needle-spined Gooseberry
291. Ribes atropurpureum . Dark-purple-flowered Black Currant
292. Ribes rubrum . . Common Red Currant
293. Ribes nigrum . . Common Black Currant
294. Ribes fragrans . . Fragrant - flowered Gooseberry

SAXIFRAGEAE

The Grossularieae is a tribe of the Saxifrageae, of which there are six, comprising 75 genera and 540 species.

295. Saxifraga flagellaris . Whip-cord Saxifrage
296. Saxifraga Hirculus . Marsh Saxifrage
297. Saxifraga melaleuca
298. Saxifraga hieracifolia . Hieracium-leaved Saxifrage
299. Saxifraga crassifolia . Thick-leaved Saxifrage
300. Saxifraga punctata
301. Saxifraga cernua . Drooping Saxifrage
302. Saxifraga sibirica
303. Saxifraga muscoides .

390 SIBERIA

304. Saxifraga oppositifolia — Purple-flowered Saxifrage
305. Saxifraga
306. Chrysosplenium Nudicaule

UMBELLIFERAE

This order embraces upwards of 150 genera and about 1500 species.

307. Eryngium planum — Flat-leaved Eryngo
308. Cicuta virosa — Common Cow-bane, Water Hemlock
309. Aegopodium alpestre
310. Carum Carvi — Common Caraway
311. Schultzia crinita
312. Schultzia compacta
313. Bupleurum aureum
314. Bupleurum multinerve
315. Bupleurum exaltatum
316. Libanotis montana
317. Libanotis condensata
318. Conioselinum Fischeri
319. Angelica sylvestris — Wild Angelica
320. Archangelica decurrens
321. Ferula soongorica
322. Ferula gracilis
323. Peucedanum officinale — Sulphur-wort
324. Peucedanum vaginatum
325. Peucedanum baicalense
326. Heracleum barbatum
327. Pachypleurum alpinum
328. Stenocoelium athamantoides
329. Anthriscus nemorosa
330. Anthriscus sylvestris — Cow-parsley
331. Chaerophyllum Prescottii
332. Pleurospermum uralense
333. Aulacospermum anomalum
334. Aulacospermum cuneatum

Caprifoliaceae

A rather large order of shrubs or herbs often twining. Flowers terminal. The Adoxa Moschatellina genus is not well known in Europe.

335. Adoxa Moschatellina . Moschatel
336. Sambucus racemosa . Hart's Elder, Scarlet-berried Elder
337. Viburnum Opulus . Guelder-Rose
338. Lonicera tartarica . Tatarian Honeysuckle
339. Lonicera hispida
340. Lonicera caerulea. . Blue-berried Honeysuckle
341. Lonicera microphylla . Small-leaved Honeysuckle
342. Linnaea borealis . . Twin-flower

Rubiaceae

A large and important natural order of erect, prostrate, or climbing trees, shrubs, or herbs, mostly tropical. Amongst the economical products of Rubiaceae, coffee and quinine take front rank. Madder, a valuable dye, may also be mentioned. The order comprises 340 genera and 4100 species. The Patrina Sibirica is a native of Siberia.

343. Asperula paniculata
344. Galium uliginosum . Swamp Bed-straw
345. Galium boreale . . Northern Bed-straw
346. Galium coriaceum
347. Galium verum . . Lady's Bed-straw
348. Galium vernum

Valerianeae

349. Patrinia sibirica
350. Patrinia intermedia
351. Valeriana capitata
352. Valeriana dubia
353. Valeriana officinalis . Cat's Valerian, All-heal

DIPSACACEAE

354. Scabiosa ochrolenca . Pale Yellow Scabious

COMPOSITAE

The most extensive order of herbs and shrubs or trees in the vegetable kingdom. There are between 700 and 800 genera, and about 10,000 species. Amongst the most important are the Aster, Chrysanthemum, Dahlia.

355. Nardosmia saxatilis
356. Nardosmia laevigata
357. Nardosmia frigida
358. Tussilago Farfara. . Common Coltsfoot
359. Aster alpinus . . Blue Alpine Daisy
360. Aster flaccidus
361. Aster Richardsonii
362. Galatella punctata
363. Galatella Hauptii
364. Calimeris tatarica
366. Erigeron acris . . Blue-flowered Flea-bane
367. Erigeron glabratus
368. Erigeron uniflorus
369. Solidaga Virgaurea . Common Golden-rod
370. Inula Helenium . . Elecampane
371. Inula salicina . . Willow-like Inula
372. Inula britannica
373. Ptarmica impatiens
374. Ptarmica alpina
375. Achillea Millefolium . Yarrow or Milfoil
376. Chrysanthemum sinuatum
377. Pyrethrum ambiguum
378. Pyrethrum pulchrum
379. Artemisia Dracunculus. Tarragon-plant
380. Artemisia campestris . Field Wormwood
381. Artemisia borealis

382. Artemisia sacrorum
383. Artemisia laciniata
384. Artemisia macrobotrys
385. Artemisia latifolia
386. Artemisia vulgaris . Mugwort
387. Artemisia sericea . . Silky-leaved Wormwood
388. Artemisia frigida . . Silky Wormwood
389. Artemisia Sieversiana
390. Tanacetum vulgare . Common Tansy
391. Gnaphalium sylvati- Chave-weed, Wood Cud-
cum . . . . weed
392. Antennaria dioica. . Cat's-foot
393. Leontopodium alpinum. Lion's-foot
394. Ligularia altaica
395. Ligularia sibirica
396. Aronicum altaicum
397. Cacalia hastata
398. Waldheimia tridactylites
399. Sececio resedaefolius
400. Senecio frigidus
401. Senecio erucaefolius . Narrow-leaved Groundsel
402. Senecio Jacobaea . Ragwort
403. Senecio nemorensis
404. Senecio sibiricus
405. Senecio alpestris . . Alpine Groundsel
406. Senecio campestris . Field Groundsel, Woolly
Groundsel
407. Senecio pratensis
408. Echinops humilis
409. Echinops Ritro . . Small Globe-thistle
410. Saussurea pygmaea . Dwarf Saw-wort
411. Saussurea
412. Saussurea crassifolia
413. Saussurea latifolia
414. Saussurea serrata
415. Saussurea discolor
416. Saussurea alpina . . Alpine Saw-wort

417. Saussurea
418. Saussurea salicifolia
419. Haplotaxis Frolowii
420. Centaurea ruthenica   .   Russian Knap-weed
421. Centaurea sibirica
422. Centaurea Marschalliana
423. Carduus nutans   .   .   Musk Thistle, Scotch Thistle
424. Carduus crispus
425. Cirsium heterophyllum
426. Cirsium esculentum   *
427. Cirsium serratulodes
428. Lappa tomentosa.
429. Leuzea carthaomides
430. Alfredia cernua
431. Serratula coronata   .   Crowned Saw-wort
432. Serratula nitida
433. Jurinea linearifolia
434. Achyrophorus maculatus
435. Tragopogon orientalis
436. Scorzonera austriaca
437. Scorzonera radiata
438. Taraxacum officinale . Dandelion
439. Taraxacum corniculatum
440. Taraxacum
441. Taraxacum glaucanthum
442. Taraxacum leucathum
443. Taraxacum palustre
444. Taraxacum Stevenii
445. Crepis multicaulis
446. Crepis Chrysantha
447. Crepis polytricha
448. Crepis praemorsa
449. Crepis sibirica
450. Crepis lyrata
451. Crepis tectorum
452. Sonchus arvensis .   .   Corn Sow-thistle
453. Youngia diversifolia

454. Youngia pygmaea
455. Mulgedium azureum
456. Mulgedium sibiricum
457. Hieracium prenanthoides Wall-lettuce Hawk-weed
458. Hieracium echioides
459. Hieracium umbellatum . Umbellate Hawk-weed
460. Hieracium virosum

CAMPANULACEAE

A bell-shaped flower, blue and white. All species are elegant when in flower. As a rule no plant is more easily cultivated in Great Britain. The strong growing kinds may be grown with the greatest success in ordinary garden soil.

461. Campanula sibirica   . Siberian Bell-flower
462. Campanula glomerata . Clustered   Bell - flower, Danesblood
463. Campanula bononiensis. Bononian Bell-flower
464. Campanula Stevenii
465. Campanula rotundifolia Hare-bell
466. Adenophora stylosa
467. Adenophora liliifolia
468. Adenophora Lamarkii

VACCINIACEAE

A natural order of erect or prostrate shrubs or trees. It comprises 26 genera and about 320 species. The three Siberian genera are not well known.

469. Vaccinium Vitis idaea . Cowberry
470. Vaccinium Myrtillus   . Whortleberry,   Bilberry, Blaeberry
471. Vaccinium uliginosum . Bog Bilberry

ERICACEAE

An extreme order widely spreading over the whole world, containing 87 genera and about 1300 species. The best known are the Rhododendron; the other two genera are not well known.

472. Arctostaphylos alpina . Alpine Bearberry, Black
                                     Bearberry
473. Rhododendron   dauri-
       cum .   .   .   . Siberian Rhododendron
474. Ledum palustre .   . March Cistus, Marsh Rose-
                                     mary

PYROLACEAE

A native of Britain and North and Central Asia. Several species are very pretty.

475. Pyrola rotundifolia   . Canker - Lettuce, False or
                                     Pear-leaved Winter-green,
                                     Larger Winter-green
476. Pyrola chlorantha
477. Pyrola minor   .   . Common   Winter - green,
                                     Wood Lily
478. Pyrola secunda   .   . Notched - leaved Winter -
                                     green
479. Moneses grandiflora

PRIMULACEAE

(From Primus—first). A genus comprising 70 or 80 species. These are mostly found in the Alps and are natives of the Altai. Five of these species are natives of Britain. These include the Primrose (Primula vulgaris). It is a charming and exceedingly useful plant. They have a great diversity of habits and growths. Some being very dwarf and slow-growing, while others develop and flower as large plants in a comparatively short time so far as Great Britain is concerned, but in Siberia these are on the large scale like all others. Many species are cultivated in Great Britain in greenhouses.

480. Primula cortusoides . Cortusa-leaved Primrose
481. Primula officinalis . Cowslip
482. Primula elatior . . Bardfield or True Ox-lip, Great Cowslip
483. Primula nivalis . . Snow-white Primrose
484. Primula auriculata . Ear-leaved Primrose
485. Primula farinosa . Bird's-eye Primrose
486. Primula longiscapa
487. Primula Sibirica . . Siberian Primrose
488. Androsace villosa
489. Androsace Gmelini
490. Androsace septentrionalis
491. Androsace filiformis
493. Cortusa Matthioli . Bear's-ear Sanicle
494. Glaux maritima . . Black Salt-wort, Sea Milk-weed, Sea Milk-wort
495. Trientalis europaea . European Chick-weed, Winter green, Star flower
496. Lysimachia (Naum-burgia) thrysiflora . Tufted Loose-strife

ASCLEPIACEAE

497. Vincetoxicum sibiricum

GENTIANEAE

The old Greek name used by Dioscorides, so called in honour of Gentus—a king of Illyricum—who imprisoned the Roman Ambassadors at the request of Peruses, King of Macedonia. He is said to have been the first who experienced the virtues of Gentian. This plant has a large genus, about 180 species. It is a perennial herb. The flowers from it in the Altai are blue, violet, purple, yellow and white. The intensity of the blue is something wonderful. In many localities these flowers are very difficult to establish, and some species (Gvera, for instance) can rarely be induced, even under artificial conditions, to increase and blossom, as it does in its natural state in the Altai. These are difficult to transplant.

498. Gentiana altaica
499. Gentiana verna . . Spring Gentian
500. Gentiana barbata
501. Gentiana tenella
502. Gentiana Amarella . Autumn Gentian, Bitter-wort, Fel-wort
503. Gentiana prostrata . Prostrate Gentian
504. Gentiana humilis
505. Gentiana decumbens . Decumbent Gentian
506. Gentiana frigida
507. Gentiana septemfida . Crested Gentian
508. Gentiana macrophylla . Large-leaved Gentian
509. Pleurogyne carinthiaca
510. Anagallidium dichoto-mum
511. Swertia obtusa

POLEMONIACEAE

512. Polemonium caeruleum. Greek Valerian, Common Jacob's-ladder
513. Polemonium pulchel-lum

CONVOLVULACEAE

An extensive order of herbs or shrubs, usually twining, and with a milky juice. This order contains 700 species.

514. Convolvulus Ammannii
515. Convolvulus arvensis . Common Bind-weed

516. Calystegia subvolubilis
517. Cuscuta europaea . . Greater Dodder, Hell-weed,
    Strangle tare

BORAGINACEAE

Sometimes called Borago. Has a blue flower, panicled,
drooping, cone-shaped. It usually grows nuts. All the
species are easily cultivated. In hot weather borage is
generally in demand for claret-cup and other drinks.

518. Anchusa myosotidiflora   Myosotideum-flowered An-
    chusa
519. Onosma Gmelini
520. Onosma simplicissimum   Very simply Golden-drop
521. Lithospermum officinale   Common Cromwell
522. Pulmonaria mollis   . Soft Lungwort
523. Myosotis palustris.   . Common Forget-me-not
524. Myosotis sylvatica   . Wood Forget-me-not
525. Myosotis intermedia
526. Eritrichium villosum
527. Eritrichium rupestre
528. Eritrichium obovatum
529. Eritrichium pectinatum
530. Echinospermum deflexum
531. Echinospermum Lappula
532. Cynoglossum officinale . Common Dog's-tongue or
    Hound's-tongue
533. Cynoglossum viridiflorum

SOLANACEAE

534. Datura Stramonium   . Common Thorn-apple
535. Hyoscyamus niger
536. Hyoscyamus physaloides Kite - flower,   Purple -
    flowered Henbane

Scrophulariaceae

This order is a most important one from a horticultural standpoint, contributing as it does so many beautiful plants to our gardens. It embraces 157 genera and nearly 1900 species, and is divided into twelve tribes.

538. Verbascum Thapsus . Mullein Dock, White Mullein
539. Verbascum phoeniceum Purple-flowered Mullein
540. Linaria macroura . Long-tailed Toad-flax
541. Linaria genistaefolia . Broom-leaved Toad-flax
542. Scrophularia incisa
543. Veronica pinnata
544. Veronica longifolia . Long-leaved Speedwell
545. Veronica spicata . . Spike-flowered Speedwell
546. Veronica spuria . . Bastard Speedwell
547. Veronica Teucrium . Hungarian or Saw-leaved Speedwell
548. Veronica macrostemon
549. Veronica densiflora
550. Castilleya pallida
551. Euphrasia officinalis . Eye-bright
552. Rhinanthus Cristagalli Yellow Rattle
553. Pedicularis verticillata Whirled Louse-wort
554. Pedicularis amoena
555. Pedicularis abrotanifolia
556. Pedicularis proboscidea
557. Pedicularis myriophylla
558. Pedicularis uncinata
559. Pedicularis compacta
560. Pedicularis lasiostachys
561. Pedicularis resupinata
562. Pedicularis elata
563. Pedicularis altaica
564. Pedicularis uliginosa
565. Pedicularis cosma . Spiked Louse-wort

566. Pedicularis versicolor . Various - coloured Louse - wort
567. Pedicularis tristis
568. Pedicularis flava . . Yellow Louse-wort

OROBANCHACEAE
569. Orobanche

SELAGINACEAE
570. Gymnandra Pallasii

· LABIATAE

An order of herbs or shrubs, a native of Siberia. Very many of this genus yield a valuable oil ; basil, hore-hound, hyssop, lavender, marjoram, mint, sage and thyme belong to this order. There are about 140 genera and 2600 species.

571. Mentha sylvestris . Brook or Water Mint, Horse Mint
572. Origanum vulgare . English, Grove or Wild Marjoram
573. Thymus Serpyllum . Wild Thyme
574. Ziziphora clinopodioides Clinopodium, like Ziziphora
575. Nepeta botryoides
576. Nepeta lavandulacea
577. Nepeta nuda
578. Nepeta macrantha . Large-flowered Cat-mint
579. Nepeta Glechoma . Ground Ivy
580. Drococephalum pinnatum
581. Dracocephalum imberbe Beardless Dragon's head
582. Dracocephalum altaiense Altaian Dragon's Head
583. Dracocephalum nutans
584. Dracocephalum pere-grinum . . . Prickly - leaved Dragon's - head, Twin - flowered Dragon's-head

585. Dracocephalum Ruy-
schiana . . . Hyssop - leaved Dragon's-
head
586. Prunella vulgaris . . Common Self-heal
587. Scutellaria alpina . Alpine Skull-cap
588. Scutellaria orientalis . Yellow - flowered Skull-cap,
Yellow Helmet-flower
589. Scutellaria scordiifolia . Scordium-leaved Skull-cap
590. Scutellaria galericulata Common Skull-cap, Hooded
Willow-herb
591. Marrubium lanatum
592. Leonurus glaucescens
595. Lamium album . . . White Dead-nettle
596. Phlomis tuberosa
597. Stachys palustris . . Clown's All-heal or Woundwort
598. Galeopsis Tetrahit . Common Hemp-nettle
599. Amethystea caerulea

PLUMBAGINEAE

600. Statice speciosa . . Showy Sea-Lavender
601. Statice congesta

PLANTAGINEAE

602. Plantago major . . Greater Plantain
603. Plantago media . . Hoary Plantain

SALSOLACEAE

An order of herbs or shrubs. There is very little
known about this flower in Europe.

604. Chenopodium acuminatum
605. Chenopodium frutescens
606. Blitum polymorphum
607. Eurotia ceratoides
608. Kochia arenaria
609. Brachylepis salsa

POLYGONEAE

A very distinct natural order of herbs, shrubs or sometimes trees, found in tropical America and the Eastern Mediterranean, but particularly in the Altai. One of the order—Rheum—is Rhubarb, and very large quantities of it grow wild in the Altai. There are 30 genera and about 600 species.

610. Rheum Rhaponticum . Garden or Tart Rhubarb
611. Oxyria reniformis . Mountain Sorrel
612. Rumex Acetosa . . Sorrel
613. Fagopyrum tataricum
614. Polygonum Bistorta . Bistort
615. Polygonum viviparum . Serpent-grass, Small Bistort
616. Polygonum polymorphum
617. Polygonum amphibium. Amphibious Knot-weed, Willow-grass
618. Tragopyrum lanceolatum . Lance-leaved Goat's-wheat

SANTALACEAE

619. Thesium repens

ELAEAGNEAE

620. Hippophae rhamnoides . Common Sea-Buckthorn

EMPETREAE

621. Empetrum nigrum . Crow-berry

EUPHORBIACEAE

A very large order of trees, shrubs, or herbs, usually abounding in milk juice. There are 200 genera and 3000 species. The 5 genera of the Altai are not well known.

622. Euphorbia alpina
623. Euphorbia macrorhiza
. Euphorbia altaica
624. Euphorbia lutescens
625. Euphorbia Esula . . Leafy Spurge

CANNABINEAE

626. Cannabis sativa . . Common Hemp
627. Humulus Lupulus . Common Hop

URTICACEAE

A natural order of trees, shrubs, or herbs. Amongst the most important members of this order, the Cannabineae is of the same tribe as this tree. It embraces 110 genera and 1500 species.

628. Urtica urens. . . Small British Nettle
629. Urtica dioica . . Common Stinging Nettle
630. Urtica canabina . . Hemp-leaved Nettle

SALICINEAE

A natural order of trees or shrubs, chiefly inhabiting northern temperate and frigid regions. There are only 2 genera, and these contribute some ornamental subjects to our gardens. The poplar wood is altogether soft, and is valued for its lightness.

631. Salix pentamdra . . Bay-leaved Willow
632. Salix amygdalina . . Almond-leaved Willow
633. Salix daphnoides . . Violet Willow
634. Salix Kochiana
635. Salix Ledebouriana
636. Salix viminalis . . Osier
637. Salix Caprea . . Common Sallow, Goat Willow
638. Salix depressa
639. Salix phylicifolia . Tea-leaved Willow
640. Salix pyrolaefolia
641. Salix repens . . . Creeping Willow
642. Salix lanata . . . Woolly Willow
643. Salix Lapponum . . Downy Willow
644. Salix glauca
645. Salix glauca
646. Salix arctica

647. Salix Myrsinites . . Whortle Willow
648. Salix Brayi
649. Salix arbuscula
650. Salix sibirica
651. Salix reticulata . . Highland or Netted-leaved
    Willow
652. Salix retusa
653. Salix herbacea . . Dwarf Willow
654. Salix
655. Salix
656. Populus tremula . . Aps, Asp or Aspen
657. Populus laurifolia . . Laurel-leaved Poplar

BETULACEAE

658. Betula alba . . . Common Birch
659. Betula microphylla
660. Betula tortuosa
661. Betula humilis
662. Betula nana . . . Dwarf Birch
663. Alnus fruticosa

MONOCOTYLEDONEAE
(Flowering Plants)

NAJADEAE

664. Potamogeton pectinatus   Fennel-leaved Pond-weed
665. Potamogeton gramineus   Grass-leaved Pond-weed

JUNCAGINEAE

666. Triglochin maritimum . Sea Arrow-grass
667. Triglochin palustre . Marsh Arrow-grass

ORCHIDEAE

A very large order of monocotyledonous plants. It is generally found growing on the trunks of trees. There are about 334 genera and 5000 species.

668. Orchis latifolia . .	Marsh Orchid
669. Orchis militaris . .	Military Orchid
670. Orchis Maculata . .	Spotted Orchid
671. Gymnadenia conopsea .	Fragrant Orchid
672 Habenaria(Platathnera) bifolia . . .	Common Butterfly Orchid
673. Herminium Monorchis	Musk Orchid
674. Goodyera repens .	Creeping Rattlesnake-Plantain
675. Cypripedium Calceolus	Lady's Slipper
676. Cypripedium macranthon	Siberian Lady's Slipper
677. Cypripedium guttatum	Hardy spotted Lady's Slipper

IRIDEAE

678. Iris ruthenica . .	Ever-blooming Iris, Russian Iris
679. Iris biglumis . .	Two-plumed Iris
680. Iris Bloudowii . .	Bloudow's Iris
681. Iris flavissima	

SMILACEAE

682. Asparagus officinalis .	Common Asparagus, Sparrow-grass
683. Polygonatum officinale	Common Solomon's-seal
684. Maianthemum bifolium	Two-leaved Lily of the Valley
685. Paris quadrifolia . .	Herb-Paris

MELANTHACEAE

676. Veratrum album . .	Lang-wort or Lyng-wort, White-flowered White Hellebore
687. Veratrum nigrum .	Dark-flowered White Hellebore

These are remarkable for the beauty of their flowers. The species Allium supplies the onion, leek, chive, shallot, rocambole and garlic. Certain species yield a bitter resinous juice. The order comprises upwards of 180 genera and about 2500 species.

688. Erythronium Denscanis   Common Dog's-tooth Violet
689. Orithyia Oxypetala
690. Gagea lutea . . . Yellow Star of Bethlehem
691. Gagea reticulata
692. Gagea minima
693. Lloydia serotina . . Mountain Spider-wort
694. Fritillaria verticillata . Verticillate Fritillary
695. Lilium Martagon . . Martagon Lily
696. Allium Schoenoprasum   Chives
697. Allium Ledebourianum
698. Allium strictum
699. Allium flavidum
700. Allium amphibolum
701. Allium nutans
702. Allium hymenorhizum
703. Allium fistilosum . . Ciboul, Stone Leek, Welsh Onion
704. Allium tenuissimum
705. Allium
706. Allium abliquum
707. Allium Stellerianum
708. Allium tulipaefolium
709. Allium Victorialis . Long-rooted Garlic
710. Allium clathratum
711. Hemerocallis flava . Yellow Day-Lily
712. Ixiolirion Ledebouri . Ledebour's Ixia-Lily

JUNCACEAE

A natural order containing about 130 species of perennial, rarely annual, herbs—principally natives of

the Arctic regions. There are 14 genera, and some of them
are represented in the British flora.

713. Luzula spadicea
714. Luzula spicata . . Spiked Wood-Rush
715. Juncus castaneus : . Black-spiked Rush
716. Juncus triglumis . . Three-flowered Rush
717. Juncus filiformis . . Thread Rush

CYPERACEAE

Is an extensive order of grass plant which bears cotton
and wool. This plant is usually confined to Arctic regions,
and according to Nicholson's *Illustrated Dictionary* there
is only one genus of about a dozen species, while there
are 18 species of the Carex genus alone found in the
Altai.

718. Eriophorum Chamissonis
719. Eriophorum augustifolium
720. Elyna Schoenoides
721. Carex capitata
722. Carex brizoides .
723. Carex obtusata
724. Carex atrata . . . Black Sedge
725. Carex ustulata
726. Carex nigra
727. Carex bicolor
728. Carex stenophylla
729. Carex saxatilis . . Highland Sedge
730. Carex tristis
731. Carex montana . . Mountain Sedge
732. Carex capillaris . . Capillary Sedge
733. Carex pediformis
734. Carex supina .
735. Carex humilis . . Dwarf Sedge
736. Carex caespitosa . . Hassock-grass, Tufted Sedge
737. Carex praecox . . Spring Sedge
738. Carex riparia . . Greater Bank Sedge.

GRAMINEAE

Normally flower-bearing; contain in their herbage, and especially in their seeds, nutritious principles which entitle them to the first rank amongst plants useful to man, and which are of the greatest importance from an economic and political point of view. Species of this order include wheat, rye, barley, oats, rice, millet. A considerable number of Gramineae are medicinal, particularly Triticum repens. There are also a number of ornamental garden plants of this order.

739.	Hordeum pratense	
740.	Elymus dasystachys	
741.	Elymus junceus	
742.	Triticum cristatum	
743.	Triticum strigosum	
744.	Triticum repens	Couch or Quitch Grass
745.	Festuca ovina	Sheep's Fescue-grass
746.	Festuca rubra	Red or Creeping Fescue grass
747.	Festuca altaica	
748.	Bromus inermis	
749.	Dactylis glomerata	Cock's-foot Grass
750.	Poa pratensis	Kentucky Blue - grass, Natural-grass, Smooth-stalked Meadow - Grass,
751.	Poa nemoralis	Wood Meadow-grass
752.	Poa attenuata	
753.	Poa serotina	
754.	Poa alpina	
755.	Poa alpina	
756.	Poa alpina	
757.	Poa bulbosa	
758.	Poa laxa	
759.	Poa altaica	
760.	Poa annua	Common Meadow-Grass
761.	Colpodium altaicum	

762. Arundo Phragmites . Common Reed, Spire Reed
763. Koeleria cristata
764. Hierochloe alpina . . Alpine Holy Grass
765. Hierochloe borealis . Northern Holy Grass
766. Hierochloe glabra
767. Anthoxanthum odor- Vernal or Sweet Vernal
atum . . . . Grass
768. Avena pubescens
769. Avena pratensis . . Oat Grass, Perennial Oat
770. Avena desertorum
771. Avena flavescens . . Yellow Oat Grass
772. Avena subspicata
773. Deschampsia caespitosa
774. Calamagrostis Epigejos Bush Grass, Common Wood-
reed
775. Calamagrostis sylvatica
776. Calamagrostis lanceolata Spear-leaved Wood-reed
777. Calamagrostis Halleriana
778. Agrostis canina
779. Milium effusum . . Millet Grass
780. Lasiagrostis splendens
781. Stipa capillata . . Long-haired Feather Grass
782. Stipa Pennata . . Feather Grass
783. Stipa orientalis
784. Beckmannia erucaeformis
785. Phleum Boehmeri
786. Phleum alpinum
787. Alopecurus pratensis . Fox-tail Grass
788. Alopecurus glaucus
789. Setaria viridis . . Bottle Grass, Green Fox-
tail Grass

GYMNOSPERMAE
CONIFERAE
A large order of trees or shrubs, mostly evergreen, and with resinous secretions.
790. Picea obovata . . Siberian Spruce

791. Abies sibirica . . Siberian Spruce Fir
792. Larix sibirica
793. Pinus Cembra . . Russian Cedar, Swiss Stone
                       Pine
794. Pinus sylvestris . . Scotch Fir
795. Juniperus Sabina . . Common Savin
796. Juniperus nana . . Dwarf Juniper
797. Juniperus davurica

GNETACEAE
798. Ephedra vulgaris
799. Ephedra procera

CRYPTOGAMAE
EQUISETACEAE
800. Equisetum arvense . Bottle Brush, False Horse-
                         tail
801. Equisetum palustre . Marsh Horse-tail

LYCOPODIACEAE
802. Lycopodium Selago . Fir Club Moss, Fir Moss,
                         Tree Moss
803. Lycopodium annotinum
804. Lycopodium alpinum . Alpine Club Moss

FILICES
There are about 70 genera and about 2500 species
known. The Polypodium is responsible for a large
number of these, while the Pteris is also responsible for a
large number.
805. Polypodium vulgare . Common Polypody
806. Polypodium Phegopteris Beech Fern
807. Polypodium Dryopteris Moss Fern, Oak Fern
808. Woodsia ilvensis .
809. Cystopteris fragilis . Brittle Bladder Fern
810. Pteris aquilina . . Adder-Spit, Bracken,Brake-
                         Fern, Eagle-Fern
811. Struthiopteris Germanica Ostrich - Fern of North
                              America

These flowers were discovered in the year 1899 in the higher Irtish and round the Irtish.

1. Clematis glauca . . Glaucous-leaved Clematis
2. Cl. integrifolia . . Entire-leaved Clematis
3. Thalictrum simplex
4. Nasturtium palustre . Marsh Water-cress
5. N. amphibium . . Great Water-cress
6. Erysimum canescens
7. Syrenia siliculosa
8. Lepidium Draba . . Hoary Cress
9. L. perfoliatum
10. L. latifolium . . . Broad-leaved Cress
11. Hymenophysa pubescens
12. Brassica campestris . Wild Cabbage
13. Dianthus pallidiflorus . Pale-flowered Pink
14. Gypsophila paniculata . Panicled Gypsophila
15. Silene Otites. . . Spanish Campion
16. S. multiflora
17. Lychnis chalcedonica . Common Rose-Campion
18. Lavatera thuringiaca
19. Althaea ficifolia . . Antwerp Hollyhock
20. Geranium collinum . Gill Crane's Bill
21. Ger. affine
22. Zygophyllum macropterum
23. Dictamnus Fraxinella . Burning Bush, Dittany, Fraxinella Gas-plant
24. Nitraria Schoberi
25. Medicago falcata . . Sickle-podded Medick
26. M. lupulina . . . Black Medick
27. Melilotus macrorhiza
28. Lotus corniculatus . Common Bird's-foot Trefoil
29. Glycyrrhiza glandulifera
30. G. asperrima
31. Caragana frutescens . Shrubby Siberian Pea-tree
32. C. pygmaea . . . Pigmy Siberian Pea-tree
33. Halimodentron argenteum . Silvery-leaved Salt-tree

34. Astragalus semibilocularis
35. A. Alopecias
36. A. roseus
37. A. consanguineus
38. Ervum tetraspermum
39. Lathyrus pratensis . Meadow-Pea
40. Hedysarum splendens
41. Sophora alopecuroices
42. Spiraea hypericifolia . Italian "May"
43. Potentilla supina
44. P. bifurca
45. Rubus caesius . . Blue Bramble, Dewberry
46. Rosa pimpinellifolia . Pimpernel-leaved Rose
47. Lythrum virgatum . Slender - branched Purple Loose-strife
48. Herniaria hirsuta
49. Eryngium planum. . Flat-leaved Eryngo
50. Sium lancifolium
51. Galium verum . . Lady's Bed-straw
52. Scabiosa isetensis
53. Erigeron acris . . Blue-flowered Flea-bane
54. E. glabratus
55. Inula britannica
56. Artemisia scoparia . Twiggy-branched Southern-wood
57. A. maritima . . . Garden Cypress, Seaside Wormwood
58. A. frigida . . . Silky Wormwood
59. Senecio Jacobaea . . Ragwort
60. Echinops Ritro . . Small Globe-thistle
61. Cirsium arvense . . Canada Thistle, Creeping Thistle
62. Acroptilon Picris
63. Tragopogon ruber . Red Goat's beard
64. Chondrilla pauciflora
65. Taraxacum palustre
66. Mulgedium tartaricum

67. Xanthium Strumarium .   Ditch-bur, Louse-bur, Small Burdock
68. Lysimachia vulgaris   .   Yellow Loose-strife
69. Apocynum venetum   .   Venetian Dog's-bane
70. Cynanchum acutum   .   Montpelier Scammony Plant
71. Gentiana decumbens   .   Decumbent Gentian
72. Lymnanthemum nymphoides
73. Convolvulus arvensis   .   Common Bind-weed
74. Calystegia sepium
75. Onosma Gmelini
76. Arnebia cornuta
77. Echinospermum deflexum
78. E. Lappula
79. Solanum persicum
80. Dodartia orientalis
81. Gratiola officinalis   .   Hedge-Hyssop, Poor-man's Herb
82. Veronica spuria   .   .   Bastard Speedwell
83. V. Anagallis .   .   .   Great Water Speedwell, Water Pimpernel
84. V. Beccabunga   .   .   Brooklime
85. Mantha sylvestris   .   Horse-mint
86. Hyssopus officinalis   .   Common Hyssop
87. Salvia sylvestris .   .   Wood Sage
88. Ziziphora clinopodioides Clinopodium, like Ziziphon
89. Nepeta nuda
90. Scutellaria orientalis   .   Yellow-flowered Skull-cap, Yellow Helmet-flower
91. Stachys palustris .   .   Clown's All-heal or Woundwort, Marsh Betony
92. Eremostachys molucelloides
93. Lagochilus hirtus
94. Statice Gmelini   .   .   Gmelin's Sea-Lavender
95. St. speciosa .   .   .   Showy Sea-Lavender
96. Plantago maxima.   .   Broad-leaved Plantain
97. P. Maritima .   .   .   Seaside Plantain
98. Atriplex laciniata

99. Chenopodium acuminatum
100. Blitum polymorphum
101. Eurotia ceratoides
102. Camphorosma ruthenica
103. Salicornia herbacea   .   Marsh Samphire
104. Colligonum rubicundum
105. Rumex Marschallianus
106. Atraphaxis lanceolata
107 Polygonum lapathifolium Pale-flowered   Knot-weed,
                                    Willow-weed
108. Cannabis sative .   . Common Hemp
109. Daphne altaica   .   . Altaian Daphne
110. Salix alba   .   . Common White Huntingdon,
                                    or Swallow-tailed Willow
111. Populus alba   .   . White Poplar
112. P. nigra   .   .   . Black Poplar
113. Sparganium ramosum . Common Bur-reed
114. Butomus umbellatus . Flowering Rush
115. Allium obliquum
116. A. angulosum
117. Asparagus officinalis . Common Asparagus
118. A. trichophyllus .   . Hair-leaved Asparagus
119. A. maritimus
120. Scirpus maritimus   . Seaside Club-rush, Spurt-
                                    grass
121. Festuca ovina   .   . Sheep's Fescue-grass
122. Lasiagrostis splendens
123. Aeluropus litoralis
124. Hordeum pratense
125. Ephedra vulgaris .   . Common Ephedra
126. Equisetum palustre   . Marsh Horse-tail
127. E. Hyemale .   .   . Dutch Rus

The best dictionary for particulars about those flowers
that are known to Europe, is Nicholson's *Illustrated
Dictionary of Gardening*, in four volumes and two
supplements.

THE BEST WINTER ROAD FROM NOVO-NICOLAËVSK TO KATUNDA.

The names of the villages are spelt in several different ways even at the villages themselves, but the difference is generally of one or two letters only, and the names can be made out easily.

From Novo-Nicolaëvsk (Obi)	to	Bersk	20 miles
„	Bersk	„	Koivsoiva	20 „
„	Koivsoiva	„	Medvedskyar	21 „
.,	Medvedskyar	„	Gangogekina	12½ „
„	Gangogekina	„	Anisimofsky	16 „
„	Anisimofsky	„	Talmanskaeyar	16 „
„	Talmanskaeyar	„	Ozjorka	16 „
„	Ozjorka	„	Povolicha	10½ „
„	Povolicha	„	Beleraska	8 „
„	Beleraska	„	Barnaoul	10½ „
„	Barnaoul	„	Chelofsky	6 „
„	Chelofsky	„	Jelenski	18½ „
„	Jelenski	.,	Ofchenikofsky	16½ „
„	Ofchenikofsky	„	Petrofsky	14 „
„	Petrofsky	„	Haruzofsky	14 „
.,	Haruzofsky	„	Bulanka	11½ „
„	Bulanka	„	Skubensky	12 „
„	Skubensky	„	Bysk	15½ „
„	Bysk	„	Krasnobaisk	16 „
„	Krasnobaisk	„	Altaiskoë	34 „
„	Altaiskoë	„	Barancha	27 „
„	Barancha	„	Tavourck	14 „
„	Tavourck	„	Chorni-Anni	24 „
„	Chorni-Anni	„	Melia	10 „
„	Melia	„	Ouskam	20 „
„	Ouskam	„	Koksa	40 „
„	Koksa	„	Ouemon	16 „
„	Ouemon	„	Katunda	10½ „

INDEX

LaVergne, TN USA
09 September 2009
157349LV00007B/63/A

9 781104 304584